808 · 3

JOH

STUDYING FICTION

WITHDRAWN

D0512583

~ok is to be returned on or before
· date stamped below.

COALVILLE TECHNICAL COLLEGE
LIBRARY

Date Recd. .....20. 5. 94......

Requisition No. .....L 11383...

Accession No. .....40243...

Location......8. 09 : 820-31

....

COALVILLE TECHNICAL COLLEGE
LIBRARY

STUDYING FICTION

A guide and study programme

Roy Johnson

MANCHESTER UNIVERSITY PRESS

MANCHESTER AND NEW YORK

*distributed exclusively in the USA
and Canada by* ST. MARTIN'S PRESS

Copyright © Roy Johnson 1992

Published by Manchester University Press
Oxford Road, Manchester M13 9PL, England
and Room 400, 175 Fifth Avenue, New York, NY 10010, USA

Distributed exclusively in the USA and Canada
by St. Martin's Press, Inc., 175 Fifth Avenue, New York,
NY 10010, USA

A catalogue record for this book is available
from the British Library

Library of Congress cataloging in publication data
Johnson, Roy, 1939–
        Studying fiction: a guide and study programme / Roy Johnson.
            p.   cm.
        Includes bibliographical references (p.   ) and index.
        ISBN 0-7190-3396-9 (hardback). — ISBN 0-7190-3397-7 (paperback)
        1. English fiction—Study and teaching—Outlines, syllabi, etc.
        I. Title
    PR824.5.J64   1991
    808.3—dc20   91-3851

ISBN 0 7190 3397 7 *paperback*

Typeset in Scala
by Koinonia Limited, Manchester
Printed in Great Britain
byBell & Bain, Glasgow

CONTENTS

ACKNOWLEDGEMENTS

The contents of this book are based upon the experience of teaching adult students over the last twenty years in classes organised by the Workers Educational Association, and my thanks are principally due to its North Western District for permission to draw upon the materials and the teaching strategies I have developed during that time. I would also like to acknowledge all my students past and present, from whom I have learned a great deal, both about methods of teaching and learning, and about the pleasures of literature itself. Then at an individual level I also wish to thank my colleagues Heather Pollitt for advice on points of grammar, Margaret Bell for fruitful discussions on pedagogy, and Pat Herman for an illustrative example which has been useful many times over.

Grateful acknowledgement is made to the following for permission to reprint copyright material:

Lawrence Pollinger Ltd and the Estate of Frieda Lawrence Ravagli, for D. H. Lawrence's 'Fanny and Annie' from *The Collected Short Stories of D. H. Lawrence* (Viking Penguin, Inc.)

Alfred A. Knopf, Inc., for Katherine Mansfield's 'The Voyage', from *The Short Stories of Katherine Mansfield*, copyright 1922 by Alfred A. Knopf, Inc. and renewed 1950 by John Middleton Murry

CHAPTER ONE

Introduction: how to use the guide

1 The study programme

This book offers you an introduction to all the *basic* skills and intellectual tools required for making a study of fiction. It also presents an explanation of the most common features of narrative prose – and it does so by using practical examples drawn from six short stories which are included as part of the study programme itself. The first two or three chapters deal with the most straightforward issues, and there is a general attempt to encourage you to pay extra close attention to what is printed on the page. This is a skill called 'Close reading', and the programme at this stage is concerned with helping you to build up an accurate *description* of the piece of writing concerned.

After that we move on to explore slightly more sophisticated techniques, into a phase where more emphasis is put upon *analysis*. That is, inspecting, comparing, and evaluating the various features and qualities we might find in a piece of writing.

Finally, we combine all the elements that have been covered to arrive at the stage of *interpretation* – which involves making judgements about a work and perhaps seeing it from various differing points of view.

So, the elements of the programme are graded, and all new concepts or technical terms are explained as we go along. There is a considerable amount of overlapping, and many of the most important features of fiction are covered more than once so as to make sure that the points at issue have been fully illustrated and explained.

2 How to use the guide

All you need in the way of materials to undertake this study programme are pencil and paper, plus the book in your hands. It is worth stressing at the outset that you should try to get used to an active manner of learning. What this means in practice is as follows.

You will see that each chapter offers a few introductory remarks about the story you will be studying, then asks you to read it through carefully – maybe more than once. This is the first stage: you do some reading. And whilst doing so you should get used to making notes and looking up the meaning of any words you do not understand.

Stage two is a discussion of the story and some of the literary devices the author has used. You will be offered various comments to consider and asked to look at some of the technical features of the story. But we approach these matters using a study method you may not have come across before.

When the text poses a question or sets a problem for you to solve and asks you to STOP – you should do so. Stop, think through your answer or responses, and *write down what you have to say* before going any further. A decorated line will remind you to pause. Instead of reading on, draft your answers to the question, even if it is only in note form.

Don't imagine that any of this will be a test of your memory. Get used to the idea of looking back into the story to find evidence for your answers. And if there are any technical terms whose meaning you are not sure of – *look them up*, using the glossary in Chapter Eight. There are also some terms from the realm of intellectual discourse which have been deliberately placed throughout the book in order to prompt you to use a good dictionary.

Each chapter ends with a graded series of self-assessment exercises designed to help you check that you have grasped the issues under examination. Just answer as many of the questions as you can, then compare your responses with those offered in the Guidance Notes at the end of the book.

Finally, for those people who might be using this book as part of a tutor–led course, there are a number of discussion topics and essay questions listed under Course work. Even if you are working alone however, you might use the topics and questions for further study practice.

3 Making notes

Most of the time when studying literature you will obviously be *reading*. You should get used to the idea that whilst doing so you should be *active*. This means not only paying close attention to the words printed on the page, but also *thinking* about them and making a note of things which seem to you particularly important or striking. Always read with a pencil in hand, then you will be able to make two types of notes – small details noted in the margins of the book, and larger observations on separate sheets of paper.

Let me try to illustrate this by suggesting a procedure you might adopt. It is based upon the most common form of note–taking techniques when tackling a piece of fiction for the first time. To start with, the notes in your own copy of the book.

TAKING NOTES WHILST READING

Always use a soft pencil. Ink is too permanent and too distracting when re-reading the story. Just note anything which strikes you as interesting – but try to get into the habit of giving a name to what it *is*. For instance when Hardy uses the word 'lorn' in his section title 'A Lorn Milkmaid' you might underline the word and make a note in the margin – 'arch.vocab' – which is *my* abbreviation for 'archaic vocabulary'.

Similarly you might underline a striking phrase – such as his description of a church as 'the ancient little pile'. It might not always be possible to say exactly *why* it is particularly striking – but if you have further thoughts you can always locate it again easily.

Do *not* underline whole sections or paragraphs. It is a complete waste of time and a distraction on subsequent readings. If a whole paragraph strikes you as significant it is better to say *why* or *how* it is so at the head or foot of the page – which will be a much more useful sort of note anyway.

You might also note cross references in the margin. For instance, if a phrase or a symbol is used more than once or a character does something twice (as happens in 'The Signalman') you might note on one page the number of the other page on which it recurs.

It is also sometimes useful to 'comment' on the story as you go along. That is, record two or three words of summary description of

MANSFIELD PARK.

pub 1814
(JA 34)

Geo III
reign 1760–1820

1780s

CHAPTER I.

Conversat^l
ironic?

class / status

(not all)

ABOUT thirty years ago, Miss Maria Ward of Huntingdon, with only seven thousand pounds, had the good luck
to captivate Sir Thomas Bertram, of Mansfield Park, in
the county of Northampton, and to be thereby raised to
the rank of a baronet's lady, with all the comforts and
consequences of an handsome house and large income.
All Huntingdon exclaimed on the greatness of the match,
and her uncle, the lawyer, himself, allowed her to be at
least three thousand pounds short of any equitable claim
to it. She had two sisters to be benefited by her eleva-
tion; and such of their acquaintance as thought Miss
Ward and Miss Frances quite as handsome as Miss Maria,
did not scruple to predict their marrying with almost
equal advantage. But there certainly are not so many
men of large fortune in the world, as there are pretty
women to deserve them. Miss Ward, at the end of half
a dozen years, found herself obliged to be attached to
the Rev. Mr. Norris, a friend of her brother-in-law, with
scarcely any private fortune, and Miss Frances fared yet
worse. Miss Ward's match, indeed, when it came to the
point, was not contemptible, Sir Thomas being happily
able to give his friend an income in the living of Mansfield,
and Mr. and Mrs. Norris began their career of conjugal
felicity with very little less than a thousand a year. But
Miss Frances married, in the common phrase, to disoblige
her family, and by fixing on a Lieutenant of Marines,
without education, fortune, or connections, did it very

£

alliter^n

£ / class

eldest sister

satirical aphorism

def. ironic.

Eccles. posn

£

income   fortune
'equitable claim'

Theme(s)
£ / class / marriage

Figure I

4

what is happening in the story, or give a name to what seem to you to be the most important events. All this will help you with the analysis which comes later.

You should also devise your own private code of abbreviations to indicate regularly recurring features – interesting figures of speech or points of style, linguistic items, features of characterisation, dramatisation, and so on. Figure 1 shows an example of my own notes to the opening page of Jane Austen's *Mansfield Park*.

MAKING SEPARATE NOTES

Most of the best readers possess books which bear the marks of several readings – because each time you read a piece of fiction you are likely to see something new in it. However, if you really are reluctant to write in a book, you have the possibility of making notes on separate sheets of paper. In which case, keep in mind the following guidelines.

☆ Use loose-leaf A4 size paper

☆ Write clearly and leave a double space between entries

☆ Use a tabulation system (as I am doing here)

☆ Don't attempt to write continuous prose

☆ Use a logical and a memorable layout

☆ Use a new page for each separate set of notes

☆ Label everything clearly

☆ Use lettering, numbering, and indentation for sections and sub-sections

☆ Use a system of abbreviations

☆ Make a note of your sources (Author, title, and publication date of any book)

☆ Use your own words: do not copy down undigested chunks of a book or a lecture

☆ Use one side of the paper only

☆ Notes should not be lengthy, and full grammatical sentences are not necessary

☆ Store your notes carefully in a loose-leaf binder or a pocket file

Detailed notes and comments should also be accompanied by page references, otherwise you will waste a lot of time locating the same point in the text at a later date. And there are some things which are best listed separately – particularly when you come to study longer works, such as novels:

☆ A list of the characters: their names, ages, and relation to each other, and whatever else might be significant about them

☆ A summary of the story or the plot. This might be no more than four or five separately tabulated sentences. These will help you keep a grasp of the story as a whole

☆ A list of notes concerning the subject and theme of the story, observations or judgements on the author's approach and style, or questions to which answers might be sought on later readings

If you are coming to literary studies for the first time all this might seem a rather cumbersome and mechanical procedure – but it is the sort of thing which distinguishes serious study from reading for pleasure. The important thing is that you should develop a system which is as clear and simple as possible to use.

4 Close reading

In the course of this study programme we will be touching repeatedly on what is undoubtedly the most important skill you will need for any form of literary studies – 'Close reading', or paying especially close attention to what is printed on the page. This is a much more subtle and complex process than such a simple term might suggest. For close reading means not only reading and understanding the meanings of the individual printed words; it also involves being sensitive to all the nuances and connotations of language as it is used by skilled writers. This can mean anything from a work's particular vocabulary, sentence construction, and imagery, to the themes that are being dealt with, the manner in which the story is being told, and the view of the world that it offers. In other words, close reading involves almost everything from the smallest linguistic items to the much larger issues of literary understanding and judgement.

The process of close reading involves both an understanding of what a particular passage is 'about' and what goes to make up its literary 'quality'. That is, you should learn to scrutinise the text as closely as possible, and be prepared to name its parts, and say what literary devices the author is using. Don't be afraid to take cognisance of even the most obvious points.

Many people, when they first encounter a piece of writing, may be vaguely aware that it has certain qualities: they can sense that it is 'good' or 'fine' writing, but they are not quite sure *why*. They are not sure *where* exactly those good qualities are located, or *how* they have been created. That is why one of the first things you need to acquire for serious literary study is a knowledge of the vocabulary, the technical language in which literature is discussed. You need to acquaint yourself with the technical vocabulary of the discipline and then go on to study how its parts work.

Close reading however is not a skill which can be developed to a sophisticated extent overnight. It requires a lot of practice in the various linguistic and literary disciplines involved – and it requires that you do a lot of reading. But the good news is that most people already *possess* the skills required. They have acquired them automatically simply through being able to read – even though they havn't been conscious of doing so. This is rather like many other things which we learn unconsciously. After all, you don't need to know the names of your leg muscles in order to walk down the street.

The list which follows in the next section is *not* a comprehensive inventory of all the critical terms you will need or the things you might look for in a piece of fiction. It is just a prompt to help us get under way. And in any case, the best way to build up your critical vocabulary is slowly and regularly – seeing the terms used in context when dealing with practical examples. You should get used to the idea of looking up and checking the meaning of terms in the same way you would any other items of vocabulary.

One important point to make about close reading is that it becomes easier if you get used to the idea of reading and *re*-reading. The Russian novelist Vladimir Nabokov (famous for *Lolita*) once observed that 'Curiously enough, one cannot read a book: one can only re–read it.' What he meant by this apparently contradictory remark is that the first time we read a book we are busy absorbing information, and we cannot *appreciate* all the subtle connections there may be between its parts – because we don't yet have the complete picture before us. Only when we read it for a second time (or even better, a third or fourth) are we in a position to assemble and compare the nuances of meaning and the significance of its details in relation to each other.

Finally, let's try to dispel a common misconception. Many people ask, when they first come into contact with close reading: 'Doesn't analysing a piece of work in close detail spoil your enjoyment of it?' The answer to this question is 'No – on the contrary – it should enhance it.' The simple fact is that we get more *out* of a piece of writing if we can appreciate all the subtleties and the intricacies which exist within it. Nabokov also suggested that 'In reading, one should notice and fondle the details.'

5 Literary terms

This section presents an introduction to some of the terms you will need for our exercises in literary appreciation. It offers a basic checklist which you can use throughout the course as a reference and an *aide-memoire*. Whenever you are asked to analyse or comment upon a passage, the checklist can be used to remind you of some of the features you might look for in it. We will be exploring the meaning and uses of these features as we go along in the study programme

Grammar. The relationships of the words in sentences, which might include such items as the use of adjectives in description, of verbs to denote action, switching between tenses to move between present and past, or any use of unusual combinations of words or phrases.

Vocabulary. The author's choice of individual words – which may be drawn from various *registers* such as slang, literary, plain speech, or journalism, and may vary from simple to complex and sophisticated.

Syntax. The arrangement and logical coherence of words in a sentence. The possibilities for re–arrangement are often used for emphasis or dramatic effect.

Figures of speech. The rhetorical devices used to give decoration and imaginative expression to literature. For example – simile, metaphor, puns, irony.

Literary devices. The devices commonly used in literature to give added depth to the work. For example – imagery, symbolism, allusion.

Tone. The author's attitude to the subject as revealed in the style and the manner of the writing.

Narrator. The person who is telling the story. This may be the author, or it may be a fictional character.

Narrative mode. This is usually either
    (a) first person singular ('I am going to tell you ...')
    (b) third person singular ('The duchess raised her head')

Narrative. The story which is being told: that is, the history of the events, characters, or whatever the narrator wishes to relate to the reader.

Characterisation. The means by which characters are depicted or created – commonly by an account of their physical or psychological characteristics and their direct speech.

Structure. The planned underlying framework or shape of a piece of work. The relationship between its parts in terms of arrangement or construction.

Theme. The underlying topic or issue, as distinct from the overt subject, with which a work deals.

Genre. The literary category or type (for instance, short story, lyric poem, or novel) to which the work belongs and with which it might be compared.

Cultural context. The historical and cultural context and the circumstances in which the work was produced, which might have some bearing on its meanings.

6 Self-assessment questions

What follow are a number of questions dealing with the technical vocabulary of literary discussion which have been mentioned in this introductory chapter. The exercise will help you make a start in looking up the meanings of such terms. To answer the questions you may need to refer to the checklist in Section 5 and the more extended glossary in Chapter Eight, which you might wish to glance through first to acquaint yourself with all these terms. Write down your answers, then check your results against the Guidance Notes at the end of the book.

    i What figure of speech is being used here? 'The young moon recurved, and shining low in the west, was like a slender shaving thrown up from a bar of gold.' (Joseph Conrad)

2 What figure of speech is being used here? 'Come into the garden, Maud, / for the black bat, Night, has flown' (Lord Tennyson)

3 Which *one* figure of speech and *two* literary devices are being used here? 'O my love is like a red, red rose' (Robert Burns)

4 What most obvious literary device is being used here? 'Fog everywhere. Fog up the river, where it flows among green aits and meadows; fog down the river, where it rolls defiled among the tiers of shipping, and the waterside pollutions of a great (and dirty) city. Fog on the Essex marshes, fog on the Kentish heights' (Charles Dickens)

5 'During the whole of a dull, dark, and soundless day in the autumn of the year, when the clouds hung oppressively low in the heavens, I had been passing alone, on horseback, through a singularly dreary tract of country; and at length found myself, as the shades of the evening drew on, within view of the melancholy House of Usher' (Edgar Allan Poe)

   (a) What literary device is most obviously being used here?
   (b) Which words create the 'atmosphere'?
   (c) Which parts of speech are 'dull', 'dark', and 'soundless'?
   (d) What part of speech is 'oppressively'?
   (e) How would you describe Poe's use of the term 'the Heavens'?

7 Course work

If you are using this study programme as part of a tutor–led course, these exercises at the end of each chapter are offered as suggestions for either classroom discussion topics or written assignments. Your tutor will offer guidance on the manner in which they can be used to develop your skills of argument and analysis. But even if you are studying alone you might use them as stimulus material. They can be regarded as exercises in making notes, or you can practise assembling your own ideas in response to the questions they raise.

1 Write a short account of your own experience of literature. Try to explain what effects books have had in your life and how your current tastes have been formed.

2 Write a short review of a book you have read recently. Imagine that you are writing a review article in a good quality news-

paper. Give a brief account of the content or the story-line, and then go on to say something about any special qualities it has, the style in which it is written, and how it might compare with other books of its type.

3 Read any one of the stories in this book, then comment on the qualities which made it enjoyable as a piece of fiction. (Try to avoid re-telling the story.)

4 Write your own short piece of imaginative prose or fiction – then, using the checklist of literary terms in Section 5, produce a close reading of your own work. Try to give a name to the various figures of speech and the literary devices you have used.

CHAPTER TWO

The basic elements of fiction

1 Introduction

We are now making a start on our first complete piece of fiction –
Arthur Conan Doyle's 'A Scandal in Bohemia'. I have chosen it as
our starting point because it represents everything that is traditional
about a short piece of fiction: there is a clear *story* to be told; it has a
plot and even *suspense*; and there is a stand-out *character* acting in a
realistic *setting*. It therefore serves as an example of what is typical in
a great deal of fiction, but I should add that it is also well written and
very entertaining.

You certainly can if you wish go straight to it now and read it for the
sake of pure enjoyment, then come back to pick up these introductory remarks and the biographical notes later. In fact when you
have developed more confidence in studying fiction I would *recommend* that you do this in order to experience your first reading of the
text uncluttered by any preconceptions. But for the time being use
the biographical note at whatever stage suits you best.

In this chapter we will be looking at some of the basic elements of
fiction – setting, characters, and story – and the emphasis of the tui-
tion notes will be on illustrating how these features are created by the
author. Then we will look at the way in which stories are told – which
is sometimes a more complex business than you might have imagined.

When you do come to read the story, don't forget to follow the
instructions on making notes (Chapter One, Section 3). Read with
pencil in hand, and make a note of anything which seems interesting
or of significance to you. 'A Scandal in Bohemia' is a very typical

Sherlock Holmes story in that it follows the pattern of establishing the detective's character and immediately posing a problem for him to solve. As the literary critic Julian Symons has remarked 'The stories often begin with the arrival of a client in trouble, and frequently [Doyle's] description of it is marked by a teasingly obscure but not necessarily criminal problem, and by a display of Holmesian intellectual fireworks'.

2 Biographical note

Arthur Conan Doyle was born in 1859 in Edinburgh and educated at Stonyhurst College in Lancashire, a public school run by Jesuits. From there he went back to Edinburgh University to study medicine, meeting in the process Doctor Joseph Bell, a consulting surgeon whose strong powers of deduction were later used as the basis for the creation of Sherlock Holmes. He also began to develop a youthful enthusiasm for writing around this time. In 1880 he signed on as ship's surgeon on an Arctic whaling expedition, then after returning several months later, completed his degree and sailed off again, this time to Africa.

He set up his first practice as a doctor in Portsmouth, and in the long periods spent waiting for patients wrote stories which were published anonymously. In 1885 he married the sister of one of his patients and the year after wrote the book in which Sherlock Holmes made his first appearance – *A Study in Scarlet*. He went on to write historical romances, but when more Sherlock Holmes stories were published in *The Strand* magazine and became increasingly popular, he gave up medicine to be a professional author.

The Sherlock Holmes phenomenon made his fame and fortune, but because he thought of himself as a 'serious novelist' he eventually killed off his by now world famous detective hero by having the villainous Professor Moriarty pull him to his death over the edge of the Reichenbach falls in the appropriately named story 'The Final Problem'. Conan Doyle travelled widely in America, Egypt, and South Africa – working for a time as a doctor in the Boer War, and in 1902 he was knighted by Edward VII for his enthusiastic contribution to the English war against the Boers.

Meanwhile the success of the Sherlock Holmes stories in America brought a renewed and very profitable demand for more. As a first move he wrote one of his best Holmes pieces – *The Hound of the Baskervilles* – but set it at a time *before* Holmes's supposed demise. The book was such an instant success however that he was forced to resurrect his hero completely, and he went on to write another series of the stories – though devotees of the cult claim that these are not quite so skilfully executed as the first.

Conan Doyle became a public figure and gave his support to a number of different causes: he stood for parliament on two occasions – both times unsuccessfully; he took up the cases of people he felt had been unjustly treated by the law; and he gave money and time to advance the cause of spiritualism. In 1912 he published his second most successful work which does *not* include Sherlock Holmes – *The Lost World*, a novel of adventure featuring a prehistoric world of dinosaurs and mammoths discovered in the jungles of South America.

During the period of 1914–1918 he occupied himself producing patriotic tracts, wrote a six-volume history of the war, and gradually transferred most of his attention to works of non-fiction. Then during the last fifteen to twenty years of his life he devoted himself almost entirely to the promotion of spiritualism. At that time this phenomenon was in its heyday of seances in which the dead were summoned back at public meetings, psychic mediums extruded ectoplasm from their mouths, and photographs of ghosts and fairies were seriously offered as evidence of the existence of a 'spirit world'. Despite the fact that these events were exposed as frauds by Harry Houdini – the escapologist whom he met and befriended in 1920 – Conan Doyle continued in his blind belief and damaged his public reputation with publications such as *The Coming of the Fairies* in 1922. In his last years he toured Australia, the United States, and Scandinavia, preaching the spiritualist cause. When he died in 1930 his grave was inscribed:

STEEL TRUE

BLADE STRAIGHT

ARTHUR CONAN DOYLE

KNIGHT

PATRIOT, PHYSICIAN & MAN OF LETTERS

A SCANDAL IN BOHEMIA
ARTHUR CONAN DOYLE

I

To Sherlock Holmes she is always *the* woman. I have seldom heard him mention her under any other name. In his eyes she eclipses and predominates the whole of her sex. It was not that he felt any emotion akin to love for Irene Adler. All emotions, and that one particularly, were abhorrent to his cold, precise, but admirably balanced mind. He was, I take it, the most perfect reasoning and observing machine that the world has seen: but, as a lover, he would have placed himself in a false position. He never spoke of the softer passions, save with a gibe and a sneer. They were admirable things for the observer – excellent for drawing the veil from men's motives and actions. But for the trained reasoner to admit such intrusions into his own delicate and finely adjusted temperament was to introduce a distracting factor which might throw a doubt upon all his mental results. Grit in a sensitive instrument, or a crack in one of his own high-power lenses, would not be more disturbing than a strong emotion in a nature such as his. And yet there was but one woman to him, and that woman was the late Irene Adler, of dubious and questionable memory.

I had seen little of Holmes lately. My marriage had drifted us away from each other. My own complete happiness, and the home-centred interests which rise up around the man who first finds himself master of his own establishment, were sufficient to absorb all my attention; while Holmes, who loathed every form of society with his whole Bohemian soul, remained in our lodgings in Baker Street, buried among his old books, and alternating from week to week between cocaine and ambition, the drowsiness of the drug, and the fierce energy of his own keen nature. He was still, as ever, deeply attracted by the study of crime, and occupied his immense faculties and extraordinary powers of observation in following out those clues, and clearing up those mysteries, which had been abandoned as hopeless by the official police. From time to time I heard some vague account of his doings: of his summons to Odessa in the case of the Trepoff murder, of his clearing up of the singular tragedy of the Atkinson brothers at Trincomalee, and finally of the mission which he had accomplished so delicately and successfully for the reigning family of Holland. Beyond these signs of his activity, however, which I merely shared with all the readers of the daily press, I knew little of my former friend and companion.

One night – it was on the 20th of March, 1888 – I was returning from a journey to a patient (for I had now returned to civil practice), when my way led me through Baker Street. As I passed the well-remembered door, which must always be associated in my mind with my wooing, and with the dark incidents of the Study in Scarlet, I was seized with a keen desire to see

Holmes again, and to know how he was employing his extraordinary powers. His rooms were brilliantly lit, and, even as I looked up, I saw his tall spare figure pass twice in

a dark silhouette against the blind. He was pacing the room swiftly, eagerly, with his head sunk upon his chest, and his hands clasped behind him. To me, who knew his every mood and habit, his attitude and manner told their own story. He was at work again. He had risen out of his drug-created dreams, and was hot upon the scent of some new problem. I rang the bell, and was shown up to the chamber which had formerly been in part my own.

His manner was not effusive. It seldom was; but he was glad, I think, to see me. With hardly a word spoken, but with a kindly eye, he waved me to an arm-chair, threw across his case of cigars, and indicated a spirit case and a gasogene in the corner. Then he stood before the fire, and looked me over in his singular introspective fashion.

'Wedlock suits you,' he remarked. 'I think, Watson, that you have put on seven and a half pounds since I saw you.'

'Seven,' I answered.

'Indeed, I should have thought a little more. Just a trifle more, I fancy, Watson. And in practice again, I observe. You did not tell me that you intended to go into harness.'

'Then, how do you know?'

'I see it, I deduce it. How do I know that you have been getting yourself very wet lately, and that you have a most clumsy and careless servant girl?'

'My dear Holmes,' said I, 'this is too much. You would certainly have been burned had you lived a few centuries ago. It is true that I had a country walk on Thursday and came home in a dreadful mess; but, as I have changed my clothes, I can't imagine how you deduce it. As to Mary Jane, she is incorrigible, and my wife has given her notice; but there again I fail to see how you work it out.'

He chuckled to himself and rubbed his long nervous hands together.

'It is simplicity itself,' said he; 'my eyes tell me that on the inside of your left shoe, just where the firelight strikes it, the leather is scored by six almost parallel cuts. Obviously they have been caused by some one who has very carelessly scraped round the edges of the sole in order to remove crusted mud from it. Hence, you see, my double deduction that you had been out in vile weather, and that you had a particularly malignant boot-slitting specimen of the London slavey. As to your practice, if a gentleman walks into my rooms smelling of iodoform, with a black mark of nitrate of silver upon his right forefinger, and a bulge on the side of his top hat to show where he has secreted his stethoscope, I must be dull indeed if I do not pronounce him to be an active member of the medical profession.'

I could not help laughing at the ease with which he explained his process of deduction. 'When I hear you give your reasons,' I remarked, 'the thing always appears to me to be so ridiculously simple that I could easily do it myself, though at each successive instance of your reasoning I am baffled, until you explain your process. And yet I believe that my eyes are as good as yours.'

'Quite so,' he answered, lighting a cigarette, and throwing hlmself down into an arm-chair. 'You see, but you do not observe. The distinction is clear. For example, you have frequently seen the steps which lead up from the hall to this room.'

'Frequently.'

'How often?'

'Well, some hundreds of times.'

'Then how many are there?'

'How many! I don't know.'

'Quite so! You have not observed. And yet you have seen. That is just my point. Now, I know that there are seventeen steps, because I have both seen and observed. By the way, since you are interested in these little problems, and since you are good enough to chronicle one or two of my trifling experiences, you may be interested in this.' He threw over a sheet of thick pink-tinted note-paper which had been lying open upon the table. 'It came by the last post,' said he. 'Read it aloud.'

The note was undated, and without either signature or address.

'There will call upon you to-night, at a quarter to eight o'clock,' it said, 'a gentleman who desires to consult you upon a matter of the very deepest moment. Your recent services to one of the Royal Houses of Europe have shown that you are one who may safely be trusted with matters which are of an importance which can hardly be exaggerated. This account of you we have from all quarters received. Be in your chamber then at that hour, and do not take it amiss if your visitor wear a mask.'

'This is indeed a mystery,' I remarked. 'What do you imagine that it means?'

'I have no data yet. It is a capital mistake to theorize before one has data. Insensibly one begins to twist facts to suit theories, instead of theories to suit facts. But the note itself. What do you deduce from it?'

I carefully examined the writing, and the paper upon which it was written.

'The man who wrote it was presumably well-to-do,' I remarked, endeavouring to imitate my companion's processes.

'Such paper could not be bought under half a crown a packet. It is peculiarly strong and stiff.'

'Peculiar – that is the very word,' said Holmes. 'It is not an English paper at all. Hold it up to the light.'

I did so, and saw a large E with a small g, a P, and a large G with a small t woven into the texture of the paper.

'What do you make of that?' asked Holmes.

'The name of the maker, no doubt; or his monogram, rather.'

'Not at all. The G with the small t stands for "Gesellschaft" which is the German for "Company". It is a customary contraction like our "Co.". P, of course, stands for "Papier". Now for the Eg. Let us glance at our Continental

Gazetteer.' He took down a heavy brown volume from his shelves. 'Eglow Eglonitz—here we are, Egria. It is in a German-speaking country – in Bohemia, not far from Carlsbad. "Remarkable as being the scene of the death of Wallenstein, and for its numerous glass factories and paper mills." Ha, ha, my boy what do you make of that?' His eyes sparkled, and he sent up a great blue triumphant cloud from his cigarette.

'The paper was made in Bohemia,' I said.

'Precisely. And the man who wrote the note is a German. Do you note the peculiar construction of the sentence – "This account of you we have from all quarters received." A Frenchman or Russian could not have written that. It is the German who is so uncourteous to his verbs. It only remains, therefore to discover what is wanted by this German who writes upon Bohemian paper, and prefers wearing a mask to showing his face. And here he comes, if I am not mistaken, to resolve all our doubts.'

As he spoke there was the sharp sound of horses' hoofs and grating wheels against the kerb, followed by a sharp pull at the bell. Holmes whistled.

'A pair by the sound,' said he. 'Yes,' he continued, glancing out of the window. 'A nice little brougham and a pair of beauties. A hundred and fifty guineas apiece. There's money in this case, Watson if there is nothing else.'

'I think that I had better go, Holmes.'

'Not a bit, Doctor. Stay where you are. I am lost without my Boswell. And this promises to be interesting. It would be a pity to miss it.'

'But your client –

'Never mind him. I may want your help, and so may he. Here he comes. Sit down in that arm-chair, Doctor, and give us your best attention.'

A slow and heavy step, which had been heard upon the stairs and in the passage, paused immediately outside the door. Then there was a loud and authoritative tap.

'Come in!' said Holmes.

A man entered who could hardly have been less than six feet six inches in height, with the chest and limbs of a Hercules. His dress was rich with a richness which would, in England, be looked upon as akin to bad taste. Heavy bands of astrakhan were slashed across the sleeves and fronts of his double-breasted coat, while the deep blue cloak which was thrown over his shoulders was lined with flame-coloured silk, and secured at the neck with a brooch which consisted of a single flaming beryl. Boots which extended half-way up his calves, and which were trimmed at the tops with a rich brown fur, completed the impression of barbaric opulence which was suggested by his whole appearance. He carried a broadbrimmed hat in his hand, while he wore across the upper part of his face, extending down past the cheek-bones, a black vizard mask, which he had apparently adjusted that very moment, for his hand was still raised to it as he entered. From the lower part of the face he appeared to be a man of strong character, with a thick, hanging lip, and a long straight chin, suggestive of resolution pushed to the length of obstinacy.

'You had my note?' he asked, with a deep, harsh voice and a strongly marked German accent. 'I told you that I would call.' He looked from one to the other of us, as if uncertain which to address. 'Pray take a seat,' said Holmes.

'This is my friend and colleague, Dr Watson, who is occasionally good enough to help me in my cases. Whom have I the honour to address?'

'You may address me as the Count von Kramm, a Bohemian nobleman. I understand that this gentleman, your friend, is a man of honour and discretion, whom I may trust with a matter of the most extreme importance. If not, I should much prefer to communicate with you alone.'

I rose to go, but Holmes caught me by the wrist and pushed me back into my chair. 'It is both, or none,' said he. 'You may say before this gentleman anything which you may say to me.'

The Count shrugged his broad shoulders. 'Then I must begin,' said he, 'by binding you both to absolute secrecy for two years, at the end of that time the matter will be of no importance. At present it is not too much to say that it is of such weight that it may have an influence upon European history.'

'I promise,' said Holmes.

'And I.'

'You will excuse this mask,' continued our strange visitor. 'The august person who employs me wishes his agent to be unknown to you, and I may confess at once that the title by which I have just called myself is not exactly my own.'

'I was aware of it,' said Holmes dryly.

'The circumstances are of great delicacy, and every precaution has to be taken to quench what might grow to be an immense scandal and seriously compromise one of the reigning families of Europe. To speak plainly, the matter implicates the great House of Ormstein, hereditary kings of Bohemia.'

'I was also aware of that,' murmured Holmes, settling himself down in his arm-chair, and closing his eyes.

Our visitor glanced with some apparent surprise at the languid, lounging figure of the man who had been no doubt depicted to him as the most incisive reasoner, and most energetic agent in Europe. Holmes slowly reopened his eyes, and looked impatiently at his gigantic client.

'If your Majesty would condescend to state your case,' he remarked, 'I should be better able to advise you.'

The man sprang from his chair, and paced up and down the room in uncontrollable agitation. Then, with a gesture of desperation, he tore the mask from his face and hurled it upon the ground. 'You are right,' he cried, 'I am the King. Why should I attempt to conceal it?'

'Why, indeed?' murmured Holmes. 'Your Majesty had not spoken before I was aware that I was addressing Wilhelm Gottsreich Sigismond von Ormstein, Grand Duke of Cassel-Felstein, and hereditary King of Bohemia.'

'But you can understand,' said our strange visitor, sitting down once more and passing his hand over his high, white forehead, 'you can understand that I am not accustomed to doing such business in my own person. Yet the matter was so delicate that I could not confide it to an agent without putting myself in his power. I have come *incognito* from Prague for the purpose of consulting you.'

'Then, pray consult,' said Holmes, shutting his eyes once more.

'The facts are briefly these: Some five years ago, during a lengthy visit to Warsaw, I made the acquaintance of the well-known adventuress Irene Adler. The name is no doubt familiar to you.'

'Kindly look her up in my index, Doctor,' murmured Holmes, without opening his eyes. For many years he had adopted a system of docketing all paragraphs concerning men and things, so that it was difficult to name a subject or a person on which he could not at once furnish information. In this case I found her biography sandwiched in between that of a Hebrew Rabbi and that of a staff-commander who had written a monograph upon the deep-sea fishes.

'Let me see,' said Holmes. 'Hum! Born in New Jersey in the year 1858. Contralto—hum! La Scala, hum! Prima donna Imperial Opera of Warsaw – Yes! Retired from operatic stage – ha! Living in London – quite so! Your Majesty, as I understand, became entangled with this young person, wrote her some compromising letters, and is now desirous of getting those letters back.'

'Precisely so. But how –'

'Was there a secret marriage?'

'None.'

'No legal papers or certificates?'

'None.'

'Then I fail to follow Your Majesty. If this young person should produce her letters for blackmailing or other purposes, how is she to prove their authenticity?'

'There is the writing.'

'Pooh, pooh! Forgery.'

'My private note-paper.'

'Stolen.'

'My own seal.'

'Imitated.'

'My photograph.'

'Bought.'

'We were both in the photograph.'

'Oh, dear! That is very bad! Your Majesty has indeed committed an indiscretion.'

'I was mad – insane.'

'You have compromised yourself seriously.'

'I was only Crown Prince then. I was young. I am but thirty now.'

'It must be recovered.'

'We have tried and failed.'

'Your Majesty must pay. It must be bought.'

'She will not sell.'

'Stolen, then.'

'Five attempts have been made. Twice burglars in my pay ransacked her house. Once we diverted her luggage when she travelled. Twice she has been waylaid. There has been no result.'

'No sign of it?'

'Absolutely none.'

Holmes laughed. 'It is quite a pretty little problem,' said he.

'But a very serious one to me,' returned the King, reproachfully.

'Very, indeed. And what does she propose to do with the photograph?'

'To ruin me.'

'But how?'

'I am about to be married.'

'So I have heard.'

'To Clotilde Lothman von Saxe-Meningen, second daughter of the King of Scandinavia. You may know the strict principles of her family. She is herself the very soul of delicacy. A shadow of a doubt as to my conduct would bring the matter to an end.'

'And Irene Adler?'

'Threatens to send them the photograph. And she will do it. I know that she will do it. You do not know her, but she has a soul of steel. She has the face of the most beautiful of women, and the mind of the most resolute of men. Rather than I should marry another woman, there are no lengths to which she would not go – none.'

'You are sure that she has not sent it yet?'

'I am sure.'

'And why?'

'Because she has said that she would send it on the day when the betrothal was publicly proclaimed. That will be next Monday.'

'Oh, then, we have three days yet,' said Holmes, with a yawn. 'That is very fortunate, as I have one or two matters of importance to look into just at present. Your Majesty will, of course, stay in London for the present?'

'Certainly. You will find me at the Langham, under the name of the Count von Kramm.'

'Then I shall drop you a line to let you know how we progress.'

'Pray do so. I shall be all anxiety.'

'Then, as to money?'

'You have *carte blanche*.'

'Absolutely?'

'I tell you that I would give one of the provinces of my kingdom to have that photograph.'

'And for present expenses?'

The King took a heavy chamois leather bag from under his cloak, and laid it on the table.

'There are three hundred pounds in gold, and seven hundred in notes,' he said.

Holmes scribbled a receipt upon a sheet of his note-book, and handed it to him.

'And mademoiselle's address?' he asked.

'Is Briony Lodge, Serpentine Avenue, St John's Wood.'

Holmes took a note of it. 'One other question,' said he. 'Was the photograph a cabinet?'

'It was.'

'Then, good night, Your Majesty, and I trust that we shall soon have some good news for you. And good night, Watson,' he added, as the wheels of the Royal brougham rolled down the street. 'If you will be good enough to call to-morrow afternoon, at three o'clock, I should like to chat this little matter over with you.'

II

At three o'clock precisely I was at Baker Street, but Holmes had not yet returned. The landlady informed me that he had left the house shortly after eight o'clock in the morning. I sat down beside the fire, however, with the intention of awaiting him, however long he might be. I was already deeply interested in his inquiry, for, though it was surrounded by none of the grim and strange features which were associated with the two crimes which I have elsewhere recorded, still, the nature of the case and the exalted station of his client gave it a character of its own. Indeed, apart from the nature of the investigation which my friend had on hand, there was something in his masterly grasp of a situation, and his keen, incisive reasoning, which made it a pleasure to me to study his system of work, and to follow the quick, subtle methods by which he disentangled the most inextricable mysteries. So accustomed was I to his invariable success that the very possibility of his failing had ceased to enter into my head.

It was close upon four before the door opened, and a drunken-looking groom, ill-kempt and side-whiskered with an inflamed face and disreputable clothes, walked into the room. Accustomed as I was to my friend's amazing powers in the use of disguises, I had to look three times before I was certain that it was indeed he. With a nod he vanished into the bedroom, whence he emerged in five minutes tweed-suited and respectable, as of old. Putting his hands into his pockets, he stretched out his legs in front of the fire, and laughed heartily for some minutes.

'Well, really!' he cried, and then he choked; and laughed again until he was obliged to lie back, limp and helpless, in the chair.

'What is it?'

'It's quite too funny. I am sure you could never guess how I employed my morning, or what I ended by doing.'

'I can't imagine. I suppose that you have been watching the habits, and perhaps the house, of Miss Irene Adler.'

'Quite so, but the sequel was rather unusual. I will tell you, however. I left the house a little after eight o'clock this morning, in the character of a groom out of work. There is a wonderful sympathy and freemasonry among horsey men. Be one of them, and you will know all that there is to know. I soon found Briony Lodge. It is a bijou villa, with a garden at the back, but built out in front right up to the road, two stories. Chubb lock to the door. Large sitting-room on the right side, well furnished, with long windows almost to the floor, and those preposterous English window fasteners which a child could open. Behind there was nothing remarkable, save that the passage window could be reached from the top of the coach-house. I walked round it and examined it closely from every point of view, but without noting anything else of interest.

'I then lounged down the street, and found, as I expected, that there was a mews in a lane which runs down by one wall of the garden. I lent the ostlers a hand in rubbing down their horses, and I received in exchange twopence, a glass of halfand-half, two fills of shag tobacco and as much information as I could desire about Miss Adler, to say nothing of half a dozen other people in the neighbourhood in whom I was not in the least interested, but whose biographies I was compelled to listen to.'

'And what of Irene Adler?' I asked.

'Oh, she has turned all the men's heads down in that part. She is the daintiest thing under a bonnet on this planet. So say the Serpentine Mews, to a man. She lives quietly, sings at concerts, drives out at five every day, and returns at seven sharp for dinner. Seldom goes out at other times, except when she sings. Has only one male visitor, but a good deal of him. He is dark, handsome, and dashing; never calls less than once a day, and often twice. He is a Mr Godfrey Norton, of the Inner Temple. See the advantages of a cabman as a confidant. They had driven him home a dozen times from Serpentine Mews, and knew all about him. When I had listened to all that they had to tell, I began to walk up and down near Briony Lodge once more, and to think over my plan of campaign.

'This Godfrey Norton was evidently an important factor in the matter. He was a lawyer. That sounded ominous. What was the relation between them, and what the object of his repeated visits? Was she his client, his friend, or his mistress? If the former, she had probably transferred the photograph to his keeping. If the latter, it was less likely. On the issue of this question depended whether I should continue my work at Briony Lodge, or turn my attention to the gentleman's chambers in the Temple. It was a delicate point, and it widened the field of my inquiry. I fear that I bore you with these details, but I have to let you see my little difficulties, if you are to understand the situation.'

'I am following you closely,' I answered.

'I was still balancing the matter in my mind when a hansom cab drove up to Briony Lodge, and a gentleman sprang out. He was a remarkably handsome man, dark, aquiline, and moustached – evidently the man of whom I had heard. He appeared to be in a great hurry, shouted to the cabman to wait, and brushed past the maid who opened the door with the air of a man who was thoroughly at home.

'He was in the house about half an hour, and I could catch glimpses of him, in the windows of the sitting-room, pacing up and down, talking excitedly and waving his arms. Of her I could see nothing. Presently he emerged, looking even more flurried than before. As he stepped up to the cab, he pulled a gold watch from his pocket and looked at it earnestly. "Drive like the devil," he shouted, "first to Gross and Hankey's in Regent Street, and then to the church of St Monica in the Edgware Road. Half a guinea if you do it in twenty minutes!'

'Away they went, and I was just wondering whether I should not do well to follow them, when up the lane came a neat little landau, the coachman with his coat only half buttoned, and his tie under his ear, while all the tags of his harness were sticking out of the buckles. It hadn't pulled up before she shot out of the hall door and into it. I only caught a glimpse of her at the moment, but she was a lovely woman, with a face that a man might die for.

'"The Church of St Monica, John," she cried, "and half a sovereign if you reach it in twenty minutes."

'This was quite too good to lose, Watson. I was just balancing whether I should run for it, or whether I should perch behind her landau, when a cab came through the street. The driver looked twice at such a shabby fare; but I jumped in before he could object. "The Church of St Monica," said I, "and half a sovereign if you reach it in twenty minutes." It was twenty-five minutes to twelve, and of course it was clear enough what was in the wind.

'My cabby drove fast. I don't think I ever drove faster, but the others were there before us. The cab and the landau with their steaming horses were in front of the door when I arrived. I paid the man and hurried into the church. There was not a soul there save the two whom I had followed, and a surpliced clergyman, who seemed to be expostulating with them. They were all three standing in a knot in front of the altar. I lounged up the side aisle like any other idler who has dropped into a church. Suddenly, to my surprise, the three at the altar faced round to me, and Godfrey Norton came running as hard as he could towards me.

'"Thank God!" he cried. "You'll do. Come! Come!"

'"What then?" I asked.

'"Come. man, come. only three minutes, or it won't be legal."

'I was half dragged up to the altar, and before I knew where I was, I found myself mumbling responses which were whispered in my ear, and vouching for things of which I knew nothing, and generally assisting in the secure tying up of Irene Adler, spinster, to Godfrey Norton, bachelor. It was all done in an instant, and there was the gentleman thanking me on the one side and the lady on the other, while the clergyman beamed on me in front. It was the most preposterous position in which I ever found myself in my life, and it was the thought of it that started me laughing just now. It seems that there had been some informality about their licence, that the clergyman absolutely refused to marry them without a witness of some sort, and that my lucky appearance saved the bridegroom from having to sally out into the streets in search of a best man. The bride gave me a sovereign, and I mean to wear it on my watch-chain in memory of the occasion.'

'This is a very unexpected turn of affairs,' said I; 'and what then?'

'Well, I found my plans very seriously menaced. It looked as if the pair might take an immediate departure, and so necessitate very prompt and energetic measures on my part. At the church door, however, they separated, he driving back to the Temple, and she to her own house. "I shall drive out in the Park at five as usual," she said as she left him. I heard no more. They drove away in different directions, and I went off to make my own arrangements.'

'Which are?'

'Some cold beef and a glass of beer,' he answered, ringing the bell. 'I have been too busy to think of food, and I am likely to be busier still this evening. By the way, Doctor, I shall want your co-operation.'

'I shall be delighted.'

'You don't mind breaking the law?'

'Not in the least.'

'Nor running a chance of arrest?'

'Not in a good cause.'

'Oh, the cause is excellent!'

'Then I am your man.'

'I was sure that I might rely on you.'

'But what is it you wish?'

'When Mrs Turner has brought in the tray I will make it clear to you. Now,' he said, as he turned hungrily on the simple fare that our landlady had provided, 'I must discuss it while I eat, for I have not much time. It is nearly five now. In two hours we must be on the scene of action. Miss Irene, or Madame, rather, returns from her drive at seven. We must be at Briony Lodge to meet her.'

'And what then?'

'You must leave that to me. I have already arranged what is to occur. There is only one point on which I must insist. You must not interfere, come what may. You understand?'

'I am to be neutral?'

'To do nothing whatever. There will probably be some small unpleasantness. Do not join in it. It will end in my being conveyed into the house. Four or five minutes afterwards the sitting-room window will open. You are to station yourself close to that open window.'

'Yes.'

'You are to watch me, for I will be visible to you.'

'Yes.'

'And when I raise my hand – so – you will throw into the room what I give you to throw, and will, at the same time, raise the cry of fire. You quite follow me?'

'Entirely.'

'It is nothing very formidable,' he said, taking a long cigar-shaped roll from his pocket. 'It is an ordinary plumber's smoke rocket, fitted with a cap at either end to make it selflighting. Your task is confined to that. When you raise your cry of fire, it will be taken up by quite a number of people. You may then walk to the end of the street, and I will rejoin you in ten minutes. I hope that I have made myself clear?'

'I am to remain neutral, to get near the window, to watch you, and, at the signal, to throw in this object, then to raise the cry of fire, and to await you at the corner of the street.'

'Precisely.'

'Then you may entirely rely on me.'

'That is excellent. I think perhaps it is almost time that I prepared for the new rôle I have to play.'

He disappeared into his bedroom, and returned in a few minutes in the character of an amiable and simple-minded Nonconformist clergyman. His broad black hat, his baggy trousers, his white tie, his sympathetic smile, and general look of peering and benevolent curiosity, were such as Mr John Hare alone could have equalled. It was not merely that Holmes changed his costume. His expression, his manner, his very soul seemed to vary with every fresh part that he assumed. The stage lost a fine actor, even as science lost an acute reasoner, when he became a specialist in crime.

It was a quarter past six when we left Baker Street, and it still wanted ten minutes to the hour when we found ourselves in Serpentine Avenue. It was already dusk, and the lamps were just being lighted as we paced up and down in front of Briony Lodge, waiting for the coming of its occupant. The house was just such as I had pictured it from Sherlock Holmes' succinct description, but the locality appeared to be less private than I expected. On the contrary, for a small street in a quiet neighbourhood, it was remarkably animated. There was a group of shabbily-dressed men smoking and laughing in a corner, a scissors-grinder with his wheel, two guardsmen who were flirting with a nurse-girl, and several well-dressed young men who were lounging up and down with cigars in their mouths.

'You see,' remarked Holmes, as we paced to and fro in front of the house, 'this marriage rather simplifies matters. The photograph becomes a double-edged weapon now. The chances are that she would be as averse to its being seen by Mr Godfrey Norton, as our client is to its coming to the eyes of his Princess. Now the question is – Where are we to find the photograph?'

'Where, indeed?'

'It is most unlikely that she carries it about with her. It is cabinet size. Too large for easy concealment about a woman's dress. She knows that the King is capable of having her waylaid and searched. Two attempts of the sort have already been made. We may take it then that she does not carry it about with her.'

'Where, then?'

'Her banker or her lawyer. There is that double possibility. But I am inclined to think neither. Women are naturally secretive, and they like to do their own secreting. Why should she hand it over to anyone else? She could trust her own guardianship, but she could not tell what indirect or political influence might be brought to bear upon a business man. Besides, remember that she had resolved to use it within a few days. It must be where she can lay her hands upon it. It must be in her own house.'

'But it has twice been burgled.'

'Pshaw! They did not know how to look.'

'But how will you look?'

'I will not look.'

'What then?'

'I will get her to show me.'

'But she will refuse.'

'She will not be able to. But I hear the rumble of wheels. It is her carriage. Now carry out my orders to the letter.'

As he spoke, the gleam of the sidelights of a carriage came round the curve of the avenue. It was a smart little landau which rattled up to the door of Briony Lodge. As it pulled up, one of the loafing men at the corner dashed forward to open the door in the hope of earning a copper, but was elbowed away by another loafer who had rushed up with the same intention. A fierce quarrel broke out, which was increased by the two guardsmen, who took sides with one of the loungers, and by the scissors-grinder, who was equally hot upon the other side. A blow was struck, and in an instant the lady, who had stepped from her carriage, was the centre of a little knot of flushed and struggling men who struck savagely at each other with their fists and sticks. Holmes dashed into the crowd to protect the lady; but just as he reached her, he gave a cry and dropped to the ground, with the blood running freely down his face. At his fall the guardsmen took to their heels in one direction and the loungers in the other, while a number of better dressed people who had watched the scuffle without taking part in it, crowded in to help the lady and to attend to the injured man. Irene Adler, as I will still call her, had hurried up the steps; but she stood at the top with her superb figure outlined against the lights of the hall, looking back into the street.

'Is the poor gentleman much hurt?' she asked.

'He is dead,' cried several voices.

'No, no, there's life in him,' shouted another. 'But he'll be gone before you can get him to hospital.'

'He's a brave fellow,' said a woman. 'They would have had the lady's purse and watch if it hadn't been for him. They were a gang, and a rough one, too. Ah, he's breathing now.'

'He can't lie in the street. May we bring him in, marm?'

'Surely. Bring him into the sitting-room. There is a comfortable sofa. This way, please!'

Slowly and solemnly he was borne into Briony Lodge, and laid out in the principal room, while I still observed the proceedings from my post by the window. The lamps had been lit, but the blinds had not been drawn, so that I could see Holmes as he lay upon the couch. I do not know whether he was seized with com- punction at that moment for the part he was playing, but I know that I never felt more heartily ashamed of myself in my life than when I saw the beautiful creature against whom I was conspiring, or the grace and kindliness with which she waited upon the injured man. And yet it would be the blackest treachery to Holmes to draw back now from the part which he had entrusted to me. I hardened my heart and took the smoke rocket from under my ulster. After all, I thought, we are not injuring her. We are but preventing her from injuring another.

Holmes had sat up upon the couch, and I saw him motion like a man who is in want of air. A maid rushed across and threw open the window. At the same instant I saw him raise his hand, and at the signal I tossed my rocket into the room with a cry of 'Fire'. The word was no sooner out of my mouth than the whole crowd of spectators, well dressed and ill – gentlemen, ostlers, and servant maids – joined in a general shriek of 'Fire'. Thick clouds of smoke curled into the room, and out at the open window. I caught a glimpse of rushing figures, and a moment later the voice of Holmes from within, assuring them that it was a false alarm. Slipping through the shouting crowd I made my way to the corner of the street, and in ten minutes was rejoiced to find my friend's arm in mine, and to get away from the scene of the uproar. He walked swiftly and in silence for some few minutes, until we had turned down one of the quiet streets which lead towards the Edgware Road.

'You did it very nicely, Doctor,' he remarked. 'Nothing could have been better. It is all right.'

'You have the photograph!'

'I know where it is.'

'And how did you find out?'

'She showed me, as I told you she would.'

'I am still in the dark.'

'I do not wish to make a mystery,' said he, laughing. 'The matter was perfectly simple. You, of course, saw that every one in the street was an accomplice. They were all engaged for the evening.'

'I guessed as much.'

'Then, when the row broke out, I had a little moist red paint in the palm of my hand. I rushed forward, fell down, clapped my hand to my face, and became a piteous spectacle. It is an old trick.'

'That also I could fathom.'

'Then they carried me in. She was bound to have me in. What else could she do? And into her sitting-room which was the very room which I suspected. It lay between that and her bedroom, and I was determined to see which. They laid me on a couch, I motioned for air, they were compelled to open the window and you had your chance.'

'How did that help you?'

'It was all-important. When a woman thinks that her house is on fire, her instinct is at once to rush to the thing which she values most. It is a perfectly overpowering impulse, and I have more than once taken advantage of it. In the case of the Darlington Substitution Scandal it was of use to me, and also in the Arnsworth Castle business. A married woman grabs at her baby – an unmarried one reaches for her jewel box. Now it was clear to me that our lady of to-day had nothing in the house more precious to her than what we are in quest of. She would rush to secure it. The alarm of fire was admirably done. The smoke and shouting was enough to shake nerves of steel. She responded beautifully. The photograph is in a recess behind a sliding panel just above the right bell-pull. She was there in an instant, and I caught a glimpse of it as she half drew it out. When I cried out that it was a false alarm she replaced it, glanced at the rocket, rushed from the room, and I have not seen her since. I rose, and, making my excuses, escaped from the house, I hesitated whether to attempt to secure the photograph at once; but the coachman had come in, and as he was watching me narrowly, it seemed safer to wait. A little over-precipitance may ruin all.'

'And now?' I asked.

'Our quest is practically finished. I shall call with the King to-morrow, and with you, if you care to come with us. We will be shown into the sitting-room to wait for the lady, but it is probable that when she comes she may find neither us nor the photograph. It might be a satisfaction to His Majesty to regain it with his own hands.'

'And when will you call?'

'At eight in the morning. She will not be up, so that we shall have a clear field. Besides, we must be prompt, for this marriage may mean a complete change in her life and habits. I must wire to the King without delay.'

We had reached Baker Street, and had stopped at the door. He was searching his pockets for the key, when some one passing said:

'Good night, Mister Sherlock Holmes.'

There were several people on the pavement at the time, but the greeting appeared to come from a slim youth in an ulster who had hurried by.

'I've heard that voice before,' said Holmes, staring the dimly lit street. 'Now, I wonder who the deuce that could have been.'

III

I slept at Baker Street that night, and we were engaged upon our toast and coffee when the King of Bohemia rushed into the room.

'You have really got it!' he cried, grasping Sherlock Holmes by either shoulder, and looking eagerly into his face.

'Not yet.'

'But you have hopes?'

'I have hopes.'

'Then, come. I am all impatience to be gone.'

'We must have a cab.'

'No, my brougham is waiting.'

'Then that will simplify matters.'

We descended, and started off once more for Briony Lodge.

'Irene Adler is married,' remarked Holmes.

'Married! When?'

'Yesterday.'

'But to whom?'

'To an English lawyer named Norton.'

'But she could not love him?'

'I am in hopes that she does.'

'And why in hopes?'

'Because it would spare Your Majesty all fear of future annoyance. If the lady loves her husband, she does not love Your Majesty. If she does not love Your Majesty there is no reason why she should interfere with Your Majesty's plan.'

'It is true. And yet – ! Well! I wish she had been of my own station! What a queen she would have made!' He relapsed into a moody silence which was not broken until we drew up in Serpentine Avenue.

The door of Briony Lodge was open, and an elderly woman stood upon the steps. She watched us with a sardonic eye as we stepped from the brougham.

'Mr Sherlock Holmes, I believe?' said she.

'I am Mr Holmes,' answered my companion, looking at her with a questioning and rather startled gaze.

'Indeed! My mistress told me that you were likely to call. She left this morning with her husband, by the 5.15, train from Charing Cross, for the Continent.'

'What!' Sherlock Holmes staggered back, white with chagrin and surprise. 'Do you mean that she has left England?'

'Never to return.'

'And the papers?' asked the King hoarsely. 'All is lost.'

'We shall see.' He pushed past the servant, and rushed into the drawing-room, followed by the King and myself. The furniture was scattered about in every direction, with dismantled shelves, and open drawers, as if the lady had hurriedly ransacked them before her flight. Holmes rushed at the bell-pull, tore back a small sliding shutter, and, plunging in his hand, pulled out a photograph and a letter. The photograph was of Irene Adler herself in evening dress, the letter was superscribed to 'Sherlock Holmes, Esq. To be left till called for.' My friend tore it open and we all three read it together. It was dated at midnight of the preceding night, and ran in this way:

My Dear Mr Sherlock Holmes, – You really did it very well. You took me in completely. Until after the alarm of fire, I had not a suspicion. But then, when I found how I had betrayed myself, I began to think. I had been warned against you months ago. I had been told that if the King employed an agent, it would certainly be you. And your address had been given me. Yet, with all this, you made me reveal what you wanted to know. Even after I became suspicious, I found it hard to think evil of such a dear, kind old clergyman But, you know, I have been trained as an actress myself. Male costume is nothing new to me. I often take advantage of the freedom which it gives. I sent John, the coachman, to watch you, ran upstairs, got into my walking clothes, as I call them, and came down just as you departed.

Well, I followed you to your door, and so made sure that I was really an object of interest to the celebrated Mr Sherlock Holmes. Then I, rather imprudently, wished you goodnight, and started for the Temple to see my husband.

We both thought the best resource was flight when pursued by so formidable an antagonist; so you will find the nest empty when you call to-morrow. As to the photograph, your client may rest in peace. I love and am loved by a better man than he. The King may do what he will without hindrance from one whom he has cruelly wronged. I keep it only to safeguard myself, and to preserve a weapon which will always secure me from any steps which he might take in the future. I leave a photograph which he might care to possess; and I remain, dear Mr Sherlock Holmes, very truly

IRENE NORTON, _née_ ADLER

'What a woman – oh, what a woman!' cried the King of Bohemia, when we had all three read this epistle. 'Did I not tell you how quick and resolute she was? Would she not have made an admirable queen? Is it not a pity she was not on my level?'

'From what I have seen of the lady, she seems, indeed, to be on a very different level to Your Majesty,' said Holmes coldly. 'I am sorry that I have not been able to bring Your Majesty's business to a more successful conclusion.'

'On the contrary, my dear sir,' cried the King. 'Nothing could be more successful. I know that her word is inviolate. The photograph is now as safe as if it were in the fire.'

I am glad to hear Your Majesty say so.'

'I am immensely indebted to you. Pray tell me in what way I can reward you. This ring –' He slipped an emerald snake ring from his finger and held it out upon the palm of his hand.

'Your Majesty has something which I could value even more highly, said Holmes.

'You have but to name it.'

'This photograph!'

The King stared at him in amazement. 'Irene's photograph!' he cried. 'Certainly, if you wish it.'

'I thank Your Majesty. Then there is no more to be done in the matter. I have the honour to wish you a very good morning.' He bowed, and, turning away without observing the hand which the King had stretched out to him, he set off in my company for his chambers.

And that was how a great scandal threatened to affect the kingdom of Bohemia, and how the best plans of Mr Sherlock Holmes were beaten by a woman's wit. He used to make merry over the cleverness of women, but I have not heard him do it of late. And when he speaks of Irene Adler, or when he refers to her photograph, it is always under the honourable title of *the* woman.

> *gasogene* — a soda syphon
> *vizard* — a half mask
> *cabinet* — decoratively framed
> *John Hare* — English actor–manager

3 The basic elements of fiction

As I mentioned in the introduction, the basic elements of most fiction are setting, character, and story. We are going to look at them now in that order – because they are progressively more complex issues. If you have not already done so, read the story before going any further, and make notes in response to the question which follows. But don't imagine that it is a test of your memory: you should get used to the practice of looking back into the story for the details around which you will build your answer. And don't forget to STOP to write notes for your responses.

SETTING

Let's go straight into our consideration of this basic feature with a question and discussion exercise.

Which elements and details in the story help to create its *setting*? List as many different *kinds* of detail as you can, and give examples of each drawn from the text. If you are not sure what to do, look ahead to just the *first* of the examples which follow, then go back to complete the rest of the exercise yourself.

───◆───

You should have had very little difficulty in listing *some* of the following, though you may not have put them in the same order.

Place Names. The story is set in London. Holmes lives in Baker Street, and Irene Adler in St John's Wood. Many other places are mentioned – Edgware Road, Regent Street, and Charing Cross – and because they actually exist they help to establish *realistic* setting.

33

Historical Details. Watson gives an exact date at the start of the story – '20th of March, 1888'; the King is from Bohemia, which had been a separate state in the nineteenth century (and still *does* exist); he arrives in a 'brougham' (a Victorian carriage); and the cab driver is paid 'Half a guinea'. These details correspond to the historical picture we have of the world at that time and therefore make the background to the story seem *credible*.

Characters. The story is populated by a married doctor, a bachelor detective, a foreign king, an 'adventuress', a lawyer, and various other minor characters. Although Holmes has unusually developed skills and Kings are not exactly commonplace, these characters form part of a world which seems reasonable, not unlike our own, and therefore acceptable. We know that such people could exist, and they thus help to make the fictional world Conan Doyle offers us *realistic*.

Environment. The story begins in the streets of London, continues in Holmes's first floor apartment, and is subsequently taken on to the mews where servants are working, a church in the Edgware Road, and the avenue where Briony Lodge is situated. It reaches its climax inside the drawing room of the 'bijou villa' from which Irene Adler has recently decamped, and it ends as Watson and Holmes take to the streets of London again. All of these locations help to create a perfectly credible *milieu*.

What I am suggesting is that the combined effect of these details of place names, historical details, credible characters, and realistic environment all help to create a setting which is vivid, immediate and convincing in being so concrete and specific. We are persuaded that such a fictional world exists – partly because it corresponds convincingly with one which we know existed at the end of the nineteenth century, and some parts of which still exist today.

That was our first real exercise in using this particular study technique. Don't worry too much if you chose different details to those listed: if yours were roughly the same *type* then you have grasped the idea of how setting is created. If not, then read through my list again and try to see how they relate to the question which was asked.

In these early stages this sort of analysis might seem rather dry and unexciting. You may be itching to consider the twists and turns of the plot and to decide how 'likeable' certain characters are – or otherwise. This is understandable – but we will come to it a little later. What we need to establish first of all is *how* and *with what means* writers construct the stories they offer us. However, we will take one step closer to human interest by going on next to consider our second important element of fiction – the creation of 'character'.

I'm sure you will agree that Conan Doyle manages to create a very memorable figure in his detective Sherlock Holmes. He was a popular fictional character one hundred years ago, and has gone on being so ever since. For the moment however you should try to forget all those screen images of him which are now almost part of the collective consciousness (the meerschaum pipe and deerstalker cap) because for the purpose of the next exercise I want you to discover *how* he is created as a fictional character purely within the pages of the printed text. The important thing to keep in mind here is that you should not just describe him but rather say what *sorts* of information we receive and *how* we receive it. You might like to use the following category headings: physical appearance, psychological character, and behaviour. So once again, going back to the story and searching in it for details to support your answers, STOP here and make notes in response to the following question:

> What elements are used to create Sherlock Holmes as a fictional character in 'A Scandal in Bohemia'? List as wide a *variety* of information as possible.

⸺⧳⸺

Physical appearance. There is not as much information of this kind as you might have imagined. He has a 'tall spare figure' and 'long nervous hands' and we learn this, as we do much else about him, from Watson's description. We are also told that he can successfully *alter* his appearance, but this is a feature of his cleverness rather than what he looks like – though of course it is *part* of his general character that he can if he wishes adopt this protean manner.

Psychological character. There is a lot more here. Watson tells us that Holmes has a 'cold, precise, and admirably balanced mind' – which seems to be confirmed when we see it being put into effect. He sneers at 'the softer passions' and is in general rather lofty and arrogant. The general impression we are given is of someone who is awesomely intellectual, and yet we notice that he is very friendly towards Watson.

One significant detail is his radical independence. We are told that 'he loathed every form of society with his whole Bohemian soul'. In other words he is an 'outsider' who rates his own intellectual pursuits above normal worldly values. He keeps himself shut away in his rooms much of the time for instance, away from other people, and when the King offers him a valuable ring as a reward Holmes chooses instead a photograph because of its symbolic value.

One rather surprising detail you may have noticed is that Holmes is in fact a cocaine addict, and obviously this stresses the unconventional nature of his character. Fortunately it does not seem to affect the exercise of a sharp intellect; for it is his powers of observation and deduction which help make him such a memorable character – and it is important to notice that we are not just *told* about those powers but are *shown* them in action. Holmes's analysis of Watson's shoe for instance, from which he is able to deduce his recent whereabouts and the efficiency of his domestic servant, is an illustration of this cleverness.

Behaviour. Watson tells us that 'His manner was not effusive' – and you can see from the dialogue that he is a man of few words. In conversation with the King he extracts the information he needs as briskly (almost brusquely) as possible. And at the end of the story he bows (*politely*) but moves on so quickly that he doesn't see the King's outstretched hand. This emphasises the impulsive, mercurial side of his nature. One moment he is slumped in an armchair, thinking; next he is a man of action.

We are shown that he is prepared to adopt disguises and court danger, and we notice how very *busy* he is once he decides to act. In fact a great deal of his physical behaviour turns out to be rather vigorous when we look closely. He *throws* a box of cigars to Watson, *throws* himself into his armchair, and quite apart from the fracas he arranges in the street, when looking for the photograph he *tears* back a shutter and *plunges* his hand into the recess.

His character is principally created by what we are shown and told about him, and the cumulative effect of these elements is also reinforced by the manner in which other people behave towards him. You may have selected different details from the story, but I hope you can see from these notes *how* a character is made up. There is far more one could say about a complex personality like Holmes, but for now it is more important to study the mechanics of fiction – that is, how it is made to work. And of course not all characters are created in the same way. Sometimes we are given a great deal of information about their inner thoughts and feelings, sometimes only an external view of them.

We will return to a study of characterisation again in further chapters, but what I want to emphasise now is that when considering fictional characters you should try to look below the surface to see *how* they are constructed. Keep a close watch on the *type* of information you are offered about a character as well as the *source* of that information. There can be a great deal of difference for instance between information which comes directly from the author ('Mr Smith was six feet tall') which we take to be a 'fact' – and that which comes from another fictional character ('Jones then remarked 'Smith is not a generous man'') – which is *opinion*, and might in fact tell us more about Jones than Smith.

STORY

In literary studies the 'story' is often referred to as a 'narrative' – that is, 'the account of a succession of events'. These events might be actions such as Holmes's attempts to retrieve the photograph, or they could just be the development of someone's *thoughts* – as they are in stories by Dostoyevski or Virginia Woolf. And the events need not be specially dramatic as they often are in detective stories; but fortunately *A Scandal in Bohemia* does offer us a good example of how writers arouse and hold our interest in relating this succession of events.

For that is what we will be doing in our study of 'story' – considering *not* how Sherlock Holmes bluffs his way into Irene Adler's villa, but how Conan Doyle arranges the events of his narrative and conveys them to us, the readers. This will be rather like our consideration of character: it will be our task to see *how it is done*, rather than what it *is*. This is because most readers have very little difficulty understanding what *happens* in a story – though putting it into words may not be quite so easy.

Nevertheless, before we get under way with our inspection of narrative I am going to invite you to try a short exercise in doing just that. STOP here, and try to summarise the main points of 'A Scandal in Bohemia' in no more than 100 words, then compare your précis with the one which follows. Be prepared to have two or three attempts at this; read the story again if necessary, and only include the most essential points. The purpose of this exercise is to help you develop the ability to analyse stories in a detached manner, without getting caught up in a detailed consideration of the characters or the events themselves.

Sherlock Holmes, a famous detective, is commissioned by the King of Bohemia to retrieve a potentially compromising photograph from Irene Adler, his former mistress. Holmes sets out in disguise to search her house but is sidetracked when he becomes caught up as a witness at her wedding. Later he returns and tricks her into revealing her hiding place. When he goes back the next day however Ms Adler, having perceived his ruse, has already left with her husband, taking the photograph with her.

Those are the bare bones of the story. Don't worry if your account is slightly different to mine, but I hope you can see that only the most important elements are necessary – not details of the King's clothes or Holmes's apartment. This is just a preliminary exercise in identifying the principal elements of a narrative. We will be looking at another example in more detail in the next chapter.

Now we will consider what strategies Conan Doyle uses in controlling this narrative and delivering it to us. The most obvious device he uses is to arouse our *interest*. We are presented straight away with a very talented and rather unusual character. As a fictional creation Sherlock Holmes is quite an achievement: we want to know more about such an intelligent and sharp–witted man. But before we get the chance Conan Doyle gives him an especially thorny problem to solve. Now our curiosity to know 'what happens next' is aroused. It would be dull and unimaginative reader who did not want to know how Holmes will set about solving the problem. So, Conan Doyle has now introduced another fundamental element of narrative – *suspense*. Will Holmes retrieve the photograph – and if so, how?

The next part of the story presents us with the answer: Holmes sets off in disguise with the intention of getting into the house. Our desire for information and a solution to the puzzle is being satisfied. But then Conan Doyle introduces a new element: Holmes is thwarted by the very person he is trying to rob – Irene Adler. This is a *plot twist*. We are back to where we started, with the tension of our suspense tightened another notch.

Curiously enough, in terms of his strategy in handling the narrative, it is interesting to note that he then 'resolves' the story with a repeat of the same procedure. The suspense is diminished and our curiosity is offered another dose of gratification when Holmes visits the house a second time and succeeds in obtaining the one piece of information he needs – the whereabouts of the concealed recess. But then when he returns to retrieve the photograph there is another and final twist to the tale: Irene Adler has guessed his intent and escaped in time. Both his expectations and our own are thwarted – but because we appreciate how skilfully Conan Doyle has arranged the elements of his story to reach this conclusion we have the compensatory satisfaction of contemplating his artifice.

This is an analysis of the story in terms of Conan Doyle's control of suspense and reader-expectation. There are no hard and fast rules about what a writer may or may not do in this respect. But the best authors do not abuse their readers' patience by raising and lowering the tension too often, or introducing too many plot twists. We feel cheated if the narrative is manipulated *too* much and too obviously to produce a certain effect – just as we usually feel it a sign of weakness if a mystery story is solved by the sudden introduction of information which has been concealed from us.

Notice how Conan Doyle plays fair in this respect. The first time we read 'A Scandal' we may be surprised by Irene Adler turning the tables on Holmes; but when we look more closely on second reading there are clues to the possible outcome earlier in the text. For instance, when Holmes tricks her into revealing the whereabouts of the photograph, we are told that 'she replaced it, *glanced at the rocket*, [and] rushed from the room' (my emphasis). This glance and her action suggest that she has uncovered the plot. And of course she follows Holmes back home in disguise. Her words 'Good night, Mister Sherlock Holmes' are delivered to check her assumption that it is him: (don't forget that he is still disguised as a clergyman at this point). And Holmes recognises her voice. The reader has enough information to know that she is likely to do *something* to outwit him – and an even more observant reader would spot that Holmes himself has only just said 'this marriage may mean a complete change in her life and habits'.

What I am trying to do here is illustrate the link between the analysis of a story and the practice of close reading, which requires that we pay very close attention to all such small details. You will see as we go along that it is a skill which can be brought to bear at almost every stage of analysis to aid our appreciation and understanding of a text.

4 How stories are told

Now we will move on to another very important aspect of the story – but once again without discussing what happens in it so much as *how it is told*. Let's tackle this by way of another question. You don't need to write anything down this time: just STOP and think about your answer to the following question:

> Obviously Conan Doyle is the *author* of 'A Scandal in Bohemia', but who *relates* the events of the story to us?

Give yourself full marks if your answer was Doctor Watson and bonus points if you spotted that Sherlock Holmes also relates quite a lot of the story during their conversations. Watson is what is known as the *narrator*. Now authors can either relate the events of their stories to us themselves as they do in a great deal of fiction ('The duchess got up and left the room') or they can invent someone who tells the story ('I watched the duchess get up and leave the room'). This brings us to another fundamental issue in the study of fiction, which is called *narrative mode*.

The majority of stories and novels are narrated, that is *told* to us by the author using what is called the *third person* (singular) *narrative mode*. This means that the author refers to the characters as 'he' or 'she' throughout. The characters act out the author's wishes, and we as readers may be given varying degrees of insight into their thoughts and feelings. In many traditional narratives the author may go from one character's innermost thoughts to another's in a different time and place altogether. We call such narrators *omniscient* – because they are all-seeing and all-knowing about their characters, in God-like control of the fictional worlds they are creating.

The alternative narrative mode is *first person* (singular) when authors have two choices. They can either tell the story themselves ('My tale begins, dear reader, one day when ...') or they can create a fictional character like Doctor Watson who will do the telling for them: ('I have seen little of Holmes lately. My marriage has drifted us away from each other').

Fortunately, the second type of first person narrative mode has brought us back to 'A Scandal in Bohemia'. Conan Doyle creates a fictional narrator, Doctor Watson, who relates the story which concerns his old friend, Sherlock Holmes. Now a short exercise on the use of this mode. STOP here and write brief notes in answer to the following two questions:

1 What are the possible *disadvantages* of using Watson as the narrator?

2 How does Conan Doyle overcome those disadvantages?

—————❊—————

1. The most obvious disadvantage of using such a fictional first person narrator is that he cannot tell us what is going on in a scene if he is not present in it himself. If Watson goes home for the night for instance, he

cannot say what is happening to Holmes back in Baker Street.

The other major limitation is that he cannot tell us what is going on inside someone else's mind. He cannot include in his story anyone else's secret fears and thoughts – only his own.

In addition to this the author is constrained to stay within the scope of the fictional narrator's intelligence and point of view. If Watson is supposed to be just an average and normal man he cannot be made to offer profound or spectacular solutions to problems. His language, behaviour, and observations must remain credible to us for a man of his type – otherwise we will cease to believe in him as a character.

2. Conan Doyle overcomes these limitations quite cleverly. Watson tells us what he sees acted out before him in scenes where he is present – but those where he is not are reported to *him* (and thus to us) by Holmes, who thus acts as a sort of secondary narrator. Watson does not therefore need to be present at every scene: he can let another character give an account of any events he has not witnessed. And of course he can give us information about the *past* – in this case Holmes's reputation and character.

Watson cannot tell us how other people feel inside, but he can report how they behave with some degree of interpretation. For example, when Holmes remarks that they have before them 'quite a pretty little problem' we are offered a glimpse of the King's offended pride when he replies '"But a very serious one to me" returned the King, *reproachfully*' (my emphasis).

Watson is reasonably intelligent, but just an ordinary person. Conan Doyle gets over this limitation simply by putting all the intellectual fireworks, the daring behaviour, and the piercing insights into the character of Sherlock Holmes. Watson just reports to us what he sees and hears: he himself fades into the background, and this leaves the detective standing out as the more memorable character of the two.

We will return to the subject of narrators and narratives again later. For the time being just try to keep in mind the fact that just as there is a difference between authors and fictional characters, there can be a difference between the author and the narrator of a story too.

5 Construction

The final topic in our consideration of some of the basic elements of fiction is *construction*. This refers to the shape of a story, the manner in which its parts are arranged, or the form its elements assume. What you need for this is an overview of the work or an ability to see it as a whole. You are *not* concerned with detail but with the architecture or the structure of the narrative. The ability to be able to perceive this is something which becomes easier as your experience of fiction grows. The more stories or novels you read, so the easier it becomes to perceive the manner in which they are built.

I am stressing the importance of experience in this matter because 'construction' is not something you can search for in the text like a symbol or a metaphor. It requires thought and reflection – a willingness to hold the events of the narrative in your head and to think carefully about the relationship between its parts, searching for any patterns or structures which might be holding the all together.

Fortunately for our first exercise in dealing with this element of story-telling, 'A Scandal in Bohemia' has its structure written large, being already split into three numbered parts. Conan Doyle has done the first part of our work for us. But now you should STOP, *think* about the story, or flick through the text to remind yourself of the events of the narrative, and then using just one or two sentences for each of the three parts, describe the essence of their content.

━━◦◉◦━━

PART I. This presents us with a character sketch of Holmes as an ace detective and then with the problem he must solve. In other words, the mystery or the problem is 'set up'.

PART II. This delivers an account of Holmes's first abortive then second more successful visit to discover the whereabouts of the photograph. The problem is *being* solved.

PART III. Holmes pounces – but has been outwitted. This presents the denouement and double twist 'resolution' to the problem.

You may have used different terms, but I hope you were able to see the relationship between the story as a whole and the three separate parts into which it is divided. And notice that their essence has nothing to do with their length. All the subterfuges and comings and goings of the longest Part II just boil down to Holmes's attempt to solve the problem. The details are not as important as the part they play or the position they hold in the narrative.

I hope you can also perceive some sort of aesthetically satisfying pattern in this simple triptych of events: Problem – Detection – Resolution. These are some of the more exquisite pleasures of literary appreciation.

6 Close reading

Close reading is not a skill which can be acquired in just five minutes: prolonged reading, observation, and thought need to be
brought together many times over – together if possible with a sheer
love of words and what they can be made to do.

What we are going to do now is look at the opening paragraph of 'A
Scandal'. I will offer a short demonstration of four types of close
reading which are possible (linguistic, semantic, structural, and cultural) and then ask you to make notes for your own observations. I
am going to begin with the opening sentence: 'To Sherlock Holmes
she is always the woman', and in fact my four types of close reading
will focus attention on just two words in that sentence – 'is' and 'the'.

Linguistic. The use of the present tense – 'she is' – strikes an interesting
note here. Most fiction is narrated in the past tense, but the present tense is
sometimes employed to give a sense of immediacy and urgency. This effect
is here reinforced by the brevity and directness of the sentence. It starts the
story on a bright note.

Semantic. The 'is' here also suggests something else – that the high regard
and rivalry between Sherlock Holmes and Irene Adler has originated in the
past but is still going on in the fictional present of the story. This is reinforced by the addition of the adverb 'always'. But their combined effect *also*
suggests that the two fictional characters somehow continue to exist into the
actual present in which we read the story.

Structural. The opening sentence of the story is rather neatly echoed by that
with which the story closes "When he speaks of Irene Adler ... it is always
under the honourable title of *the* woman.' This small structural link using
repetition introduces an element of symmetry or pattern into the narrative,
making it more coherent and satisfying. It proves that the story is well
designed.

Cultural. At the end of the Victorian and the beginning of the Edwardian
period there were a number of male writers who produced work which
featured a hero who has dealings with a woman who is idealised, inaccessi-
ble, mysterious, and often either beautiful or cruel. One thinks of Rider
Haggard's *She* or many of the stories of Somerset Maugham or Joseph
Conrad for instance. Of course it is a cultural stereotype which goes back a
long way and still exists today. And 'the woman' neatly encapsulates this
idea: Irene Adler is both attractive and dangerous as far as Holmes is
concerned.

I could say more about the 'fear of woman' which lies behind this,
but I will stop now and point out that this cultural reading has taken

us *outside* the story. Your reading and interpretation at such a level will depend upon the breadth or depth of your own cultural knowledge. This is another case where the more you read, the more you will be able to get out of something new.

Now you should make notes for your own close reading of the rest of the paragraph. Don't expect that every sentence will yield up so much from so little, but remember that you can bring to your analysis of each item anything which you know from the story as a whole. The numbering system I have used refers to the order of the sentences – of which we have just dealt with the first.

————◦◦◦◦————

2. 'I have ...'. This establishes the fact that the story is to be told in the first person narrative mode. We do not know the identity of the narrator yet – and in fact his name is not mentioned until two pages later when Holmes addresses him.

3. 'she eclipses ... the whole of her sex'. There is use of hyperbole (exaggeration) here which illustrates both the strength and consistency of Holmes's feelings and the dramatic effect Irene Adler can have on people. 'the whole of her sex' sounds rather abstract and clinical – but then Watson *is* a doctor.

4. 'it was not that he felt any emotion akin to love'. Here is our first insight into Holmes's unusual character. Women who eclipse all others are usually the objects of conventional love. *'akin'* is very much literary language and seems rather archaic in the context, but this helps to establish Watson as a rather old–fashioned figure. Notice that the *'was'* takes us back into the more conventional *past* tense for the rest of the story, which is where it stays until the final sentence returns to the present tense, echoing the first.

5. Love is 'abhorrent' to Holmes. This is a very strong term which emphasises both the curious nature of his personality and the manner in which many of his characteristics are taken to an 'extreme. 'cold, precise, but admirably balanced mind': we see all these three features illustrated in the next few pages.

6. 'the most perfect reasoning and observing machine'. This metaphor would seem to make Holmes into a slightly ludicrous robot, but fortunately we do have his reasoning and powers of observation demonstrated to us presently, making them quite credible. Conan Doyle is in the process of creating 'the detective as superman'.

7. 'the softer passions'. Watson's language is again abstract and neutrally descriptive. He sounds as if he is compiling a scientific analysis of his subject. But this is perfectly consistent with his occupation as a doctor and his being a no-nonsense ex-Army man. And notice how his own character is being created by the particular language he uses.

8. 'admirable things for the observer'. Watson is here presenting us with Holmes's point of view. Love is *useful* to the detective – because it causes people to reveal themselves, and 'drawing the veil from men's motives' is a very appropriate metaphor in the context of all the observing, peering, and snooping into people's lives that a detective does.

9. 'delicate and finely adjusted'. Watson returns to the language of science and technology to create an impression of 'Holmes as precision instrument' – something like a clock, which is of course neutral and *accurate*. 'mental results' has a similar effect, suggesting perhaps a calculator or an adding machine.

10. 'sensitive instrument'. This continues the metaphor and the addition of 'high–power lenses' brings the comparison closer to the very instrument which Holmes uses so effectively – his eyes. 'not be more' is a sort of rhetorical understatement called 'litotes' which reinforces the notion of Watson as politely old-fashioned.

11. 'but one woman'. This takes us back to the *ostensible* subject of the paragraph, Irene Adler (the *actual* subject is of course Holmes) and it echoes the opening sentence. Then 'that woman' gives emphasis by repetition. We may be surprised to discover that she is in fact the '*late* Irene Adler' (my emphasis) when the story begins – but the fact that she is dead only proves how powerful her influence has been, if she still *is*, always '*the* woman'. And then 'dubious and questionable' makes her appear somewhat racy and dangerous. But note that these are Watson's words: he is a rather conventional person – the safely married man who is likely to disapprove of such a bohemian type of woman. Yet the terms are vague and ambiguous, leaving *us*, the readers to think more approvingly of her if we wish.

Don't worry too much if your notes are not as comprehensive as mine – or if you have dealt with different features. The important thing is to get used to this technique of close reading. And notice that we are primarily involved in discovering how the story is put together, how its parts are connected, and what devices the author is using to construct the narrative. Try to keep in mind that close reading at this stage is principally a matter of discovering how a text has been put together.

7 Self-assessment questions

These questions are split into three groups – Language, Comprehension, and Analysis. The first and easiest is to give you practice in the 'naming of parts' so as to become more accustomed to the technical language of literary studies. The second group is a check that you have understood some of the finer points of what is going on in the story. Then the third and most difficult group presents questions which will give you an opportunity to put into practice some of the topics we have covered in this chapter. (Use the glossary and a dictionary to answer the questions.)

LANGUAGE

1 What does the King mean when he says that he has 'come *incognito* from Prague'?

2 What figure of speech does Holmes use when he says to Watson 'You did not tell me that you intended to go into harness'?

3 What does he mean by this expression?

4 What does the King mean when he says that Holmes has '*carte blanche*' with regard to the money?

5 What is the 'peculiar construction' in the sentence from the King's letter: 'This account of you we have from all quarters received'?

6 What part of speech is each word in the expression 'strongly marked German accent'?

7 What figure of speech is being used in the expression 'Drive like the Devil!'?

COMPREHENSION

1 How does Holmes know that Watson has been working as a doctor since they last met?

2 What is Holmes referring to when he says of Watson 'I am lost without my Boswell'?

3 What creates the effect of 'barbaric opulence' in the King's appearance?

4 What is Holmes's first disguise?

5 Why does Holmes linger to help the ostlers at Briony Lodge?

6 What does Holmes have for afternoon tea?

7 What excuses does Watson offer for taking part in the conspiracy against Irene Adler, even though he feels ashamed?

8 Why does Holmes arrange the false fire alarm at Briony Lodge?'

ANALYSIS

1 What are we to infer from the fact that Holmes gives the King a receipt for the money?

2 What do Holmes and the King have in common?

3 What do Holmes, the King, and Irene Adler all do at some point in the story?

4 Holmes says 'I am lost without my Boswell'. In what sense is this especially true in this narrative?

5 Watson is the narrator of 'A Scandal in Bohemia'. What do we learn about him as a character during the course of his narrative?

8 Course work

1 Choose a substantial paragraph – say half a page or so – from Watson's narrative (but *not* a section where characters are speaking to each other) and, using the checklists of literary terms in Chapter One, Section 5, produce a close reading of the passage. You should try to say as much as possible about both its constituent parts and any relation these may have to the story as a whole.

2 Write a character study of Sherlock Holmes: (try to avoid using the illustrative examples which are given in this chapter).

3 Discuss the existence of *humour* in 'A Scandal in Bohemia'. (Keep in mind here not only what the characters do and say to each other, but the fact that Conan Doyle creates all these effects.)

4 Authors of detective stories often rely for their effects on a certain amount of trickery, coincidence, or implausibility. Is this true of Conan Doyle in 'A Scandal in Bohemia'?

5 Discuss the manner in which Conan Doyle uses surprise, mystery, and suspense in 'A Scandal in Bohemia'.

9 Further reading

Conan Doyle's complete list of publications is enormously long. It includes historical novels, memoirs, plays, documentary reports, military histories, poems, what we would now call investigative journalism, polemical essays, and his apologies for spiritualism and other mystical beliefs. I have chosen to list only work relating to the one character for whom he will surely always be remembered. All titles listed are given as their first publication in book form.

STORIES

The Adventures of Sherlock Holmes, London: George Newnes, 1892.

The Memoirs of Sherlock Holmes, London: George Newnes, 1894.

The Return of Sherlock Holmes, London: George Newnes, 1905.

His Last Bow, London: John Murray, 1917.

The Case Book of Sherlock Holmes, London: John Murray, 1927.

NOVELS

A Study in Scarlet, London: Ward Lock & Co, 1888.

The Sign of Four, London: Spencer Blackett, 1890.

The Hound of the Baskervilles, London: George Newnes, 1902.

The Valley of Fear, London: Smith Elder & Co, 1915.

BIOGRAPHY

John Dickson Carr, *The Life of Sir Arthur Conan Doyle,* London: John Murray, 1949.
Pierre Nordon, *Conan Doyle: A Biography,* Trans. Frances Partridge, London: John Murray, 1966.
Hesketh Pearson, *Conan Doyle – His Life and Work,* London: Methuen, 1943.
Julian Symons, *Portrait of an Artist: Conan Doyle,* London: Whizzard Press, 1979.

CRITICISM

Don Richard Cox, *Arthur Conan Doyle,* New York: Ungar, 1985.

Owen Dudley Edwards, *The Quest for Sherlock Holmes,* Edinburgh, Mainstream, 1983.

Trevor Hall, *Sherlock Holmes: Ten Literary Studies,* London: Duckworth, 1969.

Michael and Mollie Hardwick, *The Sherlock Holmes Companion,* London:

John Murray, 1962.

Julian Symons, *Bloody Murder*, London: Faber, 1972.

Jaqueline A. Yaffe, *Arthur Conan Doyle*, Boston: Twayne, 1987.

CHAPTER THREE

Point of view, symbols and theme

1 Introduction

This chapter deals with a story by Katherine Mansfield, whose literary manner is quite different to that of Conan Doyle: she is much more 'modern', even though they were both writing around the same time. 'The Voyage' has no suspense or plot, no sudden twists in the story line, and it deals in a very understated manner with a relatively undramatic incident in the life of a young girl. The study programme which follows it offers further exercises in comprehension – that is, considering just what happens in the story. Then we pay special attention to another important element of narratives – *point of view* – and there is a further close reading exercise, in particular examining some of the subtleties which underpin what is apparently a very simple prose style. Then finally we move on to consider two slightly more complex literary topics – the use of *symbols* and the difference between story and *theme*.

Katherine Mansfield is now widely regarded as an outstandingly gifted writer of short stories, and a number of her best works have as their setting a sensitive evocation of the late-Victorian–early-Edwardian New Zealand in which she grew up. I make this observation in order to introduce a further note of caution on the vexed subject of the relationship between writers' *lives* and the works that they produce.

Students of literature often turn to the biographies of writers – partly out of a natural intellectual curiosity, and sometimes with the hope that The Life may throw some light on The Work. My cautionary note is to warn you that this is a dangerous practice because the two things often become confused or, even worse, equated. The fact is that a writer's *fiction* and a writer's *biography* are not the same thing at all.

Let me give an example. We read that a writer was unhappily married (as both Katherine Mansfield and Thomas Hardy were) then we read a story which features unhappy marriage (such as Mansfield's 'Bliss' or Hardy's 'The Withered Arm'). There is a strong temptation to think that the story 'illustrates' and is an accurate representation of this feature of the writer's own life. Conversely we may think that knowing some biographical tit-bit from the life of its author will help us analyse and therefore understand what a story 'really' means. These are both temptations which you should resist – for all sorts of reasons.

First of all, studying fiction is the appreciation of an art form, whereas biography is a sort of history (even though well written ones can be considered works of art as well). One involves the appreciation of artistic *qualities* whereas the other is concerned with establishing *facts* about the real world.

The second reason is that even when writers really *do* use incidents from their own lives as the subject matter of their fiction, those incidents are not just recorded; they are *transformed* via the writer's imagination into words.

The third reason is more mundane, but no less relevant. You should keep in mind that even the most gifted writers are also ordinary human beings: they get things wrong, misunderstand, are biased, misinterpret their own lives, and even tell lies. The biographies of people they have been married to are often very instructive in this respect.

So read biographies by all means, but at this stage do not use the information in them as evidence when analysing a text. Writers' private lives can sometimes be fascinating subjects of study in themselves, but for the purpose of literary studies at this stage try to keep in mind that we do best to concentrate our attention on the *fiction* they have produced – that is, the words of their narratives printed on the page.

2 Biographical note

Katherine Mansfield was born in Wellington, New Zealand in 1888. She had a somewhat insecure childhood and was raised largely by her grandmother. At school she proved to be gifted at writing even though her spelling was poor. Some of her erliest sketches appeared in her school magazine. It is obvious that even at this early stage she was interested in creating good prose style:

This evening I have sat in my chair with my reading lamp turned low, and given myself up to thoughts of the years that have passed. Like a strain of minor music they have surged across my heart, and the memory of them, sweet and fragrant as the perfume of my flowers, has sent a strange thrill of comfort through my tired brain.

She wrote this at the age of fifteen. Shortly afterwards the family moved to England, and she entered Queens College in Harley Street. There she became very passionate about writing and music, and was very influenced by her reading of OscarWilde and Chekhov. She also gave herself up to a rather bohemian life style and had love affairs with both men and women. For this reason her parents took her back home to New Zealand against her wishes.

By 1908 she had rebelled so much that she was allowed to go back to London with an allowance of £100 per year. There she married her singing teacher, left him the same evening and went to live with another man. In 1910 some of her stories were published in the *New Age* alongside writers like H. G. Wells, Arnold Bennett, Hilare Beloc, and Chekhov. At this stage she also began to suffer from severe bouts of illness, complicated by veneral disease and the ill effects of an abortion.

In 1912 she met John Middleton Murry and became co-editor with him of a magazine which caused something of a scandal by its title alone – *Rhythm*. They lived together, moving from England to France and back again, sometimes living together with her most devoted ex-lover, Ida Baker. She published stories in a number of magazines, left Murry during the war to live briefly with another man in France, then came back to live near D. H. Lawrence and his wife in Cornwall.

By 1918 she realised that she was trying to do something new with the short story as a literary form, and when she met Virginia Woolf they exchanged ideas on what was possible. When tuberculosis was diagnosed she moved to the south of France in search of the best conditions for her illness – a search which was to occupy the remainder of her short life. Even though she married Murry in 1918 she left him to live successively in France, Italy, and Switzerland.

All her greatest stories were written in this final period between 1918 and 1923. She knew she was going to die, but went on writing feverishly and seeking a cure, living alone, with Ida Baker and occaslonally with Murry. In 1922, she entered the Gurdjieff Institute at Fontainbleau, France for his mystic 'treatment' which was then fashionable. On January 9th 1923 Murry travelled from London to see her. He arrived in the afternoon and she died later the same day.

She is one of the few English writers to have established a significant reputation solely on the strength of writing short stories. This is because she refined both the form and the content of the short story in a way which has influenced many writers since. To begin with she removed any high drama or complex plot from her stories but conœentrated on giving a scrupulously *accurate* account of the world. There is often no overt drama in her stories at all. A story might simply involve a girl's visit to her piano teacher ('The Wind Blows') or to visit her grandparents (as we have in our story 'The Voyage'). There are no shocking climaxes or surprise endings. What she offers instead are stories in which all the details are very carefully arranged in a way which makes them seem almost half way between being poetry and prose. Her subjects are taken from everyday events, and the central character is often a young girl or woman trying to come to terms with the bewildering problems of life and other people.

THE VOYAGE
KATHERINE MANSFIELD

The Picton boat was due to leave at half-past eleven. It was a beautiful night, mild, starry, only when they got out of the cab and started to walk down the Old Wharf that jutted out into the harbour, a faint wind blowing off the water ruffled under Fenella's hat, and she put up her hand to keep it on. It was dark on the Old Wharf, very dark; the wool sheds, the cattle trucks, the

cranes standing up so high, the little squat railway engine,
all seemed carved out of solid darkness. Here and there on
a rounded wood-pile, that was like the stalk of a huge black
mushroom, there hung a lantern, but it seemed afraid to unfurl its timid,
quivering light in all that blackness; it burned softly, as if for itself.

Fenella's father pushed on with quick, nervous strides. Beside him her
grandma bustled along in her crackling black ulster; they went so fast that
she had now and again to give an undignified little skip to keep up with
them. As well as her luggage strapped into a neat sausage, Fenella carried
clasped to her her grandma's umbrella, and the handle, which was a swan's
head, kept giving her shoulder a sharp little peck as if it too wanted her to
hurry.... Men, their caps pulled down, their collars turned up, swung by; a
few women all muffled scurried along; and one tiny boy, only his little black
arms and legs showing out of a white woolly shawl, was jerked along angrily
between his father and mother; he looked like a baby fly that had fallen into
the cream.

Then suddenly, so suddenly that Fenella and her grandma both leapt,
there sounded from behind the largest wool shed, that had a trail of smoke
hanging over it, *Mia-oo-oo-O-O!*

'First whistle,' said her father briefly, and at that moment they came in
sight of the Picton boat. Lying beside the dark wharf, all strung, all beaded
with round golden lights, the Picton boat looked as if she was more ready to
sail among stars than out into the cold sea. People pressed along the
gangway. First went her grandma, then her father, then Fenella. There was a
high step down on to the deck, and an old sailor in a jersey standing by gave
her his dry, hard hand. They were there; they stepped out of the way of the
hurrying people, and standing under a little iron stairway that led to the
upper deck they began to say good-bye.

'There, mother, there's your luggage!' said Fenella's father, giving
grandma another strapped-up sausage.

'Thank you, Frank.'

'And you've got your cabin tickets safe?'

'Yes, dear.'

'And your other tickets?'

Grandma felt for them inside her glove and showed him the tips.

'That's right.'

He sounded stern, but Fenella, eagerly watching him, saw that he looked
tired and sad. *Mia-oo-oo-O-O!* The second whistle blared just above their
heads, and a voice like a cry shouted, 'Any more for the gangway?'

'You'll give my love to father,' Fenella saw her father's lips say. And her
grandma, very agitated, answered, 'Of course I will, dear. Go now. You'll be
left. Go now, Frank. Go now.'

'It's all right, mother. I've got another three minutes.' To her surprise
Fenella saw her father take off his hat. He clasped grandma in his arms and
pressed her to him. 'God bless you, mother!' she heard him say.

And grandma put her hand, with the black thread glove that was worn through on her ring finger, against his cheek, and she sobbed, 'God bless you, my own brave son!'

This was so awful that Fenella quickly turned her back on them, swallowed once, twice, and frowned terribly at a little green star on a mast head. But she had to turn round again; her father was going.

'Good-bye, Fenella. Be a good girl.' His cold, wet moustache brushed her cheek. But Fenella caught hold of the lapels of his coat.

'How long am I going to stay?' she whispered anxiously. He wouldn't look at her. He shook her off gently, and gently said, 'We'll see about that. Here! Where's your hand?' He pressed something into her palm. 'Here's a shilling in case you should need it.'

A shilling! She must be going away for ever! 'Father!' cried Fenella. But he was gone. He was the last off the ship. The sailors put their shoulders to the gangway. A huge coil of dark rope went flying through the air and fell 'thump' on the wharf. A bell rang; a whistle shrilled. Silently the dark wharf began to slip, to slide, to edge away from them. Now there was a rush of water between. Fenella strained to see with all her might. 'Was that father turning round?' - or waving? - or standing alone? - or walking off by himself? The strip of water grew broader, darker. Now the Picton boat began to swing round steady, pointing out to sea. It was no good looking any longer. There was nothing to be seen but a few lights, the face of the town clock hanging in the air, and more lights, little patches of them, on the dark hills.

The freshening wind tugged at Fenella's skirts; she went back to her grandma. To her relief grandma seemed no longer sad. She had put the two sausages of luggage one on top of the other, and she was sitting on them, her hands folded, her head a little on one side. There was an intent, bright look on her face. Then Fenella saw that her lips were moving and guessed that she was praying. But the old woman gave her a bright nod as if to say the prayer was nearly over. She unclasped her hands, sighed, clasped them again, bent forward, and at last gave herself a soft shake.

'And now, child,' she said, fingering the bow of her bonnet-strings, 'I think we ought to see about our cabins. Keep close to me, and mind you don't slip.'

'Yes, grandma!'

'And be careful the umbrella isn't caught in the stair rail. I saw a beautiful umbrella broken in half like that on my way over.'

'Yes, grandma.'

Dark figures of men lounged against the rails. In the glow of their pipes a nose shone out, or the peak of a cap, or a pair of surprised-looking eyebrows. Fenella glanced up. High in the air a little figure, his hands thrust in his short jacket pockets, stood staring out to sea. The ship rocked ever so little and she thought the stars rocked too. And now a pale steward in a linen coat, holding a tray high in the palm of his hand, stepped out of a lighted doorway and skimmed past them. They went through that doorway. Carefully over the high brass-bound step on to the rubber mat and then down such a terribly steep flight of stairs that grandma had to put both feet on each step, and Fenella clutched the clammy brass rail and forgot all about the swan-necked umbrella.

At the bottom grandma stopped; Fenella was rather afraid she was going to pray again. But no, it was only to get out the cabin tickets. They were in the saloon. It was glaring bright and stifling; the air smelled of paint and burnt chop-bones and india-rubber. Fenella wished her grandma would go on, but the old woman was not to be hurried. An immense basket of ham sandwiches caught her eye. She went up to them and touched the top one delicately with her finger.

'How much are the sandwiches?' she asked.

'Tuppence!' bawled a rude steward, slamming down a knife and fork.

Grandma could hardly believe it.

'Twopence *each*?' she asked.

'That's right,' said the steward, and he winked at his companion.

Grandma made a small, astonished face. Then she whispered primly to Fenella, 'What wickedness!' And they sailed out at the further door and along a passage that had cabins on either side. Such a very nice stewardess came to meet them. She was dressed all in blue and her collar and cuffs were fastened with large brass buttons. She seemed to know grandma well.

'Well, Mrs. Crane,' said she, unlocking their washstand. 'We've got you back again. It's not often you give yourself a cabin.'

'No,' said grandma. 'But this time my dear son's thoughtfulness - '

'I hope - ' began the stewardess. Then she turned round and took a long, mournful look at grandma's blackness and at Fenella's black coat and skirt, black blouse, and hat with a crape rose.

Grandma nodded. 'It was God's will,' said she.

The stewardess shut her lips and, taking a deep breath, she seemed to expand.

'What I always say is,' she said, as though it was her own discovery, 'sooner or later each of us has to go, and that's a certingty.' She paused. 'Now, can I bring you anything, Mrs. Crane? A cup of tea? I know it's no good offering you a little something to keep the cold out.'

Grandma shook her head. 'Nothing, thank you. We've got a few wine biscuits and Fenella has a very nice banana.'

'Then I'll give you a look later on,' said the stewardess; and she went out, shutting the door.

What a very small cabin it was! It was like being shut up in a box with grandma. The dark round eye above the wash-stand gleamed at them dully. Fenella felt shy. She stood against the door, still clasping her luggage and the umbrella. Were they going to get undressed in here? Already her grandma had taken off her bonnet, and, rolling up the strings, she fixed each with a pin to the lining before she hung the bonnet up. Her white hair shone like silk; the little bun at the back was covered with a black net. Fenella hardly ever saw her grandma with her head uncovered; she looked strange.

'I shall put on the woollen fascinator your dear mother crocheted for me,' said grandma, and, unstrapping the sausage, she took it out and wound it round her head; the fringe of grey bobbles danced at her eyebrows as she smiled tenderly and mournfully at Fenella. Then she undid her bodice, and something under that, and something else underneath that. Then there seemed a short, sharp tussle, and grandma flushed faintly. Snip! Snap! She had undone her stays. She breathed a sigh of relief and, sitting on the plush couch, she slowly and carefully pulled off her elastic-sided boots and stood them side by side.

By the time Fenella had taken off her coat and skirt and put on her flannel dressing-gown grandma was quite ready.

'Must I take off my boots, grandma? They're lace.'

Grandma gave them a moment's deep consideration. 'You'd feel a great deal more comfortable if you did, child,' said she. She kissed Fenella. 'Don't forget to say your prayers. Our dear Lord is with us when we are at sea even more than when we are on dry land. And because I am an experienced traveller,' said grandma briskly, 'I shall take the upper berth.'

'But, grandma, how ever will you get up there?'

Three little spider-like steps were all Fenella saw. The old woman gave a small silent laugh before she mounted them nimbly, and she peered over the high bunk at the astonished Fenella.

'You didn't think your grandma could do that, did you?' said she. And as she sank back Fenella heard her light laugh again.

The hard square of brown soap would not lather and the water in the bottle was like a kind of blue jelly. How hard it was, too, to turn down those stiff sheets; you simply had to tear your way in. If everything had been different, Fenella might have got the giggles.... At last she was inside, and while she lay there panting, there sounded from above a long, soft whispering, as though someone was gently, gently rustling among tissue paper to find something. It was grandma saying her prayers....

A long time passed. Then the stewardess came in; she trod softly and leaned her hand on grandma's bunk.

'We're just entering the Straits,' she said.

'Oh!'

'It's a fine night, but we're rather empty. We may pitch a little.'

And indeed at that moment the Picton boat rose and rose and hung in the air just long enough to give a shiver before she swung down again, and there was the sound of heavy water slapping against her sides. Fenella remembered she had left that swan-necked umbrella standing up on the little couch. If it fell over, would it break? But grandma remembered too, at the same time.

'I wonder if you'd mind, stewardess, laying down my umbrella,' she whispered.

'Not at all, Mrs. Crane.' And the stewardess, coming back to grandma, breathed, 'Your little granddaughter's in such a beautiful sleep.'

'God be praised for that!' said grandma.

'Poor little motherless mite!' said the stewardess. And grandma was still

c

telling the stewardess all about what happened when Fenella fell asleep.

But she hadn't been asleep long enough to dream before she woke up again to see something waving in the air above her head. What was it? What could it be? It was a small grey foot. Now another joined it. They seemed to be feeling about for something; there came a sigh.

'I'm awake, grandma,' said Fenella.

'Oh, dear, am I near the ladder?' asked grandma. 'I thought it was this end.'

'No, grandma, it's the other. I'll put your foot on it. Are we there?' asked Fenella.

'In the harbour,' said grandma. 'We must get up, child. You'd better have a biscuit to steady yourself before you move.'

But Fenella had hopped out of her bunk. The lamp was still burning, but night was over, and it was cold. Peering through that round eye she could see far off some rocks. Now they were scattered over with foam; now a gull flipped by; and now there came a long piece of real land.

'It's land, grandma,' said Fenella, wonderingly, as though they had been at sea for weeks together. She hugged herself; she stood on one leg and rubbed it with the toes of the other foot; she was trembling. Oh, it had all been so sad lately. Was it going to change? But all her grandma said was, 'Make haste, child. I should leave your nice banana for the stewardess as you haven't eaten it.' And Fenella put on her black clothes again and a button sprang off one of her gloves and rolled to where she couldn't reach it. They went up on deck.

But if it had been cold in the cabin, on deck it was like ice. The sun was not up yet, but the stars were dim, and the cold pale sky was the same colour as the cold pale sea On the land a white mist rose and fell. Now they could see quite plainly dark bush. Even the shapes of the umbrella ferns showed, and those strange silvery withered trees that are like skeletons.... Now they could see the landing-stage and some little houses, pale too, clustered together, like shells on the lid of a box. The other passengers tramped up and down, but more slowly than they had the night before, and they looked gloomy.

And now the landing-stage came out to meet them. Slowly it swam towards the Picton boat and a man holding a coil of rope, and a cart with a small drooping horse and another man sitting on the step, came too.

'It's Mr. Penreddy, Fenella, come for us,' said grandma. She sounded pleased. Her white waxen cheeks were blue with cold, her chin trembled, and she had to keep wiping her eyes and her little pink nose.

'You've got my - '

'Yes, grandma.' Fenella showed it to her.

The rope came flying through the air and 'smack' it fell on to the deck. The gangway was lowered. Again Fenella followed her grandma on to the wharf over to the little cart, and a moment later they were bowling away. The hooves of the little horse drummed over the wooden piles, then sank softly

into the sandy road. Not a soul was to be seen; there was
not even a feather of smoke. The mist rose and fell and
the sea still sounded asleep as slowly it turned on the
beach.

'I seen Mr. Crane yestiddy,' said Mr. Penreddy. 'He looked himself then.
Missus knocked him up a batch of scones last week.'

And now the little horse pulled up before one of the shell-like houses.
They got down. Fenella put her hand on the gate, and the big, trembling
dew-drops soaked through her glovetips. Up a little path of round white
pebbles they went, with drenched sleeping flowers on either side. Grandma's delicate white picotees were so heavy with dew that they were fallen,
but their sweet smell was part of the cold morning. The blinds were down in
the little house; they mounted the steps on to the veranda. A pair of old
bluchers was on one side of the door and a large red watering-can on the
other.

'Tut! tut! Your grandpa,' said grandma. She turned the handle. Not a
sound. She called, 'Walter!' And immediately a deep voice that sounded half
stifled called back, 'Is that you, Mary?'

'Wait, dear,' said grandma. 'Go in there.' She pushed Fenella gently into
a small dusky sitting-room.

On the table a white cat, that had been folded up like a camel, rose,
stretched itself, yawned, and then sprang on to the tips of its toes. Fenella
buried one cold little hand in the white, warm fur, and smiled timidly while
she stroked and listened to grandma's gentle voice and the rolling tones of
grandpa.

A door creaked. 'Come in, dear.' The old woman beckoned, Fenella
followed. There, lying to one side of an immense bed, lay grandpa. Just his
head with a white tuft and his rosy face and long silver beard showed over
the quilt. He was like a very old, wide-awake bird.

'Well, my girl!' said grandpa. 'Give us a kiss!' Fenella kissed him. 'Ugh!'
said grandpa. 'Her little nose is as cold as a button. What's that she's
holding? Her grandma's umbrella?'

Fenella smiled again and crooked the swan neck over the bedrail. Above
the bed there was a big text in a deep black frame:

> Lost! One Golden Hour
> Set with Sixty Diamond Minutes.
> *No* Reward Is Offered
> For It Is GONE FOR EVER!

'Yer grandma painted that,' said grandpa. And he ruffled his white tuft
and looked at Fenella so merrily she almost thought he winked at her.

3 Point of view

Right now, before we go any further, you should sit down and read 'The Voyage'. If it is the first time you have read it, then after thinking about it for a little while sit down and read it again, making notes in the manner I suggested in Chapter One. Don't worry if you are not quite sure *what* to make a note of at this stage. You will discover the best approach for yourself as we go along. And even if you have already read the story once, why not read it again, make notes, and think about the sorts of details I mentioned under the heading of 'Close Reading'.

When you have done this STOP here and write down your answers to the following straightforward comprehension questions:

1 Who is the central character in the story?
2 Why is Fenella going to live with her grandparents?
3 What object of her grandmother's does Fenella carry throughout the story?
4 How long does the voyage last?
5 Where is the story set?

I'm fairly sure you will have answered the first four questions without too much difficulty, though the fifth is much harder because the answer isn't obvious from the story. Correct answers prove that you have understood what the story is about and that you have a clear grasp of what is going on.

The answers, which I am not tabulating so as not to draw attention to them, are as follows: Fenella is the central character: this is important since most of the events are seen from her *point of view*, which we will deal with in a moment. She is going to live with her grandparents because her mother has died. She carries with her throughout the voyage, her grandmother's umbrella. The voyage lasts from half past eleven one night until dawn and early morning of the next day. The story is set in New Zealand, and the journey is from the north to the south island of that country, of which Picton is the most northerly port.

Now for two slightly more taxing questions which requre that you pay even closer attention to what is going on. STOP here, don't be tempted to look ahead at what follows – in fact why not cover it up with a piece of paper to remove the temptation and write down your answers to the following questions:

1 We eventually learn from the conversation between the stewardess and Fenella's grandmother that her mother has died. But there are plenty of clues before this. What are they?
2 Drawing your evidence from the first two or three pages, what examples are there of the story being told from Fenella's point of view? And can you say why this is important?

In answer to the first question you may have noticed that the grandmother was dressed in a 'black ulster' (a long loose overcoat), 'Nothing especially significant about that' you might say. But then Fenella too is dressed in 'black coat and skirt, black blouse, and hat with a crape rose'. In other words, they are dressed in mourning, so *somebody* close to them must have died. Notice too that the leavetaking between the grandmother and her son at the quayside is very emotional. He takes his hat off to embrace her, and she sobs in calling him 'my own brave son'. That is, he is brave to be facing the loss of his wife. He then gives Fenella a shilling which to her signifies that they must be separating for a long time: obviously something especially momentous must have occurred. And then when the stewardess appears she notices their mourning clothes and observes 'sooner or later each of us has to go'.

You may have guessed that Fenella's mother had died almost without being aware of how you knew. But these subtle clues are the means by which Mansfield lets *us* know without making it obvious, without having to make Fenella herself conscious of the fact, and therefore without distracting attention from *her* experience of the voyage.

The second question on point of view may have elicited any number of examples. The opening description of the Wharf has a number of details which seem to be seen by a child: 'the little squat railway engine' and the woodpile that is 'like the stalk of a huge black mushroom'. The umbrella 'kept giving her shoulder a sharp little peck': that is, as if brought to life by a child's imagination. And the little boy dressed in white is likened to 'a baby fly that had fallen into the cream'. The old sailor gives Fenella his 'dry, hard hand' which is just the sort of detail a child would notice in such an experience. Similarly, when her father kisses her goodbye she notices his 'cold wet moustache' on her cheek.

Perhaps the most striking and literal example of point of view is Fenella's vision of the sailors leaning on the rails of the ship. 'In the glow of their pipes a nose shone out, or the peak of a cap, or a pair of surprised-looking eyebrows'. That is – they are being viewed from *below* by someone smaller, and she notices the most striking details.

My supplementary question on why this question of point of view is important can be answered in a number of ways. The story is largely *about* Fenella, and Mansfield wants to offer us the opportunity of bringing us close to Fenella's experience – seeing and feeling things as a child might do. Secondly (and this is the point I was making about Fenella and her mother's death) this point of view must be logical and consistent in order that we find the story acceptable and credible. And I think we *do* find it credible that a child should be puzzled by her father's gift of a shilling and not be permanently conscious of the larger significance attending it.

You might also have noticed that the emotional farewell between her father and her grandmother embarrassed Fenella somewhat: she turned away and 'swallowed once, twice, and frowned'. That is, she is not yet old enough and has not the emotional maturity to cope with what is going on around her . Point of view is also important because it affects what *is* and what *can be told*. If the story had been told from the grandmother's point of view it would have been quite different. This is also connected with the underlying *themes* of the story which we shall come to shortly.

So, by controlling the point of view from which a story is narrated, the author can both direct our attention to particular details, and more importantly can bring us close to the consciousness of the character. Note that the author *must* be logically consistent – as is the case with characterisation. It would not seem credible to us if Fenella observed and understood the entire episode as an adult would – because she is young and inexperienced. Mansfield is successful in this respect precisely because she is able to present the world as Fenella sees it (plus a little more besides) – from which *we* are able to understand her thoughts and feelings *plus* what is going on around her, whilst *she* can only understand partially. The effect is a sort of double perspective: we see the world in close up as a child sees it, and at the same time we see it with the adult overview which Mansfield provides in the other parts of her narrative.

This brings us to a further subtle and important detail of narration. Just because authors can convincingly show us the world or draw us close to a character's consciousness by writing from that person's point of view, they are not obliged to continue doing so throughout an entire story or novel. They can if they wish switch to the point of view of another character, or they can revert to the point of view of the narrator. If this seems slightly confusing, here is an example from the story:'

What a very small cabin it was! It was like being shut up in a box with Grandma. The dark round eye above the washstand gleamed at them dully. Fenella felt shy. She stood against the door, still clasping her luggage and the umbrella.

The first three of these sentences present the story from Fenella's point of view – by creating an account of her thoughts and perceptions. But then in 'Fenella felt shy' we are told by someone else (the narrator) how she feels, and the following sentence continues this change to a view *of* Fenella – as if in a movie the camera shot had changed from showing what she *sees* to a different point of view, *showing Fenella herself*, from the outside, standing against the door.

It is a mark of Mansfield's skill that she controls this changing point of view so subtly and deftly that we are hardly aware of it changing at all. But we should try to become aware of it when necessary in order to know, when making our analyses and judgements, the differences between certain points of view and the weight of credibility we should give to them. But this is a fairly complex issue, and I think we have gone far enough with it just for now.

4 Close reading

For our close reading exercise on *The Voyage* I want to suggest that you use the following selection of literary terms from Chapter One, Section 5:

☆ Grammar

☆ Vocabulary

- ☆ Syntax
- ☆ Figures of speech
- ☆ Literary devices
- ☆ Tone
- ☆ Narrator
- ☆ Narrative mode
- ☆ Characterisation

Check back on the meaning of each of these terms if necessary, and use them to prompt your observations on what can be said about each in the *second paragraph* of the story, which begins 'Fenella's father' and ends 'into the cream'. Don't worry if you are not able to say something about every single topic, but do try to force yourself to think about each of these features in relation to the passage, and *do* use the Glossary in Chapter Eight to give an exact name to any of the examples you wish to list (under figures of speech for instance).

Keep in mind that your task in a close reading exercise of this kind is twofold. You should try to give a name to each example of any feature you identify, and try to say what it contributes to the effect and the quality of the story. And of course don't forget to STOP here to write down your responses.

⎯⎯⊙⎯⎯

The **grammar** throughout is quite conventional, though it is worth noting that the last three quarters of the paragraph consist of two quite long sentences, punctuated by commas and semi-colons. This seems to contribute to the fluency of the style, and it underlines the fact that although the story is 'about' a young girl and events are often presented from Fenella's point of view, it is in fact a very sophisticated and adult narrative. The one unconventional feature is Mansfield's use of three dots (...) which a number of modern writers use to indicate something like a short pause in thought or time.

The **vocabulary** of the passage is fairly plain and simple. Apart from 'ulster' which might not be familiar to readers today, most of the terms used would be known even to a reasonably well-educated child. And this seems appropriate since we already know that Mansfield is relating the story to us largely from a child's point of view. Her use of terms like *'little* skip', *'neat* sausage', and *'baby* fly' reinforce this effect.

The **syntax** is that of perfectly normal word order in written English (Subject

– Verb – Object). The only feature I can observe under this heading is that in some clauses she separates the subject from its verb by interposing dependent clauses ('Men, their caps pulled down, their collars turned up, swung by') but this is just giving variety to her sentence construction.

Under **figures of speech** you might have spotted the *simile* 'like a baby fly'. She also uses *onomatopoeia* in 'crackling black ulster': that is, the words themselves sound like what they are describing. There is *anthropomorphism* in the swan's-head umbrella giving Fenella a 'sharp little peck': that is, the inanimate object is spoken of as if it were alive – and this is entirely appropriate given that it is supposed to be a child's view. Mansfield also uses *alliteration* more than once: in 'crackling black ulster' there is repetition of the 'a', 'ck', and 'l' sounds, and in 'woolly white shawl' repetition of the soft 'w' and 'l' sounds. The use of these rhetorical devices brings a figurative inventiveness and imaginative colour to the writing.

It is sometimes difficult to say where a figure of speech ends and a **literary device** begins, but the final simile in the passage – 'he looked like a baby fly that had fallen into the cream' – is like an **image** in the sense that it creates a striking picture.

Tone is quite a difficult feature to pin down precisely or in one word, but I think that in this passage you could say that the author's attitude to her subject was *light, brisk,* almost *playful* in places, which is appropriate since we are being invited to see the world from a child's point of view. Yet the final sentence gives a hint of the emotional seriousness also present in the story.

The **narrator** must be Katherine Mansfield because she does not invent another person who stands between herself and the reader, telling the story. (This might seem rather obvious and unimportant – but narrators *can* be problematic, as we shall see.)

The **narrative** is in the traditional third–person *mode*, and the narrator is *omniscient*. That is, Fenella is referred to as 'she' throughout, and Mansfield never intrudes as an 'I' speaking to the reader directly. Moreover, she knows what is going on in the minds of her characters. She is 'all–knowing', which is what omniscient means.

In terms of **characterisation** we might observe that 'grandma bustled along' gives the impression of a lively older woman, which we know her to be from what happens later in the story. And Fenella's observations about the umbrella and the little boy, as well as the 'little skip' she is forced to make, help to establish her as a *young* girl. Notice incidentally that at this point in the story Mansfield has not actually *told* us that Fenella is a young girl: we have simply worked this out from the few clues and details which have been given about her. Information about the characters is revealed to us piecemeal as the story progresses, and we are left to put these pieces together as we wish.

I would like to draw your attention to the fact that in the notes which have just been offered, each claim is backed up with brief illustrative quotation drawn from the text itself. This is an important procedure in literary studies. You must give evidence for any arguments you make and *show* examples of what you mean *in the text*. Good readers, as we noted earlier, are those who pay attention to details.

5 Symbols

I want to look now at one particular feature which occurs in the work of many writers – the use of symbols. First, what *is* a symbol? It is one thing which is generally taken to represent something else. For intance, the cross is a symbol of christianity: as an object in itself it is an instrument of torture, but it is taken as a symbol of Christ's teaching because he died on one. Similarly, the rose has been used so often in connection with love that it is generally accepted as a symbol of it. So does the human heart – so there can be more than one symbol for the samle thing. Fire is often used as a symbol both for danger and for human passion – so a single phenomenon can sometimes symbolise more than one thing. Similarly diamonds might be said to symbolise both a hard, cold purity (because they possess those qualities) and great wealth (because they are very expensive). You can probably think of lots of others in common use: the ring as a symbol of marriage, the lilly as a symbol both of purity and death, the sun as a symbol of heat and life.

Many authors use symbols in their writing, and we will look at three of Katherine Mansfield's in a moment. But before that two items of warning about symbols and symbolism. First, there *must* be general agreement amongst users about the object and what it is supposed to symbolise. For instance, it would be no use suggesting that grass symbolised death just because your pet dog died on the lawn. Similarly, just because you once saw a lion frightened by an elephant it would be no use suggesting that the lion symbolises cowardice – because they are generally considered to be strong, fearless, and noble creatures.

Second, and this is a slightly more subtle point, many writers create their own symbols. By drawing attention to a particular object and linking it to something else or some other quality, they use the object symbolically. But this symbolic quality only exists within the particular work. It does not automatically become universally applicable. For instance, in his novel *The Golden Bowl*, Henry James uses a cracked glass bowl to symbolise a relationship which is flawed, but this doesn't mean that all bowls symbolise relationships.

So – let's go back to 'The Voyage'. We are going to consider three different types of symbol used by Katherine Mansfield, but I'll give you the opportunity of saying what you think they will be first. One is a perfectly normal symbol of the cross/fire type. The second is an object which comes to have a special significance just *within the story*. And the third is not so much an object as a phenomenon – a large scale feature if the story which has literary and mythical connections of a symbolic kind.

STOP here, glance back through the story if you wish, and *think* what these three symbols might be.

The first I had in mind was her repeated reference to stars, which are a common symbol. The second was the rather curious umbrella which Fenella is given charge of. And the third is the journey itself. You might have spotted others – the colour black as a symbol of death for instance – but it is these three which seem to me most striking. Let's deal with them one at a time.

I am going to invite you to STOP again, make a note of where stars are mentioned in the story and say what seems to be symbolic about them.

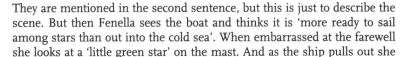

They are mentioned in the second sentence, but this is just to describe the scene. But then Fenella sees the boat and thinks it is 'more ready to sail among stars than out into the cold sea'. When embarrassed at the farewell she looks at a 'little green star' on the mast. And as the ship pulls out she feels that as the ship rocks 'the stars rocked too'.

What is happening is that the stars are being offered as a delicate symbol of Fenella's fragility and her hopes, her destiny. After all, that is what stars are commonly thought to symbolise, isn't it. Fenella is sailing off into the night, into her 'future' – so the 'rocking' of the stars reflect the uncertainty of her position. And later, when they are about to dock and dawn has not quite broken, the stars are 'dim'. That is, Fenella is safely nearing the end of her journey: her destiny is more assued: the need for 'hope' is less urgent – is becoming 'dimmer'.

I hope that this sort of argument does not seem too contrived and strained to you. But I imagine that you noticed the umbrella, so STOP again, note where it is mentioned, and try to say what you think it symbolises.

We are told in the second paragraph that Fenella is carrying the umbrella 'clasped to her' – that is, she is taking urgent care of it. Her grandmother tells her to be extra careful as they go to their cabin, but then Fenella forgets all about it when they arrive there. It is as if the grandmother has given a special task to Fenella, as if carrying the fragile umbrella is somehow being offered as a burden in the symbolic sense – a test, a mark of the extra responsibility she will have to face now that her mother has died. And at the same time it is a sort of bond between Fenella and her grandmother. Perhaps the grandmother has given her the task to keep her mind occupied and thus away from worries about the journey and separation from her father.

Later when Fenella is just about to fall asleep she remembers the umbrella and fears it might fall over and break. But her grandmother remembers it too 'at the same time'. Don't you agree that this seems to emphasise the point I have just made about its being a specially significant link between them? In fact the grandmother asks the stewardess to lay down the umbrella safely and it is thus in the same position as Fenella herself. Then next day Fenella, still in charge of the umbrella, is able to deposit it safely, crooking it over the rail of her grandmothers bed. She has carried out her-task successfully, and proved her responsibility.

Thus the umbrella, just for the duration of this story, has had a certain symbolic suggestiveness beyond its existence as an ordinary object. And it ends there. Umbrellas in the general sense don't begin to be especially symbolic again – until we enter the dream analyses of Sigmund Freud.

Now for the voyage itself, I'm just going to say very briefly that voyages and journeys are very often used to symbolise a meaningful experience or a transition from one phase of life or state of awareness into another. This is what happens to Fenella - but I want to save discussion of this for the next section on *theme*.

Finally on symbols. Many students often ask 'But did the author consciously put them there?' or 'Did the author really intend them to mean that?' And the answer to these questions is 'It doesn't matter'. So long as they *exist* in the story and we can demonstrate their relevance to it by close reference to the rest of the text – then it does not really matter if they were put there consciously or not.

And a final-final word. Don't go *hunting* for symbols. They are only of use or significance if they can be shown to reinforce the general 'meaning' of the work as a whole.

6 Theme

By now you might be thinking 'Do I have to go into all this detail?' or 'why doesn't he get on with it and consider the story?' First: yes, you do need to get used to considering fiction in far more detail than you have perhaps been used to doing before. As I tried to explain in Chapter One, this makes the difference between a casual reader and one who has the analytic skills to gain deeper insights into a piece of work. But we will be looking at different types of detail and different aspects of literary analysis with each story, so you need not worry that every Chapter will be the same.

My second reply should cheer you up. Yes, we are going to move on to the story now. And even more good news – I am quite sure you will find this part fairly easy, for a simple reason. Most people who are even only casually acquainted with literature are usually able to grasp what is going on in a story. They may not be able to spot every fine point of detail of the kind we have been practising in our close reading exercises, but they will probably be reasonable judges of character and will be able to follow the story as it unfolds. Let me try to prove this to you with one of our simple self-assessment exercises. STOP here and, using not more than fifty words, summarise the story of 'The Voyage', including what you think are its most important elements. If you wish you can begin with the simple formulation '"The Voyage" is a story about ...'.

—◁◦◉◦▷—

Don't worry if you went over the word limit slightly, and it doesn't matter if you haven't got exactly the same wording as the example I am going to offer. But you might have something like this:

'The Voyage' is a story about a young girl, Fenella, whose mother has recently died. She is taken from her father's care by a kindly grandmother and makes an overnight journey at sea to go and live at her grandparent's house.

Alternatively, you might have had something like this:

'The Voyage' is a story about a young girl's bewilderment and her relationship with her grandmother as they make a short sea trip, arriving in the early morning to be greeted by her grandfather.

This second examlle isn't *wrong* but it is not as good as my first. Can you say why?

<hr>

The answer to this question is that it misses out four important factors from the story – the fact that Fenella's mother has recently died, that she has been separated from her father, that the journey is overnight, and that she is going to *live* with her grandparents.

If your précis of the story was something like my first example, then you've done very well. But if it was more like my second, it's very important that you should give careful consideration to my next question. Don't be tempted to skim over it in a sense of frustration or impatience, because now we are approaching the most important part of our study of the story – what it *means*.

The question I want you to answer is this: why *are* the four elements present in my first and missing from my second précis so important? Why should they have been there? What significance do they have which make them necessary to a successful summary of the story?

<hr>

The fact that Fenella's mother has died is important because it means that she has suffered a major *loss* (even though she doesn't seem very conscious of it). Fenella has been dealt a cruel blow by life even whilst she is still young. This makes her more vulnerable. The next factor – separation from her father – is significant for similar reasons. She 'loses' the second most important person in her life after having just lost the first. She becomes in a sense an 'orphan'. This redoubles her vulnerability (just look at the image of the 'timid, quivering light' at the end of the first paragraph of the story and see how aptly it seems to suggest Fenella herself). The third factor – the fact that the journey is overnight – is important because the world is more mysterious and frightening at night, especially to a child. This reflects the uncertainty of the life Fenella is now facing. And the fact that she arrives at her destination early in the morning means that she starts her *new* life on a *new* day. And her going to *stay* and *live* with her grandparents means that she has a *home* and a place of security to replace the one she has lost.

These details are important because they take us closer to the deeper underlying meaning of the story – what we call its *theme*. Now first of all let's be quite sure what we think the story is most essentially *about*, what its underlying or controlling meanings are. Let me give you an example.

A story might describe a young boy going fishing, say for the first time without his father. He catches a fish, but it is so big that he panics and falls into the water. But he then recovers, lands the fish, and takes it home proudly to show his parents. The story is *about* a young boy's experiences, but its *theme* is that of *initiation* or *becoming an adult*. He has to face a problem, alone; and the fact that he eventually overcomes it and emerges the wiser for it it is a sort of an extended metaphor for the process of becoming more mature. A *theme* is the central, or underlying, or dominating idea in a literary work. It is often an abstract concept which is made concrete through the characters and the action.

So what is the central idea behind or underneath 'The Voyage'? STOP here for a moment and try to say in as few words as possible what the story is most essentially *about*.

There is not one simple answer to this question, and I certainly don't think the story can be reduced to a one-word abstract concept. But it seems to me to be concerned with an important moment of transition in Fenella's life. She has been a child, but now she must face the more complex issues of becoming an adolescent. She leaves the past (life with her parents) behind, and the journey she takes represents a break with it. Now she must begin a new life, living with her grandparents. This notion is reinforced by two things. The fact that her new life begins on a new day, which I have already mentioned, and the fact that this important experience takes place via a journey (a 'voyage') – and one over the sea at that. Journeys, and especially voyages at sea, are very often used in fiction and myths to represent an important and often educative experience . It is even possible to argue that the umbrella (you remember that odd detail?) represents a link, an element of continuity between her past and the start of her new life.

If your response was not quite the same as mine, then don't worry – because it is at this stage that the study of literature becomes a matter of argument and personal judgement. There is not a right and wrong answer to the interpretation of works of art: that is why there is often disagreement amongst critics about their relative merit and the values they contain. This may seem a little frustrating to you at this stage, but you should try to get used to the idea. It can even help you to see a single work in a number of different ways.

7 Self-assessment questions.

1 When Fenella enters the cabin with her grandma we are told: 'The dark round eye above the washstand gleamed at them dully.'
   (a) What is this 'eye'?
   (b) What figure of speech is being used here?

2 What figure of speech is being used in the expression 'her white hair shone like silk'?

3 What literary device is being used here? 'the cold pale sky was the same colour as the cold pale sea'.

4 What parts of speech are each word in 'cold pale sea'?

5 Which two figures of speech are being used here? 'The hooves of the little horse drummed over the wooden piles, then sank softly into the sandy road.'

6 What figure of speech is being used in the expression 'there was not even a feather of smoke'?

7 What figure of speech is being used here? 'a white cat, that had been folded up like a camel'.

8 What are 'picotees' and 'bluchers'?

COMPREHENSION

1 Why does Fenella's father look 'tired and sad'?

2 The stewardess 'seemed to know Grandma well'. Can you suggest any reasons *why* she does?

3 What does the stewardess mean by offering Fenella's grandmother 'a little something to keep out the cold'?

4 'You've got my – ' 'Yes, Grandma.' Fenella showed it to her. What is 'it' here?

5 Explain what Mansfield means by 'And now the landing stage came out to meet them.'

ANALYSIS

1 What elements are used to create the character of the grand-

mother? (Remember: don't just describe her, but say how she is created as a fictional character.)

2 What is the possible symbolic significance of the framed motto mentioned at the end of the story?

3 The story appears to be told throughout largely from Fenella's point of view, yet at one point the stewardess says 'Your little granddaughter's in such a beautiful sleep'. If Fenella is asleep, has the point of view changed here?

4 Is there any symmetry or pattern discernable in the narrative which gives it a clear sense of *construction?*

5 There are a number of small details evident throughout the story which create the impression of a difficult, even hostile world from Fenella's point of view. Can you say what some of them are?

8 Course work

1 Choose a substantial paragraph from the story (which does *not* include conversation) and, using the checklist of literary terms (Chapter One, Section 5) produce a close reading of the passage. Try to say as much as possible about its constituent parts and any relation these might have to the story as a whole.

2 Discuss the means used to create the *setting* of the story.

3 Write an appreciation of Katherine Mansfield's literary style in 'The Voyage'. Use the checklist of *literary terms* if necessary, and remember to first of all offer your own argument and then provide *very brief* quotations from the text to illustrate each of the claims that you make.

4 Discuss Katherine Mansfield's control of *point of view* in 'The Voyage'. (Choose examples *other* than those discussed in this chapter.)

5 Write a page of narrative which depicts events from a particular character's point of view – but *without* naming or saying directly who the character is. The selection of details should reveal the identity of the character.

9 Further reading

All of the stories Katherine Mansfield published in her own lifetime, together with her other uncollected stories, are now available in one volume:

Anthony Alpers (ed), *The Stories of Katherine Mansfield*, London: Oxford University Press, 1984.

Her journals are available as

John Middleton Murry (ed), *The Journal of Katherine Mansfield*, London: Constable, 1954.

Her letters are available as

John Middleton Murry (ed), *The Letters of Katherine Mansfield*, London: Constable, 1928.

(though these are now being re-edited because Murry suppressed and excluded so much).

The definitive biography is

Anthony Alpers, *The Life of Katherine Mansfield*, London: Oxford University Press, 1982.

Two more recent biographies are:

Gillian Boddy, *Katherine Mansfield; The Woman and the Writer*, London: Penguin, 1988.

Claire Tomalin, *Katherine Mansfield: a Secret Life*, London: Viking, 1989.

The most comprehensive bibliography (that is, books, articles, literary criticism, and historical materials related to Katherine Mansfield) is that given in Anthony Alpers's biography.

CHAPTER FOUR

Language and appreciation

1 Introduction

We come next to a writer whose work you may have already encountered – in either his novels or some of the television dramas and full length films based on books such as *Tess of the d'Urbervilles* or *Far from the Madding Crowd*. Hardy has had a popular following with the general reading public ever since the last quarter of the nineteenth century. This is largely because he possesses those skills which general readers often admire in writers: he tells an interesting story, creates memorable characters, and he is particularly good at evoking rural atmosphere and constructing vividly dramatic scenes.

Hardy's reputation in academic circles however has only recently become well established. He used to be thought of as rather old-fashioned and melodramatic; but now he is widely admired for the power of his writing, the vividness of his language, and the searching honesty with which he portrays the universal problems of love, work, and human conflict in his poetry and fiction.

In our discussion of this story, quite apart from understanding what goes on in it, we are going to consider two aspects of what seem to me his outstanding skill as a writer – his feeling for language and its possibilities, and his insights into human nature – in particular his portrayal of sub-conscious motivation in human affairs. You might, if you wish, keep these in mind whilst you read the story, but don't let this prejudice your own responses to it.

There will therefore be one fairly straightforward discussion of what happens in the story followed by a more concentrated inspection of the range and variety of language it contains. To assist you with this I have offered a glossary of some of the more unusual and antiquated terms which Hardy uses. Then later we will be touching upon some of the issues of psychological analysis which the story seems to raise.

This is followed by three items offering assistance to those readers who wish to develop their writing skills. As a gentle introduction to the subject, a typical student essay on 'The Withered Arm' will give you something with which you can compare any work of your own. Then the next two sections offer guidance on how to write a general appreciation of a piece of fiction, followed by a brief note outlining the conventions for quoting from a piece of work you are discussing.

2 Biographical note

Hardy was born in 1840 in Dorchester. His father was a bricklayer who later became a builder, and his mother was hard-working, ambitious, and very literate. Both parents, despite prosperity in their later life, shared anxieties about social class and a fear of being pulled back down into poverty. Hardy was influenced by both these concerns of his parents.

Dorset at the time of Hardy's childhood still incorporated facets and practices of rural life which pre-dated the Industrial Revolution. (It is instructive to think that Jane Austen had died only just over twenty years and Walter Scott eight years prior to Hardy's birth.) Hardy was thus able to witness the death of old pastoral traditions and the rise of the new industrialisation.

He was educated in Dorchester schools and had a musical, church-going social background. Because of his lower-class origins, higher education was closed to him but under the influence of a sympathetic schoolmaster he continued to educate himself after he left school. His first job was as clerk to an architect.

In 1862 he moved to London to earn his living as an architectural draughtsman and was actually a prize-winner in competitions. Here too his literary ambitions began. He wrote poetry, all of which was rejected when he submitted it for publication. After five years he felt he had failed in his ambitions and returned to Dorset.

There he began his first novel (*Desperate Remedies*) published in 1871 at Hardy's own expense: but it did not sell. His second novel, *Under the Greenwood Tree* (1872) was more successful, and it gave him the confidence to consider novel-writing as a profession. He married Emma Gifford with whom he had fallen in love, wrote his first major success, *Far from the Madding Crowd* (1874), as a serial for a magazine, and moved back to London.

The marriage was not a success. Emma seemed to Hardy a cold and unresponsive woman. But on her part it should be said that she had literary aspirations of her own – which Hardy discouraged. They spent most of their summers in London for 'the season' and the rest of the time in Dorset where Hardy designed and built the house at Max Gate in which he was to spend the rest of his life.

His ties with and his feeling for Dorset were very strong, and his fictionalised version of the county (Wessex) is the setting for all his major novels. These were published, as was common practice at that time, first in magazines as serials in both England and America, and then in three volumes.

Even though his fame spread and his success increased, Hardy felt irritated by the limitations imposed on late Victorian writers by the prudish conventions of the time. His novels dealt with passionate relationships between the sexes and he felt frustrated that he could not deal as honestly and openly with such matters as he wished. *Tess of the d'Urbervilles* (1891) was first rejected then censured for obscenity and blasphemy. When a similar outcry followed the publication of *Jude the Obscure* (1896) he gave up writing novels altogether and concentrated on poetry.

In the last three decades of his long life he produced several volumes of poetry, and when his wife died in 1912 much of his imaginative output was focused on recapturing their youth together. Two years later he married his secretary, who was almost forty years younger than him. He was given many public awards, honorary degrees from both Oxford and Cambridge University, and he became the great old man of English letters who many people travelled to visit. But fame did not make him happy. As he got older he became more and more pessimistic about the nature of human kind. The First World War fuelled this pessimism. His second marriage was no more successful than the first, and he became increasingly cantankerous and reclusive. In the last years of his life he dictated his autobiography to his wife and burned all his notebooks, letters and private papers. He died in 1928 and his ashes were installed in Poet's Corner at Westminster

Abbey with full public honours. However his heart, which had been cut out of his body first, was put in a biscuit tin and buried alongside his first wife in Stinsford churchyard, Dorset.

THE WITHERED ARM
THOMAS HARDY

I A LORN MILKMAID

It was an eighty-cow dairy, and the troop of milkers, regular and supernumerary, were all at work; for, though the time of year was as yet but early April, the feed lay entirely in water-meadows, and the cows were 'in full pail'. The hour was about six in the evening, and three fourths of the large, red, rectangular animals having been finished off, there was opportunity for a little conversation.

'He do bring home his bride to-morrow, I hear. They've come as far as Anglebury to-day.'

The voice seemed to proceed from the belly of the cow called Cherry, but the speaker was a milking-woman, whose face was buried in the flank of that motionless beast.

'Hav' anybody seen her?' said another.

There was a negative response from the first. 'Though they say she's a rosy-cheeked, tisty-tosty little body enough,' she added; and as the milkmaid spoke she turned her face so that she could glance past her cow's tail to the other side of the barton, where a thin, fading woman of thirty milked somewhat apart from the rest.

'Years younger than he, they say,' continued the second, with also a glance of reflectiveness in the same direction.

'How old do you call him, then?'

'Thirty or so.'

'More like forty,' broke in an old milkman near, in a long white pinafore or 'wropper', and with the brim of his hat tied down, so that he looked like a woman. ''A was born before our Great Weir was builded, and I hadn't man's wages when I laved water there.'

The discussion waxed so warm that the purr of the milk-streams became jerky, till a voice from another cow's belly cried with authority, 'Now then, what the Turk do it matter to us about Farmer Lodge's age, or Farmer Lodge's new mis'ess? I shall have to pay him nine pound a year for the rent of every one of these milchers, whatever his age or hers. Get on with your work, or 'twill be dark afore we have done. The evening is pinking in a'ready.' This speaker was the dairyman himself, by whom the milkmaids and men were employed.

Nothing more was said publicly about Farmer Lodge's wedding, but the first woman murmured under her cow to her next neighbour, ''Tis hard for *she*,' signifying the thin worn milkmaid aforesaid.

'O no,' said the second. 'He ha'n't spoke to Rhoda Brook for years.'

When the milking was done they washed their pails and hung them on a many-forked stand made as usual of the peeled limb of an oak-tree, set upright in the earth, and resembling a colossal antlered horn. The majority then dispersed in various directions homeward. The thin woman who had not spoken was joined by a boy of twelve or thereabout, and the twain went away up the field also.

Their course lay apart from that of the others, to a lonely spot high above the water-meads, and not far from the border of Egdon Heath, whose dark countenance was visible in the distance as they drew nigh to their home.

'They've just been saying down in barton that your father brings his young wife home from Anglebury to-morrow,' the woman observed. 'I shall want to send you for a few things to market, and you'll be pretty sure to meet 'em.'

'Yes, mother,' said the boy. 'Is father married then?'

'Yes.... You can give her a look, and tell me what she's like, if you do see her.'

'Yes, mother.'

'If she's dark or fair, and if she's tall – as tall as I. And if she seems like a woman who has ever worked for a living, or one that has been always well off, and has never done anything, and shows marks of the lady on her, as I expect she do.'

'Yes.'

They crept up the hill in the twilight and entered the cottage. It was built of mud-walls, the surface of which had been washed by many rains into channels and depressions that left none of the original flat face visible; while here and there in the thatch above a rafter showed like a bone protruding through the skin.

She was kneeling down in the chimney-corner, before two pieces of turf laid together with the heather inwards, blowing at the red-hot ashes with her breath till the turves flamed. The radiance lit her pale cheek, and made her dark eyes, that had once been handsome, seem handsome anew. 'Yes,' she resumed, 'see if she is dark or fair, and if you can, notice if her hands be white; if not, see if they look as though she had ever done housework, or are milker's hands like mine.'

The boy again promised, inattentively this time, his mother not observing that he was cutting a notch with his pocket-knife in the beech-backed chair.

2 THE YOUNG WIFE

The road from Anglebury to Holmstoke is in general level; but there is one place where a sharp ascent breaks its monotony. Farmers homeward-bound from the former market-town, who trot all the rest of the way, walk their horses up this short incline.

The next evening while the sun was yet bright a handsome new gig, with a lemon-coloured body and red wheels, was spinning westward along the level highway at the heels of a powerful mare. The driver was a yeoman in the prime of life, cleanly shaven like an actor, his face being toned to that bluish-vermilion hue which so often graces a thriving farmer's features when returning home after successful dealings in the town. Beside him sat a woman, many years his junior – almost, indeed, a girl. Her face too was fresh in colour, but it was of a totally different quality – soft and evanescent, like the light under a heap of rose-petals.

Few people travelled this way, for it was not a main road, and the long white riband of gravel that stretched before them was empty, save of one small scarce-moving speck, which presently resolved itself into the figure of a boy, who was creeping on at a snail's pace, and continually looking behind him – the heavy bundle he carried being some excuse for, if not the reason of, his dilatoriness. When the bouncing gig-party slowed at the bottom of the incline above mentioned, the pedestrian was only a few yards in front. Supporting the large bundle by putting one hand on his hip, he turned and looked straight at the farmer's wife as though he would read her through and through, pacing along abreast of the horse.

The low sun was full in her face, rendering every feature, shade, and contour distinct, from the curve of her little nostril to the colour of her eyes. The farmer, though he seemed annoyed at the boy's persistent presence, did not order him to get out of the way; and thus the lad preceded them, his hard gaze never leaving her, till they reached the top of the ascent, when the farmer trotted on with relief in his lineaments – having taken no outward notice of the boy whatever.

'How that poor lad stared at me!' said the young wife.

'Yes, dear; I saw that he did.'

'He is one of the village, I suppose?'

'One of the neighbourhood. I think he lives with his mother a mile or two off.'

'He knows who we are, no doubt?'

'O yes. You must expect to be stared at just at first, my pretty Gertrude.'

'I do, – though I think the poor boy may have looked at us in the hope we might relieve him of his heavy load, rather than from curiosity.'

'O no,' said her husband off-handedly. 'These country lads will carry a hundredweight once they get it on their backs; besides, his pack had more size than weight in it. Now, then, another mile and I shall be able to show you our house in the distance – if it is not too dark before we get there.' The wheels spun round, and particles flew from their periphery as before, till a white house of ample dimensions revealed itself, with farm-buildings and ricks at the back.

Meanwhile the boy had quickened his pace, and turning up a by-lane some mile and half short of the white farmstead, ascended towards the leaner pastures, and so on to the cottage of his mother.

She had reached home after her day's milking at the outlying dairy, and was washing cabbage at the doorway in the declining light. 'Hold up the net a moment,' she said, without preface, as the boy came up.

He flung down his bundle, held the edge of the cabbage-net, and as she filled its meshes with the dripping leaves she went on, 'Well, did you see her?'

'Yes; quite plain.'

'Is she ladylike?'

'Yes; and more. A lady complete.'

'Is she young?'

'Well, she's growed up, and her ways be quite a woman's.'

'Of course. What colour is her hair and face?'

'Her hair is lightish, and her face as comely as a live doll's.'

'Her eyes, then, are not dark like mine?'

'No – of a bluish turn, and her mouth is very nice and red; and when she smiles, her teeth show white.'

'Is she tall?' said the woman sharply.

'I couldn't see. She was sitting down.'

'Then do you go to Holmstoke church to-morrow morning: she's sure to be there. Go early and notice her walking in, and come home and tell me if she's taller than I.'

'Very well, mother. But why don't you go and see for yourself?'

'*I* go to see her! I wouldn't look up at her if she were to pass my window this instant. She was with Mr Lodge, of course. What did he say or do?'

'Just the same as usual.'

'Took no notice of you?'

'None.'

Next day the mother put a clean shirt on the boy, and started him off for Holmstoke church. He reached the ancient little pile when the door was just being opened and he was the first to enter. Taking his seat by the font, he watched all the parishioners file in. The well-to-do Farmer Lodge came nearly last, and his young wife, who accompanied him, walked up the aisle with the shyness natural to a modest woman who had appeared thus for the first time. As all other eyes were fixed upon her, the youth's stare was not noticed now.

When he reached home his mother said, 'Well?' before he had entered the room.

'She is not tall. She is rather short,' he replied.

'Ah!' said his mother, with satisfaction.

'But she's very pretty – very. In fact, she's lovely.' The youthful freshness of the yeoman's wife had evidently made an impression even on the somewhat hard nature of the boy.

'That's all I want to hear,' said his mother quickly. 'Now, spread the tablecloth. The hare you wired is very tender; but mind that nobody catches

you. – You've never told me what sort of hands she had.'
'I have never seen 'em. She never took off her gloves.'
'What did she wear this morning?'

'A white bonnet and a silver-coloured gownd. It whewed and whistled so loud when it rubbed against the pews that the lady coloured up more than ever for very shame at the noise, and pulled it in to keep it from touching; but when she pushed into her seat, it whewed more than ever. Mr Lodge, he seemed pleased, and his waistcoat stuck out, and his great golden seals hung like a lord's; but she seemed to wish her noisy gownd anywhere but on her.'

'Not she! However, that will do now.'

These descriptions of the newly-married couple were continued from time to time by the boy at his mother's request, after any chance encounter he had had with them. But Rhoda Brook, though she might easily have seen young Mrs Lodge for herself by walking a couple of miles, would never attempt an excursion towards the quarter where the farmhouse lay. Neither did she, at the daily milking in the dairyman's yard on Lodge's outlying second farm, ever speak on the subject of the recent marriage. The dairyman, who rented the cows of Lodge, and knew perfectly the tall milkmaid's history, with manly kindliness always kept the gossip in the cow-barton from annoying Rhoda. But the atmosphere thereabout was full of the subject during the first days of Mrs Lodge's arrival, and from her boy's description and the casual words of the other milkers, Rhoda Brook could raise a mental image of the unconscious Mrs Lodge that was realistic as a photograph.

3 A VISION

One night, two or three weeks after the bridal return, when the boy was gone to bed, Rhoda sat a long time over the turf ashes that she had raked out in front of her to extinguish them. She contemplated so intently the new wife, as presented to her in her mind's eye over the embers, that she forgot the lapse of time. At last, wearied with her day's work, she too retired.

But the figure which had occupied her so much during this and the previous days was not to be banished at night. For the first time Gertrude Lodge visited the supplanted woman in her dreams. Rhoda Brook dreamed – since her assertion that she really saw, before falling asleep, was not to be believed – that the young wife, in the pale silk dress and white bonnet, but with features shockingly distorted, and wrinkled as by age, was sitting upon her chest as she lay. The pressure of Mrs Lodge's person grew heavier; the blue eyes peered cruelly into her face, and then the figure thrust forward its left hand mockingly, so as to make the wedding-ring it wore glitter in Rhoda's eyes. Maddened mentally, and nearly suffocated by pressure, the sleeper struggled; the incubus, still regarding her, withdrew to the foot of the bed, only, however, to come forward by degrees, resume her seat, and flash her left hand as before.

Gasping for breath, Rhoda, in a last desperate effort, swung out her right hand, seized the confronting spectre by its obtrusive left arm, and whirled it backward to the floor, starting up herself as she did so with a low cry.

'O, merciful heaven!' she cried, sitting on the edge of the bed in a cold sweat; 'that was not a dream – she was here!'

She could feel her antagonist's arm within her grasp even now – the very flesh and bone of it, as it seemed. She looked on the floor whither she had whirled the spectre, but there was nothing to be seen.

Rhoda Brook slept no more that night, and when she went milking at the next dawn they noticed how pale and haggard she looked. The milk that she drew quivered into the pail: her hand had not calmed even yet, and still retained the feel of the arm. She came home to breakfast as wearily as if it had been supper-time.

'What was that noise in your chimmer, mother, last night?' said her son. 'You fell off the bed, surely?'

'Did you hear anything fall? At what time?'

'Just when the clock struck two.'

She could not explain, and when the meal was done went silently about her household work, the boy assisting her, for he hated going afield on the farms, and she indulged his reluctance. Between eleven and twelve the garden-gate clicked, and she lifted her eyes to the window. At the bottom of the garden, within the gate, stood the woman of her vision. Rhoda seemed transfixed.

'Ah, she said she would come!' exclaimed the boy, also observing her.

'Said so – when? How does she know us?'

'I have seen and spoken to her. I talked to her yesterday.'

'I told you,' said the mother, flushing indignantly, 'never to speak to anybody in that house, or go near the place.'

'I did not speak to her till she spoke to me. And I did not go near the place. I met her in the road.'

'What did you tell her?'

'Nothing. She said, "Are you the poor boy who had to bring the heavy load from market?" And she looked at my boots, and said they would not keep my feet dry if it came on wet, because they were so cracked. I told her I lived with my mother, and we had enough to do to keep ourselves, and that's how it was; and she said then, "I'll come and bring you some better boots, and see your mother." She gives away things to other folks in the meads besides us.'

Mrs Lodge was by this time close to the door – not in her silk, as Rhoda had dreamt of in the bed-chamber, but in a morning hat, and gown of common light material, which became her better than silk. On her arm she carried a basket.

The impression remaining from the night's experience was still strong. Brook had almost expected to see the wrinkles, the scorn, and the cruelty on her visitor's face. She would have escaped an interview had escape been possible. There was, however, no backdoor to the cottage, and in an instant the boy had lifted the latch to Mrs Lodge's gentle knock.

'I see I have come to the right house,' said she, glancing at the lad, and smiling. 'But I was not sure till you opened the door.'

The figure and action were those of the phantom; but her voice was so indescribably sweet, her glance so winning, her smile so tender, so unlike that of Rhoda's midnight visitant, that the latter could hardly believe the evidence of her senses. She was truly glad that she had not hidden away in sheer aversion, as she had been inclined to do. In her basket Mrs Lodge brought the pair of boots that she had promised to the boy, and other useful articles.

At these proofs of a kindly feeling towards her and hers Rhoda's heart reproached her bitterly. This innocent young thing should have her blessing and not her curse. When she left them a light seemed gone from the dwelling. Two days later she came again to know if the boots fitted, and less than a fortnight after that paid Rhoda another call. On this occasion the boy was absent.

'I walk a good deal,' said Mrs Lodge, 'and your house is the nearest outside our own parish. I hope you are well. You don't look quite well.'

Rhoda said she was well enough, and, indeed, though the paler of the two, there was more of the strength that endures in her well-defined features and large frame than in the soft-cheeked young woman before her. The conversation became quite confidential as regarded their powers and weaknesses; and when Mrs Lodge was leaving, Rhoda said, 'I hope you will find this air agree with you, ma'am, and not suffer from the damp of the water-meads.'

The younger one replied that there was not much doubt of it, her general health being usually good. 'Though, now you remind me,' she added, 'I have one little ailment which puzzles me. It is nothing serious, but I cannot make it out.'

She uncovered her left hand and arm, and their outline confronted Rhoda's gaze as the exact original of the limb she had beheld and seized in her dream. Upon the pink round surface of the arm were faint marks of an unhealthy colour, as if produced by a rough grasp. Rhoda's eyes became riveted on the discolorations; she fancied that she discerned in them the shape of her own four fingers.

'How did it happen?' she said mechanically.

'I cannot tell,' replied Mrs Lodge, shaking her head. 'One night when I was sound asleep, dreaming I was away in some strange place, a pain suddenly shot into my arm there, and was so keen as to awaken me. I must have struck it in the daytime, I suppose, though I don't remember doing so.' She added, laughing, 'I tell my dear husband that it looks just as if he had flown into a rage and struck me there. O, I daresay it will soon disappear.'

'Ha, ha! Yes.... On what night did it come?'

Mrs Lodge considered, and said it would be a fortnight ago on the morrow. 'When I awoke I could not remember where I was,' she added, 'till the clock striking two reminded me.'

She had named the night and the hour of Rhoda's spectral encounter, and Brook felt like a guilty thing. The artless disclosure startled her; she did not reason on the freaks of coincidence, and all the scenery of that ghastly night returned with double vividness to her mind.

'O, can it be,' she said to herself, when her visitor had departed, 'that I exercise a malignant power over people against my own will?' She knew that she had been slily called a witch since her fall; but never having understood why that particular stigma had been attached to her, it had passed disregarded. Could this be the explanation, and had such things as this ever happened before?

4 A SUGGESTION

The summer drew on, and Rhoda Brook almost dreaded to meet Mrs Lodge again, notwithstanding that her feeling for the young wife amounted wellnigh to affection. Something in her own individuality seemed to convict Rhoda of crime. Yet a fatality sometimes would direct the steps of the latter to the outskirts of Holmstoke whenever she left her house for any other purpose than her daily work, and hence it happened that their next encounter was out of doors. Rhoda could not avoid the subject which had so mystified her, and after the first few words she stammered, 'I hope your – arm is well again, ma'am?' She had perceived with consternation that Gertrude Lodge carried her left arm stiffly.

'No; it is not quite well. Indeed, it is no better at all; it is rather worse. It pains me dreadfully sometimes.'

'Perhaps you had better go to a doctor, ma'am.'

She replied that she had already seen a doctor. Her husband had insisted upon her going to one. But the surgeon had not seemed to understand the afflicted limb at all; he had told her to bathe it in hot water, and she had bathed it, but the treatment had done no good.

'Will you let me see it?' said the milkwoman.

Mrs Lodge pushed up her sleeve and disclosed the place, which was a few inches above the wrist. As soon as Rhoda Brook saw it, she could hardly preserve her composure. There was nothing of the nature of a wound, but the arm at that point had a shrivelled look, and the outline of the four fingers appeared more distinct than at the former time. Moreover, she fancied that they were imprinted in precisely the relative position of her clutch upon the arm in the trance: the first finger towards Gertrude's wrist, and the fourth towards her elbow.

What the impress resembled seemed to have struck Gertrude herself since their last meeting. 'It looks almost like finger-marks,' she said; adding with a faint laugh, 'My husband says it is as if some witch, or the devil himself, had taken hold of me there, and blasted the flesh.'

Rhoda shivered. 'That's fancy,' she said hurriedly. 'I wouldn't mind it, if I were you.'

'I shouldn't so much mind it,' said the younger, with hesitation, 'if if I hadn't a notion that it makes my husband – dislike me – no, love me less. Men think so much of personal appearance.'

'Some do – he for one.'

'Yes; and he was very proud of mine, at first.'

'Keep your arm covered from his sight.'

'Ah – he knows the disfigurement is there!' She tried to hide the tears that filled her eyes.

'Well, ma'am, I earnestly hope it will go away soon.'

And so the milkwoman's mind was chained anew to the subject by a horrid sort of spell as she returned home. The sense of having been guilty of an act of malignity increased, affect as she might to ridicule her superstition. In her secret heart Rhoda did not altogether object to a slight diminution of her successor's beauty, by whatever means it had come about; but she did not wish to inflict upon her physical pain. For though this pretty young woman had rendered impossible any reparation which Lodge might have made Rhoda for his past conduct, everything like resentment at the unconscious usurpation had quite passed away from the elder's mind.

If the sweet and kindly Gertrude Lodge only knew of the dreamscene in the bed-chamber, what would she think? Not to inform her of it seemed treachery in the presence of her friendliness; but tell she could not of her own accord – neither could she devise a remedy.

She mused upon the matter the greater part of the night, and the next day, after the morning milking, set out to obtain another glimpse of Gertrude Lodge if she could, being held to her by a gruesome fascination. By watching the house from a distance the milkmaid was presently able to discern the farmer's wife in a ride she was taking alone – probably to join her husband in some distant field. Mrs Lodge perceived her, and cantered in her direction.

'Good morning, Rhoda!' Gertrude said, when she had come up. 'I was going to call.'

Rhoda noticed that Mrs Lodge held the reins with some difficulty.

'I hope – the bad arm,' said Rhoda.

'They tell me there is possibly one way by which I might be able to find out the cause, and so perhaps the cure, of it,' replied the other anxiously. 'It is by going to some clever man over in Egdon Heath. They did not know if he was still alive – and I cannot remember his name at this moment; but they said that you knew more of his movements than anybody else hereabout, and could tell me if he were still to be consulted. Dear me – what was his name? But you know.'

'Not Conjuror Trendle?' said her thin companion, turning pale.

'Trendle – yes. Is he alive?'

'I believe so,' said Rhoda, with reluctance.

'Why do you call him conjuror?'

'Well – they say – they used to say he was a – he had powers other folks have not.'

'O, how could my people be so superstitious as to recommend a man of that sort! I thought they meant some medical man. I shall think no more of him.'

Rhoda looked relieved, and Mrs Lodge rode on. The milkwoman had inwardly seen, from the moment she heard of her having been mentioned as a reference for this man, that there must exist a sarcastic feeling among the workfolk that a sorceress would know the whereabouts of the exorcist. They suspected her, then. A short time ago this would have given no concern to a woman of her common sense. But she had a haunting reason to be superstitious now; and she had been seized with sudden dread that this Conjuror Trendle might name her as the malignant influence which was blasting the fair person of Gertrude and so lead her friend to hate her for ever, and to treat her as some fiend in human shape.

But all was not over. Two days after, a shadow intruded into the window-pattern thrown on Rhoda Brook's floor by the afternoon sun. The woman opened the door at once, almost breathlessly.

'Are you alone?' said Gertrude. She seemed to be no less harassed and anxious than Brook herself.

'Yes,' said Rhoda.

'The place on my arm seems worse, and troubles me!' the young farmer's wife went on. 'It is so mysterious! I do hope it will not be an incurable wound. I have again been thinking of what they said about Conjuror Trendle. I don't really believe in such men, but I should not mind just visiting him, from curiosity – though on no account must my husband know. Is it far to where he lives?'

'Yes – five miles,' said Rhoda backwardly. 'In the heart of Egdon.'

'Well, I should have to walk. Could not you go with me to show me the way – say to-morrow afternoon?'

'O, not I – that is,' the milkwoman murmured, with a start of dismay. Again the dread seized her that something to do with her fierce act in the dream might be revealed, and her character in the eyes of the most useful friend she had ever had be ruined irretrievably.

Mrs Lodge urged, and Rhoda finally assented, though with much misgiving. Sad as the journey would be to her, she could not conscientiously stand in the way of a possible remedy for her patron's strange affliction. It was agreed that, to escape suspicion of their mystic intent, they should meet at the edge of the heath at the corner of a plantation which was visible from the spot where they now stood.

5 CONJUROR TRENDLE

By the next afternoon Rhoda would have done anything to escape this inquiry. But she had promised to go. Moreover, there was a horrid fascination at times in becoming instrumental in throwing such possible light on her own character as would reveal her to be something greater in the occult world than she had ever herself suspected.

She started just before the time of day mentioned between them, and half-an-hour's brisk walking brought her to the south-eastern extension of the Egdon tract of country, where the fir plantation was. A slight figure, cloaked and veiled, was already there. Rhoda recognized, almost with a shudder, that Mrs Lodge bore her left arm in a sling.

They hardly spoke to each other, and immediately set out on their climb into the interior of this solemn country, which stood high above the rich alluvial soil they had left half-an-hour before. It was a long walk; thick clouds made the atmosphere dark, though it was as yet only early afternoon; and the wind howled dismally over the slopes of the heath – not improbably the same heath which had witnessed the agony of the Wessex King Ina, presented to after-ages as Lear. Gertrude Lodge talked most, Rhoda replying with monosyllabic preoccupation. She had a strange dislike to walking on the side of her companion where hung the afflicted arm, moving round to the other when inadvertently near it. Much heather had been brushed by their feet when they descended upon a cart-track, beside which stood the house of the man they sought.

He did not profess his remedial practices openly, or care anything about their continuance, his direct interests being those of a dealer in furze, turf, 'sharp sand', and other local products. Indeed, he affected not to believe largely in his own powers, and when warts that had been shown him for cure miraculously disappeared – which it must be owned they infallibly did – he would say lightly, 'O, I only drink a glass of grog upon 'em at your expense – perhaps it's all chance,' and immediately turn the subject.

He was at home when they arrived, having in fact seen them descending into his valley. He was a grey-bearded man, with a reddish face, and he looked singularly at Rhoda the first moment he beheld her. Mrs Lodge told him her errand; and then with words of self-disparagement he examined her arm.

'Medicine can't cure it,' he said promptly. ' 'Tis the work of an enemy.

Rhoda shrank into herself, and drew back.

'An enemy? What enemy?' asked Mrs Lodge.

He shook his head. 'That's best known to yourself,' he said. 'If you like, I can show the person to you, though I shall not myself know who it is. I can do no more; and don't wish to do that.'

She pressed him; on which he told Rhoda to wait outside where she stood, and took Mrs Lodge into the room. It opened immediately from the door; and, as the latter remained ajar, Rhoda Brook could see the proceedings without taking part in them. He brought a tumbler from the dresser, nearly filled it with water, and fetching an egg, prepared it in some private way; after which he broke it on the edge of the glass, so that the white went in and the yolk remained. As it was getting gloomy, he took the glass and its contents to the window, and told Gertrude to watch the mixture closely. They leant over the table together, and the milkwoman could see the opaline hue of the egg-fluid changing form as it sank in the water, but she was not near enough to define the shape that it assumed.

'Do you catch the likeness of any face or figure as you look?' demanded the conjuror of the young woman.

She murmured a reply, in tones so low as to be inaudible to Rhoda, and continued to gaze intently into the glass. Rhoda turned, and walked a few steps away.

When Mrs Lodge came out, and her face was met by the light, it appeared exceedingly pale – as pale as Rhoda's – against the sad dun shades of the upland's garniture. Trendle shut the door behind her, and they at once started homeward together. But Rhoda perceived that her companion had quite changed.

'Did he charge much?' she asked tentatively.

'O no – nothing. He would not take a farthing,' said Gertrude.

'And what did you see?' inquired Rhoda.

'Nothing I – care to speak of.' The constraint in her manner was remarkable; her face was so rigid as to wear an oldened aspect, faintly suggestive of the face in Rhoda's bed-chamber.

'Was it you who first proposed coming here?' Mrs Lodge suddenly inquired, after a long pause. 'How very odd, if you did!'

'No. But I am not sorry we have come, all things considered,' she replied. For the first time a sense of triumph possessed her, and she did not altogether deplore that the young thing at her side should learn that their lives had been antagonized by other influences than their own.

The subject was no more alluded to during the long and dreary walk home. But in some way or other a story was whispered about the many-dairied lowland that winter that Mrs Lodge's gradual loss of the use of her left arm was owing to her being 'overlooked' by Rhoda Brook. The latter kept her own counsel about the incubus, but her face grew sadder and thinner; and in the spring she and her boy disappeared from the neighbourhood of Holmstoke.

6 A SECOND ATTEMPT

Half a dozen years passed away, and Mr and Mrs Lodge's married experience sank into prosiness, and worse. The farmer was usually gloomy and silent; the woman whom he had wooed for her grace and beauty was contorted and disfigured in the left limb; moreover, she had brought him no child, which rendered it likely that he would be the last of a family who had occupied that valley for some two hundred years. He thought of Rhoda Brook and her son; and feared this might be a judgment from heaven upon him.

The once blithe-hearted and enlightened Gertrude was changing into an irritable, superstitious woman, whose whole time was given to experimenting upon her ailment with every quack remedy she came across. She was honestly attached to her husband, and was ever secretly hoping against hope to win back his heart again by regaining some at least of her personal beauty. Hence it arose that her closet was lined with bottles, packets, and ointment-pots of every description – nay, bunches of mystic herbs, charms, and books of necromancy, which in her schoolgirl time she would have ridiculed as folly.

'Damned if you won't poison yourself with these apothecary messes and witch mixtures some time or other,' said her husband, when his eye chanced to fall upon the multitudinous array.

She did not reply, but turned her sad, soft glance upon him in such heart-swollen reproach that he looked sorry for his words, and added, 'I only meant it for your good, you know, Gertrude.'

'I'll clear out the whole lot, and destroy them,' said she huskily, 'and try such remedies no more!'

'You want somebody to cheer you,' he observed. 'I once thought of adopting a boy; but he is too old now. And he is gone away I don't know where.'

She guessed to whom he alluded; for Rhoda Brook's story had in the course of years become known to her; though not a word had ever passed between her husband and herself on the subject. Neither had she ever spoken to him of her visit to Conjuror Trendle, and of what was revealed to her, or she thought was revealed to her, by that solitary heathman.

She was now five-and-twenty; but she seemed older. 'Six years of marriage, and only a few months of love,' she sometimes whispered to herself. And then she thought of the apparent cause, and said, with a tragic glance at her withering limb, 'If I could only again be as I was when he first saw me!'

She obediently destroyed her nostrums and charms; but there remained a hankering wish to try something else – some other sort of cure altogether. She had never revisited Trendle since she had been conducted to the house of the solitary by Rhoda against her will; but it now suddenly occurred to Gertrude that she would, in a last desperate effort at deliverance from this seeming curse, again seek out the man, if he yet lived. He was entitled to a certain credence, for the indistinct form he had raised in the glass had undoubtedly resembled the only woman in the world who – as she now knew, though not then – could have a reason for bearing her ill-will. The visit should be paid.

This time she went alone, though she nearly got lost on the heath, and roamed a considerable distance out of her way. Trendle's house was reached at last, however; he was not indoors, and instead of waiting at the cottage, she went to where his bent figure was pointed out to her at work a long way off. Trendle remembered her, and laying down the handful of furze-roots which he was gathering and throwing into a heap, he offered to accompany her in her homeward direction, as the distance was considerable and the days were short. So they walked together, his head bowed nearly to the earth, and his form of a colour with it.

'You can send away warts and other excrescences, I know,' she said; 'why can't you send away this?' And the arm was uncovered.

'You think too much of my powers!' said Trendle; 'and I am old and weak now, too. No, no; it is too much for me to attempt in my own person. What have ye tried?'

She named to him some of the hundred medicaments and counterspells which she had adopted from time to time. He shook his head.

'Some were good enough,' he said approvingly; 'but not many of them for such as this. This is of the nature of a blight, not of the nature of a wound, and if you ever do throw it off, it will be all at once.'

'If I only could!'

'There is only one chance of doing it known to me. It has never failed in kindred afflictions – that I can declare. But it is hard to carry out, and especially for a woman.'

'Tell me!' said she.

'You must touch with the limb the neck of a man who's been hanged.'

She started a little at the image he had raised.

'Before he's cold – just after he's cut down,' continued the conjuror impassively.

'How can that do good?'

'It will turn the blood and change the constitution. But, as I say, to do it is hard. You must go to the jail when there's a hanging, and wait for him when he's brought off the gallows. Lots have done it, though perhaps not such pretty women as you. I used to send dozens for skin complaints. But that was in former times. The last I sent was in '13 – near twelve years ago.'

He had no more to tell her, and, when he had put her into a straight track homeward, turned and left her, refusing all money as at first.

7 A RIDE

The communication sank deep into Gertrude's mind. Her nature was rather a timid one; and probably of all remedies that the white wizard could have suggested there was not one which would have filled her with so much aversion as this, not to speak of the immense obstacles in the way of its adoption.

Casterbridge, the county-town, was a dozen or fifteen miles off; and though in those days, when men were executed for horse-stealing, arson, and burglary, an assize seldom passed without a hanging, it was not likely that she could get access to the body of the criminal unaided. And the fear of her husband's anger made her reluctant to breathe a word of Trendle's suggestion to him or to anybody about him.

She did nothing for months, and patiently bore her disfigurement as before. But her woman's nature, craving for renewed love, through the medium of renewed beauty (she was but twenty-five), was ever stimulating her to try what, at any rate, could hardly do her any harm. 'What came by a spell will go by a spell surely,' she would say. Whenever her imagination pictured the act she shrank in terror from the possibility of it; then the words of the conjuror, 'It will turn your blood,' were seen to be capable of a scientific no less than a ghastly interpretation; the mastering desire returned, and urged her on again.

There was at this time but one county paper, and that her husband only occasionally borrowed. But old-fashioned days had old-fashioned means, and news was extensively conveyed by word of mouth from market to market, or from fair to fair, so that, whenever such an event as an execution was about to take place, few within a radius of twenty miles were ignorant of the coming sight; and, so far as Holmstoke was concerned, some enthusiasts had been known to walk all the way to Casterbridge and back in one day, solely to witness the spectacle. The next assizes were in March; and when Gertrude Lodge heard that they had been held, she inquired stealthily at the inn as to the result, as soon as she could find opportunity.

She was, however, too late. The time at which the sentences were to be carried out had arrived, and to make the journey and obtain admission at such short notice required at least her husband's assistance. She dared not tell him, for she had found by delicate experiment that these smouldering village beliefs made him furious if mentioned, partly because he half entertained them himself It was therefore necessary to wait for another opportunity.

Her determination received a fillip from learning that two epileptic children had attended from this very village of Holmstoke many years before with beneficial results, though the experiment had been strongly condemned by the neighbouring clergy. April, May, June passed; and it is no overstatement to say that by the end of the last-named month Gertrude wellnigh longed for the death of a fellow-creature. Instead of her formal prayers each night, her unconscious prayer was, 'O Lord, hang some guilty or innocent person soon!'

This time she made earlier inquiries, and was altogether more systematic in her proceedings. Moreover, the season was summer, between the haymaking and the harvest, and in the leisure thus afforded him her husband had been holiday-taking away from home.

The assizes were in July, and she went to the inn as before. There was to be one execution – only one – for arson.

Her greatest problem was not how to get to Casterbridge, but what means she should adopt for obtaining admission to the jail. Though access for such purposes had formerly never been denied, the custom had fallen into desuetude; and in contemplating her possible difficulties, she was again almost driven to fall back upon her husband. But, on sounding him about the assizes, he was so uncommunicative, so more than usually cold, that she did not proceed, and decided that whatever she did she would do alone.

Fortune, obdurate hitherto, showed her unexpected favour. On the Thursday before the Saturday fixed for the execution, Lodge remarked to her that he was going away from home for another day or two on business at a fair, and that he was sorry he could not take her with him.

She exhibited on this occasion so much readiness to stay at home that he looked at her in surprise. Time had been when she would have shown deep disappointment at the loss of such a jaunt. However, he lapsed into his usual taciturnity, and on the day named left Holmstoke.

It was now her turn. She at first had thought of driving, but on reflection held that driving would not do, since it would necessitate her keeping to the turnpike-road, and so increase by tenfold the risk of her ghastly errand being found out. She decided to ride, and avoid the beaten track, notwithstanding that in her husband's stables there was no animal just at present which by any stretch of imagination could be considered a lady's mount, in spite of his promise before marriage to always keep a mare for her. He had, however, many cart-horses, fine ones of their kind; and among the rest was a serviceable creature, an equine Amazon, with a back as broad as a sofa, on which Gertrude had occasionally taken an airing when unwell. This horse she chose.

On Friday afternoon one of the men brought it round. She was dressed, and before going down looked at her shrivelled arm. 'Ah!' she said to it, if it had not been for you this terrible ordeal would have been saved me!'

When strapping up the bundle in which she carried a few articles of clothing, she took occasion to say to the servant, 'I take these in case I should not get back to-night from the person I am going to visit. Don't be alarmed if I am not in by ten, and close up the house as usual. I shall be at home to-morrow for certain.' She meant then to tell her husband privately; the deed accomplished was not like the deed projected. He would almost certainly forgive her.

And then the pretty palpitating Gertrude Lodge went from her husband's homestead; but though her goal was Casterbridge she did not take the direct route thither through Stickleford. Her cunning course at first was in precisely the opposite direction. As soon as she was out of sight, however, she turned to the left, by a road which led into Egdon, and on entering the heath wheeled round, and set out in the true course, due westerly. A more private way down the county could not be imagined; and as to direction, she had merely to keep her horse's head to a point a little to the right of the sun. She knew that she would light upon a firze-cutter or cottager of some sort from time to time, from whom she might correct her bearing.

Though the date was comparatively recent, Egdon was much less fragmentary in character than now. The attempts – successful and otherwise – at cultivation on the lower slopes, which intrude and break up the original heath into small detached heaths, had not been carried far; Enclosure Acts had not taken effect, and the banks and fences which now exclude the cattle of those villagers who formerly enjoyed rights of commonage thereon, and the carts of those who had turbary privileges which kept them in firing all the year round, were not erected. Gertrude, therefore, rode along with no other obstacles than the prickly furze bushes, the mats of heather, the white water-courses, and the natural steeps and declivities of the ground.

Her horse was sure, if heavy-footed and slow, and though a draught. animal, was easy-paced; had it been otherwise, she was not a woman who could have ventured to ride over such a bit of country with a half-dead arm. It was therefore nearly eight o'clock when she drew rein to breathe her bearer on the last outlying high point of heath-land towards Casterbridge, previous to leaving Egdon for the cultivated valleys.

She halted before a pool called Rushy-pond, 'flanked by the ends of two hedges; a railing ran through the centre of the pond, dividing it in half. Over the railing she saw the low green country; over the green trees the roofs of the town; over the roofs a white flat façade, denoting the entrance to the county jail. On the roof of this front specks were moving about; they seemed to be workmen erecting something. Her flesh crept. She descended slowly, and was soon amid corn-fields and pastures. In another half-hour, when it was almost dusk, Gertrude reached the White Hart, the first inn of the town on that side.

Little surprise was excited by her arrival; farmers' wives rode on horseback then more than they do now; though, for that matter, Mrs Lodge was not imagined to be a wife at all; the innkeeper supposed her some harumskarum young woman who had come to attend 'hang-fair' next day. Neither her husband nor herself ever dealt in Casterbridge market, so that she was unknown. While dismounting she beheld a crowd of boys standing at the door of a harness-maker's shop just above the inn, looking inside it with deep interest.

'What is going on there?' she asked of the ostler.

'Making the rope for to-morrow.'

She throbbed responsively, and contracted her arm.

''Tis sold by the inch afterwards,' the man continued. 'I could get you a bit, miss, for nothing, if you'd like?'

She hastily repudiated any such wish, all the more from a curious creeping feeling that the condemned wretch's destiny was becoming interwoven with her own; and having engaged a room for the night, sat down to think.

Up to this time she had formed but the vaguest notions about her means of obtaining access to the prison. The words of the cunning-man returned to her mind. He had implied that she should use her beauty, impaired though it was, as a pass-key. In her inexperience she knew little about jail functionaries; she had heard of a high-sheriff and an undersheriff, but dimly only. She knew, however, that there must be a hangman, and to the hangman she determined to apply.

8 A WATER-SIDE HERMIT

At this date, and for several years after, there was a hangman to almost every jail. Gertrude found, on inquiry, that the Casterbridge official dwelt in a lonely cottage by a deep slow river flowing under the cliff on which the prison buildings were situate – the stream being the selfsame one, though she did not know it, which watered the Stickleford and Holmstoke meads lower down in its course.

Having changed her dress, and before she had eaten or drunk – for she could not take her ease till she had ascertained some particulars – Gertrude pursued her way by a path along the water-side to the cottage indicated. Passing thus the outskirts of the jail, she discerned on the level roof over the gateway three rectangular lines against the sky, where the specks had been moving in her distant view; she recognized what the erection was, and passed quickly on. Another hundred yards brought her to the executioner's house, which a boy pointed out. It stood close to the same stream, and was hard by a weir, the waters of which emitted a steady roar.

While she stood hesitating the door opened, and an old man came forth, shading a candle with one hand. Locking the door on the outside, he turned to a flight of wooden steps fixed against the end of the cottage, and began to ascend them, this being evidently the staircase to his bedroom. Gertrude hastened forward, but by the time she reached the foot of the ladder he was at the top. She called to him loudly enough to be heard above the roar of the weir; he looked down and said, 'What d'ye want here?'

'To speak to you a minute.'

The candlelight, such as it was, fell upon her imploring, pale, upturned face, and Davies (as the hangman was called) backed down the ladder. 'I was just going to bed,' he said. '"Early to bed and early to rise", but I don't mind stopping a minute for such a one as you. Come into house.' He reopened the door, and preceded her to the room within.

The implements of his daily work, which was that of a jobbing gardener, stood in a corner, and seeing probably that she looked rural, he said, 'If you want me to undertake country work I can't come, for I never leave Casterbridge for gentle nor simple – not I. My real calling is officer of justice, he added formally.

'Yes, yes! That's it. To-morrow!'

'Ah! I thought so. Well, what's the matter about that? 'Tis no use to come here about the knot – folks do come continually, but I tell 'em one knot is as merciful as another if ye keep it under the ear. Is the unfortunate man a relation; or, I should say, perhaps' (looking at her dress) 'a person who's been in your employ?'

'No. What time is the execution?'

'The same as usual – twelve o'clock, or as soon after as the London mail-coach gets in. We always wait for that, in case of a reprieve.'

'O – a reprieve – I hope not!' she said involuntarily.

'Well, – hee, hee! – as a matter of business, so do I! But still, if ever a young fellow deserved to be let off, this one does; only just turned eighteen, and only present by chance when the rick was fired. Howsomever, there's not much risk of it, as they are obliged to make an example of him, there having been so much destruction of property that way lately.'

'I mean,' she explained, 'that I want to touch him for a charm, a cure of an affliction, by the advice of a man who has proved the virtue of the remedy.'

'O yes, miss! Now I understand. I've had such people come in past years. But it didn't strike me that you looked of a sort to require bloodturning. What's the complaint? The wrong kind for this, I'll be bound.'

'My arm.' She reluctantly showed the withered skin.

'Ah! – 'tis all a-scram!' said the hangman, examining it.

'Yes,' said she.

'Well,' he continued, with interest, 'that is the class o' subject, I'm bound to admit! I like the look of the wound; it is truly as suitable for the cure as any I ever saw. 'Twas a knowing-man that sent 'ee, whoever he was.'

'You can contrive for me all that's necessary?' she said breathlessly.

'You should really have gone to the governor of the jail, and your doctor with 'ee, and given your name and address – that's how it used to be done, if I recollect. Still, perhaps, I can manage it for a trifling fee.'

'O, thank you! I would rather do it this way, as I should like it kept private.'

'Lover not to know, eh?'

'No – husband.'

'Aha! Very well. I'll get 'ee a touch of the corpse.'

'Where is it now?' she said, shuddering.

'It? – he, you mean; he's living yet. Just inside that little small winder up there in the glum.' He signified the jail on the cliff above.

She thought of her husband and her friends. 'Yes, of course,' she said; 'and how am I to proceed?'

He took her to the door. 'Now, do you be waiting at the little wicket in the wall, that you'll find up there in the lane, not later than one o'clock. I will open it from the inside, as I shan't come home to dinner till he's cut down. Good-night. Be punctual; and if you don't want anybody to know 'ee, wear a veil. Ah – once I had such a daughter as you!'

She went away, and climbed the path above, to assure herself that she would be able to find the wicket next day. Its outline was soon visible to her – a narrow opening in the outer wall of the prison precincts. The steep was so great that, having reached the wicket, she stopped a moment to breathe; and, looking back upon the water-side cot, saw the hangman again ascending his outdoor staircase. He entered the loft or chamber to which it led, and in a few minutes extinguished his light. The town clock struck ten, and she returned to the White Hart as she had come.

9 A RENCOUNTER

It was one o'clock on Saturday. Gertrude Lodge, having been admitted to the jail as above described, was sitting in a waiting-room within the second gate, which stood under a classic archway of ashlar, then comparatively modern, and bearing the inscription, 'COVNTY JAIL: 1793'. This had been the façade she saw from the heath the day before. Near at hand was a passage to the roof on which the gallows stood.

The town was thronged, and the market suspended; but Gertrude had seen scarcely a soul. Having kept her room till the hour of the appointment, she had proceeded to the spot by a way which avoided the open space below the cliff where the spectators had gathered; but she could, even now, hear the multitudinous babble of their voices, out of which rose at intervals the hoarse croak of a single voice uttering the words, 'last dying speech and confession!' There had been no reprieve, and the execution was over; but the crowd still waited to see the body taken down.

Soon the persistent woman heard a trampling overhead, then a hand beckoned to her, and, following directions, she went out and crossed the inner paved court beyond the gatehouse, her knees trembling so that she could scarcely walk. One of her arms was out of its sleeve, and only covered by her shawl.

On the spot at which she had now arrived were two trestles, and before she could think of their purpose she heard heavy feet descending stairs somewhere at her back. Turn her head she would not, or could not, and, rigid in this position, she was conscious of a rough coffin passing her shoulder, borne by four men. It was open, and in it lay the body of a young man, wearing the smockfrock of a rustic, and fustian breeches. The corpse had been thrown into the coffin so hastily that the skirt of the smockfrock was hanging over. The burden was temporarily deposited on the trestles.

By this time the young woman's state was such that a gray mist seemed to float before her eyes, on account of which, and the veil she wore, she could scarcely discern anything: it was as though she had nearly died, but was held up by a sort of galvanism.

'Now!' said a voice close at hand, and she was just conscious that the word had been addressed to her.

By a last strenuous effort she advanced, at the same time hearing persons approaching behind her. She bared her poor curst arm; and Davies, uncovering the face of the corpse, took Gertrude's hand, and held it so that her arm lay across the dead man's neck, upon a line the colour of an unripe blackberry, which surrounded it.

Gertrude shrieked: 'the turn o' the blood', predicted by the conjuror, had taken place. But at that moment a second shriek rent the air of the enclosure: it was not Gertrude's, and its effect upon her was to make her start round.

Immediately behind her stood Rhoda Brook, her face drawn, and her eyes red with weeping. Behind Rhoda stood Gertrude's own husband; his countenance lined, his eyes dim, but without a tear.

'D—n you! what are you doing here?' he said hoarsely.

'Hussy – to come between us and our child now!' cried Rhoda. 'This is the meaning of what Satan showed me in the vision! You are like her at last!' And clutching the bare arm of the younger woman, she pulled her unresistingly back against the wall. Immediately Brook had loosened her hold the fragile young Gertrude slid down against the feet of her husband. When he lifted her up she was unconscious.

The mere sight of the twain had been enough to suggest to her that the dead young man was Rhoda's son. At that time the relatives of an executed convict had the privilege of claiming the body for burial, if they chose to do so; and it was for this purpose that Lodge was awaiting the inquest with Rhoda. He had been summoned by her as soon as the young man was taken in the crime, and at different times since; and he had attended in court during the trial. This was the 'holiday' he had been indulging in of late. The two wretched parents had wished to avoid exposure; and hence had come themselves for the body, a waggon and sheet for its conveyance and covering being in waiting outside.

Gertrude's case was so serious that it was deemed advisable to call to her the surgeon who was at hand. She was taken out of the jail into the town; but she never reached home alive. Her delicate vitality, sapped perhaps by the paralyzed arm, collapsed under the double shock that followed the severe strain, physical and mental, to which she had subjected herself during the previous twenty-four hours. Her blood had been 'turned' indeed – too far. Her death took place in the town three days after.

Her husband was never seen in Casterbridge again; once only in the old market-place at Anglebury, which he had so much frequented, and very seldom in public anywhere. Burdened at first with moodiness and remorse, he eventually changed for the better, and appeared as a chastened and thoughtful man. Soon after attending the funeral of his poor young wife he took steps towards giving up the farms in Holmstoke and the adjoining parish, and, having sold every head of his stock, he went away to Port-Bredy, at the other end of the county, living there in solitary lodgings till his death two years later of a painless decline. It was then found that he had bequeathed the whole of his not inconsiderable property to a reformatory for boys, subject to the payment of a small annuity to Rhoda Brook, if she could be found to claim it.

For some time she could not be found; but eventually she reappeared in her old parish, – absolutely refusing, however, to have anything to do with the provision made for her. Her monotonous milking at the dairy was resumed, and followed for many long years, till her form became bent, and her once abundant dark hair white and worn away at the forehead – perhaps by long pressure against the cows. Here, sometimes, those who knew her experiences would stand and observe her, and wonder what sombre thoughts were beating inside that impassive, wrinkled brow, to the rhythm of the alternating milk-streams.

SECTION 1: *lorn* – forlorn; *tisty-tosty* – like a ball; *laved* – drew water; *Turk* – devil; *aforesaid* – said before; *twain* – two; *barton* – cow shed.

SECTION 2: *yeoman* – landowner; *whewed* – out-of-breath noise.

SECTION 3: *incubus* – evil spirit; *spectre* – ghost; *chimmer* – room; *meads* – meadows; *parish* – district; *morrow* – next day; *stigma* – mark.

SECTION 4: *usurpation* – seizure; *sorceress* – female wizard; *exorcist* – one who removes evil spirits.

SECTION 5: *occult* – mystic, secret; *alluvial* – riverflood; *furze* – gorse; *sharpsand* – building sand; *grog* – alcohol and water; *opaline* – milky white; *overlooked* – bewitched.

SECTION 6: *blithe* – gay; *quack* – ignorant of medicine; *necromancy* – magic; *nostrum* – cure; *ye* – you; *blight* – disease.

SECTION 7: *assize* – trial; *spell* – magic; *fillip* – stimulus; *epileptic* – nervous disease; *obdurate* – stubborn; *equine* – of horses; *Amazon* – female warrior; *palpitating* – throbbing; *commonage* – access to land; *turbary* – right to cut turf; *firing* – fuel; *draught* – work; *harum-scarum* – reckless; *cunning* – crafty; *sherrif* – officer.

SECTION 8: *situate* – placed; *howsomever* – however; *a-scram* – withered; *glum* – gloom; *cot* – cottage.

SECTION 9: *ashlar* – square stone; *fustian* – rough cloth; *galvanism* – electricity; *countenance* – face; *annuity* – yearly grant.

3 Understanding the story

What I want to do with this story is to discuss various elements of it which are common to most stories, and then concentrate on just two aspects in particular – language (in Section 4) and psychology (Section 5). The elements which I think appropriate to this and most other stories are its

- ☆ construction
- ☆ dramatisation
- ☆ characterisation
- ☆ setting
- ☆ subject
- ☆ treatment

Let's consider these one at a time. You may find that items in one category sometimes overlap into another. It is not always possible to keep these issues absolutely separate. But first I will assist you by reminding you briefly what these terms *mean*.

Construction. This refers to the *shape* of a story, the way its parts are arranged, the *form* its elements assume. It refers to the 'architecture' of a piece of work rather than its contents or subject.

Dramatisation. This refers to the manner in which our interest in what is going on is *created* and *held*. It refers to the way the story unfolds, and although it is a term taken from the theatre the events need not necessarily be 'dramatic' in the sense of being startling or shocking.

Characterisation. This refers to the manner in which credible people are created in fiction, how the author makes a character come to life, or how characters are made memorable or different from each other.

Setting. This refers to the creation of a world in which the characters of the story and the events in it take place. It might be realistic or totally imaginary and fantastic.

Subject. This term refers to what the story is *about*. It is a term close to 'theme' but is broader and allows for a fuller description of what is the central point of interest in the story.

Treatment. This refers to the manner in which the author deals with his subject. It is the attitude of the author towards the events of the story.

What I want you to do now is STOP, think about each one of these features of the story in turn, and make notes of your responses and observations. You will need to *think* about these features: they are not something which can be looked up or just 'spotted' in the story like individual names or words. You will need to focus your thoughts on to the single feature itself and separate it from other considerations. In this way you will be exercising discrimination and developing your powers of critical analysis.

And remember that you need evidence to support any claims you wish to make: these will come from specific references in the story. For instance if you want to claim that character X is wicked you need to give examples of what X *does* that is wicked.

Be disciplined, and do *write down* your notes. There is quite a lot to get through here – certainly too much to try holding in your memory. When you have completed your notes you can compare them with my own observations.

CONSTRUCTION

You will have perhaps noted that it is quite a long story and Hardy has split it up into nine numbered and titled sections (he did this with many of his longer stories). But these are more than just a device to make the events 'manageable' for us. Note that each section is focused onto a separate character, topic, or incident. So, in the first 'A Lorn Milkmaid' – we are introduced to Rhoda Brook, and in the second – 'The Young Wife' – to Gertrude Lodge. Hardy thus constructs his story from a series of portraits, tableaux, or dramatic episodes. (Personally, I think this is one of the reasons his work is so readily adapted for the cinema and for television.)

At a deeper level you may have noted that the story is in two parts. The first part (Sections 1 to 5) establishes the characters and the dramatic problem. This part ends with Gertrude's unsuccessful first visit to Conjuror Trendle. But then six years pass in the space of the opening paragraph of Section 6. The affliction has become worse; she makes a second visit to Trendle, and the remainder of the story (Sections 6 to 9) deals with the dramatic finale.

Because it is such an exciting story we are hardly aware of this structure, but it exists nevertheless, giving a sort of architectural strength and beauty to the work.

DRAMATISATION

There are several features which contribute to the drama of the story. The first is the sheer human interest of the relationships between the characters. We want to know what has happened to Lodge, Rhoda, and the boy (his son) in the past, that they are so separate now. So the story *begins* with a dramatic situation. Then there is the psychological interest in the principal characters. Why *is* Rhoda so concerned about Gertrude's physical appearance? This compounds the dramatic tension or interest. Next comes Rhoda's shocking dream and its mysterious connection with Gertrude's affected arm. These three features alone would create enough dramatic interest for most writers, but Hardy piles on still more.

For instance, the two women begin to develop a curious relationship which has elements of both friendship and rivalry. Then there is the element of superstitious beliefs and practices introduced with the visits to Trendle. We are not told explicitly what Gertrude sees in the glass of water, but it has a powerful effect on her. What follows is an intensification of all that has gone before. Gertrude changes and becomes even *more* desperate; she makes the *second* visit to Trendle, and then finally makes her gruesome trip to the jail.

You will notice that Hardy at this point draws together every single one of these elements of mystery, suspense, psychological tension, human interest, and superstitious belief in his vividly dramatic final scene. All the main characters are present – Rhoda, Gertrude, Lodge, and the (dead) boy. The tensions between them are heightened by the addition of two further pieces of drama – the sudden appearance of her husband to Gertrude, and the tragic irony that the dead body is that of Rhoda's son.

The drama and the construction of the story reinforce each other at this point rather as they do in classical Greek drama. Every element of dramatic interest is focused in this heart-stopping finale.

CHARACTERISATION

If we look at the three main characters – Rhoda, Gertrude, and Lodge – we can see that they are created and given life by the fairly conventional manner of combining physical description with their reported speech and actions. Rhoda is 'thin', 'pale', and she has 'dark eyes'; Gertrude is short and pretty, her clothes are described, and her 'colouring' is rendered in very poetic terms: 'soft and evanescent, like the light under a heap of rose-petals'. You might have noted that we learn *less* about Lodge – just that he is 'in the prime of life' and that he is clean-shaven. This is perfectly consistent with his secondary role in the story. And we go on to learn a great deal more about the two women on whom the drama centres.

First we are presented with Rhoda's curiosity regarding Gertrude's appearance, and then her innermost thoughts when her dream is revealed to us. Similarly we learn of Gertrude's personal fears regarding her arm and her secret hopes in trying to win back Lodge's regard when she feels her beauty is fading. In other words we know these characters from both the outside *and* the inside. Note that we know hardly anything of Lodge's secret hopes and fears.

We might add that these characters are convincing or acceptable to us because they are complex and full of fears, doubts, and contradictions just like real human beings. Hardy makes them psychologically credible.

You might also have noted that some of the other characters in the story are made to seem realistic and credible by Hardy's use of dialect. His country folk speak as we believe real people might have done.

SETTING

The setting of the story is very realistic indeed. Notice how at the start of the story the detail of the working conditions in the dairy are all rendered very specifically and concretely. There is no attempt to glamourise either the geographical or the physical environment throughout the story. And the setting is perfectly ordinary and homespun – a dairy, Rhoda's humble cottage, the moors, a country town and its prison. There is more emphasis given than you might normally expect to the *work* people do and the tough conditions of their lives. This sense of *realism* in the setting makes the events of the story which is told more credible and acceptable.

Notice too how Hardy creates historical depth in his setting. The story was published in 1888 but the events take place in 1825 (we know this from Trendle's remarks 'The last I sent was in '13 near twelve years ago') And as Rhoda and Gertrude walk across Egdon Heath Hardy makes reference to the fact that this was the 'same heath which had witnessed the agony of the Wessex King Ina, represented to after-ages as Lear'. This brings both a historical-mythical dimension and the force of Shakespeare's tragedy *King Lear* to reinforce Hardy's picture and give it a long historical 'perspective'.

SUBJECT

The decision concerning what a story is most essentially *about* comes close to the business of interpretation, but here I think the most important issues are the unconscious sexual rivalry between the two women, the physical and moral decline of Gertrude, and what might be called the tragedy of the war between the sexes. If you also mentioned the power of superstition I can well understand you doing so; but personally I think this is a side-issue in the story, even though it seems to be quite important. Let me explain my choices.

It should be clear from the moment we are told of Rhoda's interest in Gertrude's physical appearance that she thinks of her as a sexual rival (after all, the younger woman has supplanted her in Lodge's affection). The violent dream reveals her unconscious desire to overthrow this rival, and even though they later appear to become quite friendly the final scene exposes her antagonism quite explicitly. You will notice that in the jail Rhoda re-enacts her dream, clutching Gertrude by the arm until she falls to the floor. Rhoda is the stronger of the two women – morally, physically and imaginatively. She has been fertile enough to produce a son – which Gertrude has not. And she *endures*: she is still milking cows at the end of the story.

Gertrude's moral decline is more subtly delineated and less obvious because we feel a certain sympathy for her predicament. She comes into the story pretty and well dressed, she treats Rhoda and the boy generously, but before long she has a physical affliction and an unhappy marriage. She then grows increasingly desperate in seeking a cure, and when she learns of Trendle's 'gallows cure' she begins to wish for someone's death to achieve her ends; she 'well-nigh longed for the death of a fellow-creature'. To reinforce the theme of unconscious wishes Hardy then adds 'instead of her formal prayers each night, her unconscious prayer was "O Lord, hang some guilty *or innocent* person soon!"' (my emphasis, drawing attention to how low she has sunk).

In terms of the war of the sexes we might consider Lodge's role in the story.

Gertrude has been his mistress in the past and borne him a son; but he has cast her off and married instead a younger, prettier woman. But then Gertrude is 'disfigured' and begins to lose her prettiness; she becomes 'irritable' and 'older' and worries about winning back Lodge's affection. She also fails to bear him a son, something which Lodge regrets. Yet Lodge already *has* a son – but one whom he has refused to acknowledge. The tragedy of their relationship is that it is based upon her physical attractiveness for him; this is the only means by which she can 'win back his heart'. Hardy reinforces this notion when he mentions 'her woman's nature, craving for renewed love, through the medium of renewed beauty'. In this sense, Hardy is offering us a 'tragedy of everyday life'.

TREATMENT

This is a more difficult feature to define in a single work, because to do so with conviction you are best equipped with experience of an author's *other* works. In other words, it is easier if you are used to the author's way of seeing the world and arranging fictional characters and events. But here I think it should be readily apparent that Hardy presents a fairly bleak view of the world and human destiny in it. He is often described as a 'tragic pessimist' because his stories, like this one, show human beings failing to achieve their wishes for personal happiness.

The characters seem to be blighted by forces outside their own control – although here you could argue that most of the tragedy originates in or has lying behind it Lodge's original rejection of Rhoda and their son which has already taken place when the story opens. This is an understandable human weakness even if we think it reprehensible, but from it flows a great deal of personal unhappiness. The boy is left fatherless and is forced to live on the fringes of legality – which eventually leads to his execution. Rhoda has a harsh life of hard work. Lodge loses first his son and then his second wife, and then he himself dies soon afterwards.

You might notice as well that the setting of the story reinforces this harsh view of the world. The dairy is a place of *work*; Rhoda's cottage is poor and rudimentary; as the two women walk over Egdon Heath 'the wind howled dismally over the slopes'; and of course the story *ends* in a prison in the shadow of the gallows.

Many of Hardy's later works present this somewhat tragic view of life, and some readers argue that he is therefore unduly pessimistic. I do not share this view – partly because I think we are invited to *pity* the characters and their plight, and partly because it is open to us to admire the artistic construction of the drama.

It would be remarkable indeed if your responses were exactly the same as mine. Just so long as they were roughly similar and dealt with the same topics you can content yourself that you are on the right lines. No two responses to a work of art are ever quite the same – nor need they be. This is what makes comparisons and discussion of our responses so interesting. However, this does not mean that *any* response is valid. If you wanted to argue that Conjuror Trendle or Davies the hangman were the two most important characters in the story, then you would be taking so perverse a line on the story that it would amount to a mis-reading of it.

But I'm fairly sure you have not done this. What is important at this stage is that you understand the nature of the various elements of the story we have just been discussing (construction, dramatisation, characterisation, setting, subject, and treatment). If you can grasp the significance of these concepts, then you have at your disposal some important skills for the purpose of literary analysis. For the first thing we need to be able to do in order to understand literature more fully is 'take it apart' to see what it is made of. And we will be moving on next to inspect one of the most fundamental elements of literature – the very thing of which it made: *words*.

4 Hardy's language

I want to turn next to one particular aspect of Hardy's literary style – his vocabulary or language – for no other reason than that it strikes me as worthy of comment. As I mentioned in my biographical note Hardy had a strongly autodidactic impulse – that is, he went on educating *himself* long after others might have stopped, and I think this is reflected in the very *wide-ranging* vocabulary he uses. Then too his love for the countryside and its people is reflected in his confident use of *colloquial* language and even *dialect*. And thirdly there seems to me a strong element of *literary* language in Hardy's work – that is, he uses terms which we only normally come across in *books* rather than in spoken language.

What I want you to do next is to look at six aspects of the vocabulary Hardy uses. I will explain the six categories, then you should find examples of such usage – limiting your search to the *first three sections* of the story (so that your examples are more likely to coincide with those offered for discussion). Then you should in addition try to say what is significant about such vocabulary. Why does Hardy use these terms? What effect do they have? Do they have any special significance for the story?

These are the six categories, with a few words of explanation:

Archaisms. Words which at the time of being employed have long since passed out of normal usage.

Literary language. Words which are more commonly used in the province of the written – rather than the spoken language

Poetic language. Words which are most commonly used in the province of poetry (rather than prose).

Colloquialisms. The language of the everyday spoken word, with the emphasis on its irregularity or slanginess.

Dialect. Terms which are particular to an individual geographical locality.

Technical language. Terms which are special to a particular activity or phenomenon.

STOP here, find examples from the first three sections of the story, *write down* the examples you find, and then make notes on what you think significant about Hardy's use of these terms.

The purpose of this exercise, once again, is to force you to consider language in more detail than you may have been used to before.

———⋙•◉•⋘———

Here are my own examples. Do not worry if your own are different. There are many instances in each category. And you may also have discovered that some terms may belong to more than one single category.

Archaisms. 'lorn' (forlorn), 'twain' (two), 'lineaments' (distinctive features).

Hardy's use of archaisms is quite justified here. After all, his story is set in the early years of the nineteenth century; so these terms help to create that historical distance or depth. But in fact they are a part of his general literary style. It seems to me that they reflect both his keen historical consciousness and a sort of archaeological manner in his writing. He wants to bring these terms back into use, and they certainly add a richness and complexity to his style – though it should be said that some readers find them a little mannered and irritating.

Literary language. 'supernumerary', 'dilatoriness', 'whewed', 'ample', 'incubus', 'visitant', 'spectral', 'supplanted', 'antagonist', 'malignant', 'stigma'.

The literary nature of these terms is very much a matter of their tone and the manner in which they are used. They are certainly not the sort of terms used in everyday speech, and some of them may have had you reaching for your dictionary. Many of them are foreign in origin or are given latinate endings, like *–ant*. Once again I think this is Hardy consciously striving to heighten his prose style. And after all that's what the best literature often is – a heightened form of language, more dense and highly wrought (that is, 'worked on') than plain prose. If he were to use *only* literary terms like these his prose might seem a little stilted or stiff, but it is the fact that he uses them alongside the other verbal registers that we are discussing here (colloquialisms, dialect, technical language) and in a context which is highly dramatic that makes his prose so vivid and rich.

Poetic language. 'whither', 'anew', 'twain', 'thereabout', 'graces', 'beheld', 'morrow'.

This category should be easier to distinguish than the others. These terms are quite simply ones we would normally expect to encounter only in poetry. You will perhaps remember that Hardy was a poet as well as a writer of prose fiction, and I think that his use of such terms reflects his desire to inject some 'poetry' into his writing of fiction. You might also notice that most of these terms could have also been included in the category of archaisms. I doubt if people even in the late nineteenth century said 'twain' for 'two' – except in poetry.

Colloquialisms. 'he do', 'she do'.

You may have had a little difficulty in distinguishing these from instances of dialect. They represent the irregularities (not 'mistakes') of everyday speech. You might notice that Hardy puts these terms into the mouths of his characters. The significance of this is that Hardy was one of the first writers to bring ordinary working people into the foreground of fiction. He believed in and took seriously the lives of what had previously been thought of as simple country folk. So he put their lives on record – including the language that they spoke.

Dialect. 'tisty-tosty', 'chimmer', 'Turk'.

These are terms which form a separate language in the region that they are used – although 'chimmer' may just be a corruption of 'chamber' and 'Turk' (a euphemism for 'Devil') might have been used outside Wessex. The point here is that as I have argued in earlier sections, Hardy is obviously enriching his prose and making a deliberate effort to give these terms a wider circulation. Their use makes his characters more psychologically credible, and it represents a sort of democratic attitude to language in Hardy.

Technical language. 'barton', 'periphery', 'wropper', 'yeoman', 'gig'.

If something has a name of its own, Hardy obviously believes in using it. This reflects the specificity of his approach. He deals in the real, the concrete, the specific world rather than some vague, abstract invention. And I think as readers we *trust* Hardy because of such usage. He seems to know what he is talking about, and he brings vividness and life to what he is saying as well as adding another layer of linguistic depth to his prose. As I have argued in the other sections, it is also obvious that he *likes* to use such terms when they are appropriate. He clearly has a love of language for its own sake – but then that is true of many great writers.

Do not worry if you put some words in different categories to mine, or if you were not quite sure what their significance might have been. The important thing here was to be aware of the range and variety of Hardy's language. If you go on to read any of Hardy's novels you will certainly need a dictionary to hand, and many editions of his work now include glossaries of his dialect and unusual words. Some critics argue that Hardy is showing off rather in this respect. That is, they argue that he is parading his erudition because he felt a class inferiority or lack of confidence in not having received a formal university education. He educated himself instead and therefore felt a need to over-compensate – they claim.

I will leave you to make up your own mind on this point, though to do so you will need to read a lot more of Hardy than just this one story. I mention the point just to alert you to the fact that in literary criticism there are no absolute rights and wrongs. What one person sees as a commendable feature in a writer's work (as I think you will have guessed I feel about the richness of Hardy's language) others may see as a weakness. The important point is that you need *evidence* to support your argument. It cannot just be based on prejudice or 'personal taste'.

5 A sample essay

If at some future date you wish to make any academic progress with literary studies you will have to be prepared to articulate your responses to questions in written form. This will mean writing essays – which are used as exercises to test your understanding of works and your ability to construct arguments. What follows is an example of a very typical student essay in response to a very typical essay question. It is offered here because in my experience many students worry unnecessarily about their ability to produce written work, and they are often very uncertain about what levels of accomplishment are expected of them. And more often than not they *overestimate* what is expected of them and *underestimate* their own abilities. It is also the case that very often students never see other people's work, so they have nothing against which to compare their own. I am not suggesting that the essay is perfect or that it is a model against which you should measure your own efforts. It is offered to show you what, with a little thought and effort, *can* be done.

What you should do is read through the essay carefully and then answer the questions which follow it.

———◦◦◦———

☆ How does Hardy handle the supernatural element in 'The Withered Arm'? Is it the main subject of the story?

This story is about the eternal tragedy of the older woman supplanted by a younger rival and the terrible revenge she takes. It is a very interesting story, though hard to believe, and like many of Hardy's stories very gloomy.

The older woman, Rhoda Brook is a milkmaid who has had a child by the farmer, Mr Lodge, who is now getting older. The farmer marries a younger women, Gertrude, who does not know about Rhoda and her child and who appears to Rhoda one night, flashing her wedding ring and gloating. This is the supernatural in the story. We are not quite sure if she is real or if Rhoda is dreaming, for Hardy gives us hints both ways. Rhoda asserts that she really saw Gertrude before falling asleep – but Hardy as narrator casts doubt on this: it 'was not to be believed'. Yet on the other hand the boy hears the noise of the struggle at the same time (two o'clock, in the night) that it takes place, and Gertrude's arm is afflicted at exactly the same moment.

Gertrude's arm begins to wither just where Rhoda has grasped it in her dream (or *was* it a dream?) until she is driven to see a 'conjuror' whom Rhoda knows who will cure it. She doesn't know if her injury is natural or not, though she reports that her husband says 'it is the Devil himself who has taken hold of it' and eventually she comes to believe this. And Rhoda herself is worried that she may be suspected, for she herself doesn't know whether she did it or not, or whether Trendle can tell. So Hardy keeps us in doubt about the arm and the supernatural, never quite telling us enough either way to be sure. We could be dealing with peasant superstition all the time, in which case the story is really about how people's beliefs control their actions and bring about their doom. But that doesn't really explain the withered arm, and there is always the feeling of 'what if...?' which deepens the story and makes it mysterious, like life itself. Did Gertrude really see Rhoda in the egg-and-water (p. 88) or did she harbour this suspicion unconsciously and use this way of bringing her suspicions to the surface of her mind?

The last event takes place in 1825 and so was in the distant past when Hardy wrote it, so he could use strange things like 'conjurors' and public hangings but still seem to be writing a true story – or realistic might be a better word.

He even gives us a little history and geographical information to emphasise the time past.

Gertrude is so anxious to touch a corpse that she prays for someone to be executed 'guilty or innocent', so her soul is withered like her arm, which Hardy might be saying is the real injury.

But then she doesn't 'deserve' the injury when it happens: it is acquired through no fault of her own as a result of human conflicts which took place years before her arrival. This seems to reinforce Hardy's view of life as tragic. Gertrude's testing is bound up with the Rhoda–Lodge conflict just as she herself realises that 'the condemned wretch's destiny was becoming interwoven with her own' (p. 94).

Hardy is presenting us with a very modern view here for he is saying that we are what we are because of what we *do* and what happens to us – *not* because of the 'nature' we were born with as some Christians might argue.

So the subject of the story is the withering of arms, and people, and lives – but whether this is affected by the supernatural or a belief in it Hardy leaves us to decide for ourselves.

Now here are a few questions I would like you to consider. If you have any difficulty at all, do not hesitate to go back and read the sample essay again. In fact it will probably be a good thing if you read it more than once anyway – just so that you take a firmer mental grasp of its arguments and its structure.

1 Has the student answered the question satisfactorily? If so, how?

2 Is there any discernible *structure* to the essay? Does it have a shape or follow a plan?

3 What are some of the good features of the essay?

4 Is the argument backed up with supporting evidence?

⋙◦◉◦⋘

Here are my own responses to those questions:

1. The question is answered in a satisfactory manner on three counts. The essay *begins* with a direct answer; the substance of the argument deals almost exclusively with the topic of the supernatural (that is, it doesn't digress from the subject in hand); and it *concludes* with a response to the question. It may be possible to argue that the topic could have been covered more comprehensively, but for an essay of this length it is admirably concentrated and focused to deal with what was asked for.

2. You will have to believe me when I tell you that I did not write this essay myself, and it was not written by one of my students. Yet it follows exactly

the structure I suggest in my model essay plan in Section 7 of this chapter. That is, it is organised around the following structure:

Brief personal response

Brief précis

Argument and evidence

Conclusion

This is a successful structure because it allows the arguments to be presented as clearly and directly as possible.

3. Some other good features are:

It is written in a simple and unpretentious style.

It is not cluttered up with topics and discussion which are not relevant to the question.

It considers both 'sides' of the argument on belief in the supernatural in a way which shows that the writer has thought carefully about the subject and is not being hasty or dogmatic.

It is neatly organised into separate paragraphs, each one dealing with a separate aspect of the question.

4. Yes, the argument is well supported by evidence drawn from the text and occasionally backed up with brief quotations. This is done in just about the right proportions and the important thing is that the argument comes *first*.

The question of how to use quotation and the conventions for presenting it causes so much confusion (even though it is a relatively simple matter) that I am now going to offer you another reference guide which you can use throughout this course – 'The conventions of quotation'.

6 The conventions of quotation

☆ Quotation is used to illustrate a point in your argument or to give an example of a feature or characteristic of the text which you have identified.

☆ Do not use quotation as a substitute for your own argument or fill out your essay with lengthy quotations from the text.

☆ Do not string together a plot summary with long quotations. This gives the impression that you are just trying to fill up space. Select just those few words which illustrate the point you are making.

☆ Keep quotations as short as possible (three lines maximum).

☆ Remember that your own argument must come *first*. Any quotation should come after it.

☆ Each point of your argument (one paragraph) should need no more than one quotation to support it.

☆ There must be grammatical continuity and sense maintained between any quotation and your own argument.

EXAMPLES

☆ You might need to quote a list of stylistic features: (do not give more than two or three examples).

> Hardy's insistent use of adverbs in this passage – 'shockingly', 'cruelly', 'mockingly' (p. 82) – create the impression of a world which ...

☆ The three dots '...' are used to denote an omission *within* the quoted passage:

> 'He had even a kind of assurance on his face ... the assurance of a common man deliberately entrenched in his commonness.' (p. 161)

☆ If the quotation will be less than two lines of your text, run it in thus 'as if she were *loved* by him' (p. 224 – my emphasis) and then carry on with what you wish to say ...

☆ If the quotation will run to more than two lines of your argument you should indent it thus:

> as if she were loved by him, but notwithstanding this she regarded the man as no more than a casual acquaintance who occasionally made her laugh (p. 226)

Only use this practice occasionally, and note that page references are given immediately *after* the quotation.

☆ When quoting conversation follow the same rules, but if it makes things easier put the words spoken within double quote marks thus:

> Kayerts is being hypocritical and self-deceiving when he 'observe[s] with a sigh: "It had to be done."' (p. 131)

Note that any changes to the text (to preserve grammatical logic) should be shown in square brackets.

7 Writing an appreciation

In literary studies you will often be asked to write a general appreciation of a piece of work. Most students are able to see good qualities in a piece of writing and they usually have something interesting to say about it – but many are not quite sure what an appreciation calls for, or they are not confident of the best order in which to offer their observations. What follows is an essay plan which you can use if you are not sure. It will be suitable for *most* questions where you are invited to give your general response to or your appreciation of a work. (If however you are asked a specific question about one particular aspect of it you will have to devise your own essay plan.) This plan will not solve the problem of what to say about a work, but it might help you to give order and shape to what you write.

There is no fixed order in which you should present your observations, but you will see from the manner in which the six headings are arranged that there is a 'shape' or a logic created in the plan. The topics move from an introductory general response, on to an examination of details, and then back to a general conclusion. In fact you will eventually see that this is a good model for most essay writing:

- ☆ Brief introduction
- ☆ Detailed argument and examination of the text
- ☆ Brief conclusion

'APPRECIATION' ESSAY PLAN

Brief personal response to the work. This will help you get started in writing if you are at a beginner's level. If you are at a more advanced stage you can leave it out. (One paragraph maximum)

Brief précis of the work. This will demonstrate that you have understood the work and it will provide a basis for the observations which follow. (One or two paragraphs maximum)

The literary qualities of the work. Use the checklist of literary terms if you wish. Concentrate on those qualities which seem most important. Illustrate your argument with brief quotations from the text to prove your points. (Several paragraphs)

The theme(s) of the work. Discuss what you think are the most important underlying subjects the work is dealing with. (This is more difficult and can be left out if you are not sure.)

The author's treatment of the subject. Discuss what seems to be the author's attitude to the subject and theme(s). (Two or three paragraphs.)

Conclusion. Your overall assessment of the author's achievement plus any general judgement of the issues dealt with in the work. (One paragraph.)

8 Self-assessment questions

LANGUAGE

1 What is a 'yeoman'?

2 What figures of speech are being used here:

> not far from the border of Egdon Heath, whose dark countenance was visible in the distance

> here and there in the thatch above a rafter showed like a bone protruding through the skin

> [Her dress] whewed and whistled so loud when it rubbed against the pews

3 Paraphrase the following sentence. That is, re–write it to express the same meaning, but using your own words

> For though this pretty young woman had rendered impossible any reparation which Lodge might have made Rhoda for his past conduct, everything like resentment at the unconscious usurpation had quite passed away.

4 What is meant by 'the sad dun shades of the upland's garniture'?

5 When Gertrude arrives at Casterbridge for the assizes she senses 'a curious creeping feeling that the condemned wretch's destiny was becoming interwoven with her own'. Say what literary device is being used here, and explain how it is operating.'

COMPREHENSION

1 How old are Lodge, Rhoda, Gertrude, and the boy at the start of the story? (Not all these ages are given directly, but there is enough evidence in the story to be able to work them out.)

2 What does Rhoda see in the glass of water and egg white presented by Conjurer Trendle? What *proof* do you have for your answer – drawn from the text?

3 Why is Rhoda's son executed?

4 To whom does Lodge bequeath his property when he dies?

5 When Gertrude wants to go to Casterbridge assizes she asks Lodge about them but finds him 'so uncommunicative, so more than usually cold' that she does not proceed. Why does Lodge behave in this way?

ANALYSIS

1 'The summer drew on, and Rhoda Brook almost dreaded to meet Mrs Lodge again, notwithstanding that her feeling for the young wife amounted well-nigh to affection. Something in her own individuality seemed to convict Rhoda of a crime.'

Say in your own words what this passage means, and explain the apparent contradiction in Rhoda's feelings.

2 In what sense might we see Rhoda's son as an outsider and a victim. Trace the development of his life through the story with this notion in mind.

3 What are we to make of the changes in Lodge's behaviour following the death of his wife and son?

4 What is the significance of the various settings or locations in their relation to the story?

5 What part do the secondary characters Trendle and Davies play in the story?

9 Course work

1 Choose a substantial paragraph from the story (which does not include conversation) and, using the checklist of literary terms (Chapter One, Section 5) produce a close reading of the passage. Try to say as much as possible about its constituent parts and any relation these may have to the story as a whole.

2 Make an analysis of the three main characters in the story (Rhoda, Gertrude, and Lodge). Say both what we know about

them and how we know it. Illustrate your account with brief examples quoted from the text.

3 Write a general appreciation of 'A Withered Arm' using the guidance notes in Section 7.

4 Give an account of the characters of the story in their relationship to the setting – that is, the physical environment in which they live and work.

5 Using the checklist of literary terms (Chapter One, Section 7) and the general glossary (Chapter Eight) produce an analysis of Hardy's literary style in 'A Withered Arm'. Illustrate your argument with brief examples quoted from the text.

10 Further reading

FICTION AND POETRY

Hardy is one of the few writers (another is D. H. Lawrence) to be highly regarded as a poet, a writer of short stories, and as a novelist.

David Wright (ed), *Thomas Hardy: Selected Poems*, London: Penguin, 1978.

James Gibson (ed), *Thomas Hardy: The Complete Poems*, London: Macmillan, 1976.

F. B. Pinion (ed), *Thomas Hardy: The Complete Short Stories*, London: Macmillan, 1977.

His greatest novels, many of which have been successfully filmed and turned into television dramas are, by common consent:

Far from the Madding Crowd, London: Smith, Elder, 1874.

The Return of the Native, London: Smith, Elder, 1878.

The Mayor of Casterbridge, London: Smith, Elder, 1885.

The Woodlanders, London: Macmillan, 1887.

Tess of the d'Urbervilles, London: Osgood, McIlvaine, 1891.

Jude the Obscure, London: Osgood, McIlvaine, 1896.

BIOGRAPHY

There are two standard and fairly easily available biographies:

Robert Gittings, *The Younger Hardy*, London: Heinemann,1975.

—, *The Older Hardy*, London: Heinemann, 1978.

Michael Millgate, *Thomas Hardy: A Biography*, London: Oxford University Press, 1982.

There is also a 'biography' of Hardy by his second wife:

Florence Hardy, *The Life of Thomas Hardy*, London: Macmillan, 1962.

but since this was written largely at Hardy's own dictation, it counts as autobiography.

CRITICISM

The following are general approaches to Hardy:

John Bayley, *An Essay on Hardy*, London: Cambridge University Press, 1978.

Kirstin Brady, *The Short Stories of Thomas Hardy*, London: Macmillan, 1982.

David Cecil, *Hardy the Novelist: An Essay in Criticism*, London: Constable, 1942.

Raymond Chapman, *The Language of Thomas Hardy*, London: Macmillan, 1990.

R. G. Cox (ed), *Thomas Hardy: The Critical Heritage*, London: Routledge and Kegan Paul, 1970.

Irving Howe, *Thomas Hardy*, London: Weidenfeld and Nicolson, 1966.

Norman Page, *Thomas Hardy*, London: Routledge, 1977.

Merryn Williams, *A Preface to Hardy*, London: Longman, 1976.

CHAPTER FIVE

Close reading and irony

1 Introduction

We come next to a story which has several layers of complexity. It is full of drama, suspense, and sensational events; it deals with the large scale political issues of colonialism and racial inequality; it is written in a very dense prose style; and the author has a rather lofty, scathing, and sometimes bitterly ironic attitude to the characters he creates. You will not be alone if you feel that it is the toughest piece of writing we have tackled so far.

In many ways it is also the most modern. Conrad's manner of writing and his choice of very negative protagonists are both typical features of the modernist phase of literary experimentation which took place between the end of the last century and the 1920s. If you are not used to reading modern fiction you may be a little shocked at finding stupidity and moral decay as its subject matter.

And if you have not read anything by Joseph Conrad before you may even experience a little difficulty in understanding what he means. This is because he sometimes writes very long sentences; he uses lots of abstract language (terms such as 'unfathomable', 'fateful', and 'profound') and he often discusses social and quasi-philosophical ideas at the same time as 'telling the story'. The answer to this potential difficulty is to be patient, look up the meanings of any words you might not understand, and be prepared to read more slowly than you normally might. You will be rewarded for this effort by the pleasure of contemplating a very entertaining and accomplished work of fiction.

It is at this stage of the study programme that we begin to consider issues and critical approaches of a slightly more complex nature than before. Here we will be looking closely at the text in relationship to its historical and cultural context. And the feature of so much irony in the story gives us the chance to practise a form of analysis in which we explore the text on two or three levels at the same time. The issues become more complex, but I hope you will find the outcomes more rewarding.

2 Biographical note

Since he is now regarded as a master of English prose style, the first and most remarkable thing to say about Conrad is that he was Polish. He was born in 1857 in one of the Ukranian provinces then under Russian Tsarist rule. His name was Josef Teodor Konrad Nalecz Korzeniowski. His parents were landowners, and his father was a man of both literary and political interests. For a time he was involved with the secret Polish nationalist movement. Because of this he was arrested when Conrad was three years old, and the whole family was exiled to Northern Russia. His mother died there and on return to Crakow his father died four years later, leaving Conrad to be raised by an uncle.

As a boy Conrad had read widely from his father's library, including adventure stories. Partly inspired by these he decided when he was seventeen to become a sailor. He spoke French fluently, and so travelled to Marseilles, joined the merchant navy, and subsequently became involved in smuggling in the West Indies. There he had his first love affair, ran up gambling debts, and attempted suicide.

He then transferred to the English merchant navy and spent the next fifteen years at sea, sailing all over the world, and eventually becoming a captain. His adventures at sea form the basis for many of his later books – *An Outcast of the Islands*, *Typhoon*, *The Rescue*, *Victory*, and many others. He became a naturalised British subject in 1886. Meanwhile he had begun writing, and following his last trips up the Congo river into Africa and round the world to Australia and back, he settled in England, married, and became a professional writer.

His first books were largely adventure stories, but then around the turn of the century, with the publication of *Heart of Darkness* and *Lord Jim* his work became more serious and profound. The themes he repeatedly deals with in his work are moral fortitude and discrimination, the complex and sometimes evil nature of man, the relationship between politics and society, and the possibility of moral redemption through acts of courage and bravery.

He settled in Kent and became a friend of many other writers living there at that time – Galsworthy, Henry James and Ford Madox Ford. He had two sons and the family travelled frequently throughout Europe. With the publication of *Chance* in 1913 he became both famous and financially successful. This novel is typical of the extremely complex narrative methods he developed in his later works, with their stories-within-stories, fractured time schemes, and multiple narrators.

Like many other great writers of this period (Tolstoy, Hardy, Joyce, Woolf) he never received the Nobel Prize, but was highly regarded both critically and by the general public. It is generally thought that the standard of his work declined in the last ten years of his life and that his greatest creative period was in the first fourteen years of the century. He died in 1924 and is buried in Canterbury, and the stone on his grave bears his Polish name.

Since that time his literary reputation has risen steadily in the academic world (amongst critics, teachers and students, that is). The influential Cambridge critic F. R. Leavis made a major contribution to the establishment of Conrad as a modern English classic by including him in his choice of the great English novelists (the others were George Eliot and Henry James) which he discusses in *The Great Tradition*.

AN OUTPOST OF PROGRESS
JOSEPH CONRAD

I

There were two white men in charge of the trading station. Kayerts, the chief, was short and fat; Carlier, the assistant, was tall, with a large head and a very broad trunk perched upon a long pair of thin legs. The third man on the staff was a Sierra Leone nigger, who maintained that his name was Henry Price. However, for some reason or other, the natives down the river had given him the name of Makola, and it stuck to him through all his wanderings about the country. He spoke English and French with a warbling accent, wrote a beautiful hand, understood book-keeping, and cherished in his innermost heart the worship of evil spirits. His wife was a negress from Loanda, very large and very noisy. Three children rolled about in sunshine before the door of his low, shed-like dwelling. Makola, taciturn and impenetrable, despised the two white men. He had charge of a small clay storehouse with a dried-grass roof, and pretended to keep a correct account of beads, cotton cloth, red kerchiefs, brass wire, and other trade goods it contained. Besides the storehouse and Makola's hut, there was only one large building in the cleared ground of the station. It was built neatly of reeds, with a verandah on all the four sides. There were three rooms in it. The one in the middle was the living-room, and had two rough tables and a few stools in it. The other two were the bedrooms for the white men. Each had a bedstead and a mosquito net for all furniture. The plank floor was littered with the belongings of the white men; open half-empty boxes, torn wearing apparel, old boots; all the things dirty, and all the things broken, that accumulate mysteriously round untidy men. There was also another dwelling-place some distance away from the buildings. In it, under a tall cross much out of the perpendicular, slept the man who had seen the beginning of all this; who had planned and had watched the construction of this outpost of progress. He had been, at home, an unsuccessful painter who, weary of pursuing fame on an empty stomach, had gone out there through high protections. He had been the first chief of that station. Makola had watched the energetic artist die of fever in the just finished house with his usual kind of 'I told you so' indifference. Then, for a time, he dwelt alone with his family, his account books, and the Evil Spirit that rules the lands under the equator. He got on very well with his god. Perhaps he had propitiated him by a promise of more white men to play with, by and by. At any rate the director of the Great Trading Company, coming up in a steamer that resembled an enormous sardine box with a flat-roofed shed erected on it, found the station in good order, and Makola as usual quietly diligent. The director had the cross put up over the first agent's grave, and appointed Kayerts to the post. Carlier was told off as second in charge. The director was a man ruthless and efficient, who at times, but very imperceptibly, indulged in grim humour. He made a speech to Kayerts and Carlier, pointing out to them the promising aspect of their station. The nearest trading-post was about three hundred miles away. It was an exceptional opportunity for them to distinguish themselves and to earn percentages on the trade. This appointment was a favour done to beginners. Kayerts was moved almost to tears by his director's kindness. He would he said, by doing his best, try to justify the flattering confidence, etc., etc. Kayerts had been in the Administration of the Telegraphs, and knew how to express himself correctly. Carlier, an ex non-commissioned officer of cavalry in an army guaranteed from harm by several European Powers, was less impressed. If there were commissions to get, so much the better; and, trailing a sulky glance over the river, the forests, the impenetrable bush that seemed to cut off the station from the rest of the world, he muttered

E

between his teeth, 'We shall see, very soon.'

Next day, some bales of cotton goods and a few cases of provisions having been thrown on shore, the sardine-box steamer went off, not to return for another six months. On the deck the director touched his cap to the two agents, who stood on the bank waving their hats, and turning to an old servant of the Company on his passage to headquarters, said, 'Look at those two imbeciles. They must be mad at home to send me such specimens. I told those fellows to plant a vegetable garden, build new storehouses and fences, and construct a landing-stage. I bet nothing will be done! They won't know how to begin. I always thought the station on this river useless, and they just fit the station!'

'They will form themselves there,' said the old stager with a quiet smile.

'At any rate, I am rid of them for six months,' retorted the director.

The two men watched the steamer round the bend, then, ascending arm in arm the slope of the bank, returned to the station. They had been in this vast and dark country only a very short time, and as yet always in the midst of other white men, under the eye and guidance of their superiors. And now, dull as they were to the subtle influences of surroundings, they felt themselves very much alone, when suddenly left unassisted to face the wilderness; a wilderness rendered more strange, more incomprehensible by the mysterious glimpses of the vigorous life it contained. They were two perfectly insignificant and incapable individuals, whose existence is only rendered possible through the high organisation of civilised crowds. Few men realise that their life, the very essence of their character, their capabilities and their audacities, are only the expression of their belief in the safety of their surroundings. The courage, the composure, the confidence; the emotions and principles; every great and every insignificant thought belongs not to the individual but to the crowd: to the crowd that believes blindly in the irresistible force of its institutions and of its morals, in the power of its police and of its opinion. But the contact with pure unmitigated savagery, with primitive nature and primitive man, brings sudden and profound trouble into the heart. To the sentiment of being alone of one's kind, to the clear perception of the loneliness of one's thoughts, of one's sensations – to the negation of the habitual, which is safe, there is added the affirmation of the unusual, which is dangerous; a suggestion of things vague, uncontrollable, and repulsive, whose discomposing intrusion excites the imagination and tries the civilised nerves of the foolish and the wise alike.

Kayerts and Carlier walked arm in arm drawing close to one another as children do in the dark; and they had the same, not altogether unpleasant, sense of danger which one half suspects to be imaginary. They chatted persistently in familiar tones. 'Our station is prettily situated,' said one. The other assented with enthusiasm, enlarging volubly on the beauties of the situation. Then they passed near the grave. ' Poor devil!' said Kayerts. He died of fever, didn't he?' muttered Carlier, stopping short. 'Why,' retorted Kayerts, with indignation, 'I've been told that the fellow exposed himself recklessly to the sun. The climate here, everybody says, is not at all worse than at home, as long as you keep out of the sun. Do you hear that, Carlier? I am chief here, and my orders are that you should not expose yourself to the sun!' He assumed his superiority jocularly, but his meaning was serious. The idea that he would, perhaps, have to bury Carlier and remain alone, gave him an inward shiver. He felt suddenly that this Carlier was more precious to him here, in the centre of Africa, than a brother could be anywhere else. Carlier, entering into the spirit of the thing, made a military salute and answered in a brisk tone, 'Your orders shall be attended to, chief!' Then he burst out laughing, slapped Kayerts on the back, and shouted, 'We shall let life run easily here! Just sit still and gather in the ivory those savages will bring. This country has its good points, after all!' They both laughed loudly while Carlier thought: That poor Kayerts; he is so fat and unhealthy. It would be awful if I had to bury him here. He is a man I respect.... Before they reached the verandah of their house they called one another my dear fellow.'

The first day they were very active, pottering about with hammers and nails and red calico, to put up curtains, make their house habitable and pretty; resolved to settle down comfortably to their new life. For them an impossible task. To grapple effectually with even purely material problems requires more serenity of mind and more lofty courage than people generally imagine. No two beings could have been more unfitted for such a struggle. Society, not from any tenderness, but because of its strange needs, had taken care of those two men, forbidding them all independent thought, all initiative, all departure from routine; and forbidding it under pain of death. They could only live on condition of being machines. And now, released from the fostering care of men with pens behind the ears, or of men with gold lace on the sleeves, they were like those lifelong prisoners who, liberated after many years, do not know what use to make of their freedom. They did not know what use to make of their faculties, being both, through want of practice, incapable of independent thought.

At the end of two months Kayerts often would say, 'If it was not for my Melie, you wouldn't catch me here.' Melie was his daughter. He had thrown up his post in the Administration of the Telegraphs, though he had been for seventeen years perfectly happy there, to earn a dowry for his girl. His wife was dead, and the child was being brought up by his sisters. He regretted the streets, the pavements, the cafés, his friends of many years; all the things he used to see, day after day; all the thoughts suggested by familiar things – the thoughts effortless, monotonous, and soothing of a Government clerk; he regretted all the gossip, the small enmities, the mild venom, and the little jokes of Government offices. 'If I had had a decent brother-in-law,' Carlier would remark, 'a fellow with a heart, I would not be here.' He had left the army and had made himself so obnoxious to his family by his laziness and impudence, that an exasperated brother-in-law had made superhuman efforts to procure him an appointment in the Company as a second-class agent. Having not a penny in the world, he was compelled to accept this means of livelihood as soon as it became quite clear to him that there was nothing more to squeeze out of his relations. He, like Kayerts, regretted his old life. He regretted the clink of sabre and spurs on a fine afternoon, the barrack-room witticisms, the girls of garrison towns; but, besides, he had also a sense of grievance. He was evidently a much ill-used man. This made him moody, at times. But the two men got on well together in the fellowship of their stupidity and laziness. Together they did nothing, absolutely nothing, and enjoyed the sense of the idleness for which they were paid. And in time they came to feel something resembling affection for one another.

They lived like blind men in a large room, aware only of what came in contact with them (and of that only imperfectly), but unable to see the general aspect of things. The river, the forest, all the great land throbbing with life, were like a great emptiness. Even the brilliant sunshine disclosed nothing intelligible. Things appeared and disappeared before their eyes in an unconnected and aimless kind of way. The river seemed to come from nowhere and flow nowhither. It flowed through a void. Out of that void, at times, came canoes, and men with spears in their hands would suddenly crowd the yard of the station. They were naked, glossy black, ornamented with snowy shells and glistening brass wire, perfect of limb. They made an uncouth babbling noise when they spoke, moved in a stately manner, and sent quick, wild glances out of their startled, never-resting eyes. Those warriors would squat in long rows, four or more deep, before the verandah, while their chiefs bargained for hours with Makola over an elephant tusk. Kayerts sat on his chair and looked down on the proceedings, understanding nothing. He stared at them with his round blue eyes, called out to Carlier, 'Here, look! look at that fellow there – and that other one, to the left. Did you ever see such a face? Oh, the funny brute!'

Carlier, smoking native tobacco in a short wooden pipe, would swagger up twirling his moustaches, and, surveying the warriors with haughty indulgence, would say –

'Fine animals. Brought any bone? Yes? It's not any too soon. Look at the muscles of that fellow – third from the end. I wouldn't care to get a punch on the nose from him. Fine arms, but legs no good below the knee. Couldn't make cavalry men of them.' And after glancing down complacently at his own shanks, he always concluded: 'Pah! Don't they stink! You, Makola! Take that herd over to the fetish' (the storehouse was in every station called the fetish, perhaps because of the spirit of civilisation it contained) 'and give them up some of the rubbish you keep there. I'd rather see it full of bone than full of rags.'

Kayerts approved.

'Yes, yes! Go and finish that palaver over there, Mr. Makola. I will come round when you are ready, to weigh the tusk. We must be careful.' Then, turning to his companion: 'This is the tribe that lives down the river; they are rather aromatic. I remember, they had been once before here. D'ye hear that row? What a fellow has got to put up with in this dog of a country! My head is split.'

Such profitable visits were rare. For days the two pioneers of trade and progress would look on their empty
courtyard in the vibrating brilliance of vertical sunshine.

Below the high bank, the silent river flowed on glittering and steady. On the
sands in the middle of the stream, hippos and alligators sunned themselves
side by side. And stretching away in all directions, surrounding the insignificant cleared spot of the trading post, immense forests, hiding fateful complications of fantastic life, lay in the eloquent silence of mute greatness. The
two men understood nothing, cared for nothing but for the passage of days
that separated them from the steamer's return. Their predecessor had left
some torn books. They took up these wrecks of novels, and, as they had
never read anything of the kind before, they were surprised and amused.
Then during long days there were interminable and silly discussions about
plots and personages. In the centre of Africa they made the acquaintance of
Richelieu and of d'Artagnan, of Hawk's Eye and of Father Goriot, and of
many other people. All these imaginary personages became subjects for
gossip as if they had been living friends. They discounted their virtues,
suspected their motives, decried their successes; were scandalised at their
duplicity or were doubtful about their courage. The accounts of crimes filled
them with indignation, while tender or pathetic passages moved them
deeply. Carlier cleared his throat and said in a soldierly voice, 'What nonsense!' Kayerts, his round eyes suffused with tears, his fat cheeks quivering,
rubbed his bald head, and declared, 'This is a splendid book. I had no idea
there were such clever fellows in the world.' They also found some old
copies of a home paper. That print discussed what it was pleased to call 'Our
Colonial Expansion' in high-flown language. It spoke much of the rights
and duties of civilisation, of the sacredness of the civilising work, and
extolled the merits of those who went about bringing light, and faith, and
commerce to the dark places of the earth. Carlier and Kayerts read, wondered, and began to think better of themselves. Carlier said one evening,
waving his hand about, 'In a hundred years, there will be perhaps a town
here. Quays, and warehouses, and barracks, and – and – billiard-rooms.
Civilisation, my boy, and virtue – and all. And then, chaps will read that two
good fellows, Kayerts and Carlier, were the first civilised men to live in this
very spot!' Kayerts nodded, 'Yes, it is a consolation to think of that.' They
seemed to forget their dead predecessor; but, early one day, Carlier went out
and replanted the cross firmly. 'It used to make me squint whenever I
walked that way,' he explained to Kayerts over the morning coffee. 'It made
me squint, leaning over so much. So I just planted it upright. And solid, I
promise you! I suspended myself with both hands to the cross-piece. Not a
move. Oh, I did that properly.'

At times Gobila came to see them. Gobila was the chief of the neighbouring villages. He was a grey-headed savage, thin and black, with a white cloth
round his loins and a mangy panther skin hanging over his back. He came
up with long strides of his skeleton legs, swinging a staff as tall as himself,
and, entering the common room of the station, would squat on his heels to

the left of the door. There he sat, watching Kayerts, and now and then making a speech which the other did not understand. Kayerts, without interrupting his occupation, would from time to time say in a friendly manner: 'How goes it, you old image?' and they would smile at one another. The two whites had a liking for that old and incomprehensible creature, and called him Father Gobila. Gobila's manner was paternal, and he seemed really to love all white men. They all appeared to him very young, indistinguishably alike (except for stature), and he knew that they were all brothers, and also immortal. The death of the artist, who was the first white man whom he knew intimately, did not disturb this belief, because he was firmly convinced that the white stranger had pretended to die and got himself buried for some mysterious purpose of his own, into which it was useless to inquire. Perhaps it was his way of going home to his own country? At any rate, these were his brothers, and he transferred his absurd affection to them. They returned it in a way. Carlier slapped him on the back, and recklessly struck off matches for his amusement. Kayerts was always ready to let him have a sniff at the ammonia bottle. In short, they behaved just like that other white creature that had hidden itself in a hole in the ground. Gobila considered them attentively. Perhaps they were the same being with the other – or one of them was. He couldn't decide – clear up that mystery; but he remained always very friendly. In consequence of that friendship the women of Gobila's village walked in single file through the reedy grass, bringing every morning to the station, fowls, and sweet potatoes, and palm wine, and sometimes a goat. The Company never provisions the stations fully, and the agents required those local supplies to live. They had them through the good-will of Gobila, and lived well. Now and then one of them had a bout of fever, and the other nursed him with gentle devotion. They did not think much of it. It left them weaker, and their appearance changed for the worse. Carlier was hollow-eyed and irritable. Kayerts showed a drawn, flabby face above the rotundity of his stomach, which gave him a weird aspect. But being constantly together, they did not notice the change that took place gradually in their appearance, and also in their dispositions.

Five months passed in that way.

Then, one morning, as Kayerts and Carlier, lounging in their chairs under the verandah, talked about the approaching visit of the steamer, a knot of armed men came out of the forest and advanced towards the station. They were strangers to that part of the country. They were tall, slight, draped classically from neck to heel in blue fringed cloths, and carried percussion muskets over their bare right shoulders. Makola showed signs of excitement, and ran out of the storehouse (where he spent all his days) to meet these visitors. They came into the courtyard and looked about them with steady, scornful glances. Their leader, a powerful and determined-looking negro with bloodshot eyes, stood in front of the verandah and made a long speech. He gesticulated much, and ceased very suddenly.

There was something in his intonation, in the sounds of the long sentences he used, that startled the two whites. It was like a reminiscence of something not exactly familiar, and yet resembling the speech of civilised men. It sounded like one of those impossible languages which sometimes we hear in our dreams.

'What lingo is that?' said the amazed Carlier. 'In the first moment I fancied the fellow was going to speak French. Anyway, it is a different kind of gibberish to what we ever heard.'

'Yes,' replied Kayerts. 'Hey, Makola, what does he say? Where do they come from? Who are they?'

But Makola, who seemed to be standing on hot bricks, answered hurriedly, 'I don't know. They come from very far. Perhaps Mrs. Price will understand. They are perhaps bad men.'

The leader, after waiting for a while, said something sharply to Makola, who shook his head. Then the man, after looking round, noticed Makola's hut and walked over there. The next moment Mrs. Makola was heard speaking with great volubility. The other strangers – they were six in all – strolled about with an air of ease, put their heads through the door of the store-room, congregated round the grave, pointed understandingly at the cross, and generally made themselves at home. 'I don't like those chaps – and, I say, Kayerts, they must be from the coast; they've got firearms,' observed the sagacious Carlier.

Kayerts also did not like those chaps. They both, for the first time, became aware that they lived in conditions where the unusual may be dangerous, and that there was no power on earth outside of themselves to stand between them and the unusual. They became uneasy, went in and loaded their revolvers. Kayerts said, 'We must order Makola to tell them to go away before dark.'

The strangers left in the afternoon, after eating a meal prepared for them by Mrs. Makola. The immense woman was excited, and talked much with the visitors. She rattled away shrilly, pointing here and pointing there at the forests and at the river. Makola sat apart and watched. At times he got up and whispered to his wife. He accompanied the strangers across the ravine at the back of the station-ground, and returned slowly looking very thoughtful. When questioned by the white men he was very strange, seemed not to understand, seemed to have forgotten French – seemed to have forgotten how to speak altogether. Kayerts and Carlier agreed that the nigger had had too much palm wine.

There was some talk about keeping a watch in turn, but in the evening everything seemed so quiet and peaceful that they retired as usual. All night they were disturbed by a lot of drumming in the villages. A deep, rapid roll near by would be followed by another far off – then all ceased. Soon short appeals would rattle out here and there, then all mingle together, increase, become vigorous and sustained, would spread out over the forest, roll through the night, unbroken and ceaseless, near and far, as if the whole land had been one immense drum booming out steadily an appeal to heaven. And through the deep and tremendous noise sudden yells that resembled snatches of songs from a madhouse darted shrill and high in discordant jets of sound which seemed to rush far above the earth and drive all peace from under the stars.

Carlier and Kayerts slept badly. They both thought they had heard shots fired during the night – but they could not agree as to the direction. In the morning Makola was gone somewhere. He returned about noon with one of yesterday's strangers, and eluded all Kayerts' attempts to close with him: had become deaf apparently. Kayerts wondered. Carlier, who had been fishing off the bank, came back and remarked while he showed his catch, 'The niggers seem to be in a deuce of a stir; I wonder what's up. I saw about fifteen canoes cross the river during the two hours I was there fishing.' Kayerts, worried, said, 'Isn't this Makola very queer to-day?' Carlier advised, 'Keep all our men together in case of some trouble.'

II

There were ten station men who had been left by the Director. Those fellows, having engaged themselves to the Company for six months (without having any idea of a month in particular and only a very faint notion of time in general), had been serving the cause of progress for upwards of two years. Belonging to a tribe from a very distant part of this land of darkness and sorrow, they did not run away, naturally supposing that as wandering strangers they would be killed by the inhabitants of the country; in which they were right. They lived in straw huts on the slope of a ravine overgrown with reedy grass, just behind the station buildings. They were not happy, regretting the festive incantations, the sorceries, the human sacrifices of their own land; where they also had parents, brothers, sisters, admired chiefs, respected magicians, loved friends, and other ties supposed generally to be human. Besides, the rice rations served out by the Company did not agree with them, being a food unknown to their land, and to which they could not get used. Consequently they were unhealthy and miserable. Had they been of any other tribe they would have made up their minds to die – for nothing is easier to certain savages than suicide – and so have escaped from the puzzling difficulties of existence. But belonging, as they did, to a warlike tribe with filed teeth, they had more grit, and went on stupidly living through disease and sorrow. They did very little work, and had lost their splendid physique. Carlier and Kayerts doctored them assiduously without being able to bring them back into condition again. They were mustered every morning and told off to different tasks – grass-cutting, fence-building, tree-felling, etc., etc., which no power on earth could induce them to execute efficiently. The two whites had practically very little control over them.

In the afternoon Makola came over to the big house and found Kayerts watching three heavy columns of smoke rising above the forests. 'What is that?' 'asked Kayerts. 'Some villages burn,' answered Makola, who seemed to have regained his wits. Then he said abruptly: 'We have got very little ivory; bad six months' trading. Do you like get a little more ivory?'

'Yes,' said Kayerts eagerly. He thought of percentages which were low.

'Those men who came yesterday are traders from Loanda who have got more ivory than they can carry home. Shall I buy? I know their camp.'

'Certainly,' said Kayerts, 'What are those traders?'

'Bad fellows,' said Makola indifferently. 'They fight with people, and catch women and children. They are bad men, and got guns. There is a great disturbance in the country. Do you want ivory?'

'Yes,' said Kayerts. Makola said nothing for a while. Then: 'Those workmen of ours are no good at all,' he muttered, looking round. 'Station in very bad order, sir. Director will growl. Better get a fine lot of ivory, then he say nothing.'

'I can't help it; the men won't work,' said Kayerts. 'When will you get that ivory?'

'Very soon,' said Makola. 'Perhaps tonight. You leave it to me, and keep indoors, sir. I think you had better give some palm wine to our men to make a dance this evening. Enjoy themselves. Work better to-morrow. There's plenty palm wine – gone a little sour.'

Kayerts said yes, and Makola, with his own hands, carried the big calabashes to the door of his hut. They stood there till the evening, and Mrs. Makola looked into every one. The men got them at sunset. When Kayerts and Carlier retired, a big bonfire was flaring before the men's huts. They could hear their shouts and drumming. Some men from Gobila's village had joined the station hands, and the entertainment was a great success.

In the middle of the night, Carlier waking suddenly, heard a man shout loudly; then a shot was fired. Only one. Carlier ran out and met Kayerts on the verandah. They were both startled. As they went across the yard to call Makola, they saw shadows moving in the night. One of them cried, 'Don't shoot! It's me, Price.' Then Makola appeared close to them. 'Go back, go back, please,' he urged, 'you spoil all.' 'There are strange men about,' said Carlier. 'Never mind; I know,' said Makola. Then he whispered, 'All right. Bring ivory. Say nothing! I know my business.' The two white men reluctantly went back to the house, but did not sleep. They heard footsteps, whispers, some groans. It seemed as if a lot of men came in, dumped heavy things on the ground, squabbled a long time, then went away. They lay on their hard beds and thought: 'This Makola is invaluable.' In the morning Carlier came out, very sleepy, and pulled at the cord of the big bell. The station hands mustered every morning to the sound of the bell. That morning nobody came. Kayerts turned out also, yawning. Across the yard they saw Makola come out of his hut, a tin basin of soapy water in his hand. Makola, a civilised nigger, was very neat in his person. He threw the soapsuds skilfully over a wretched little yellow cur he had, then turning his face to the agent's house, he shouted from the distance, 'All the men gone last night!'

They heard him plainly, but in their surprise they both yelled out together: 'What!' Then they stared at one another. 'We are in a proper fix now,' growled Carlier. 'It's incredible!' muttered Kayerts. 'I will go to the huts and see,' said Carlier, striding off. Makola coming up found Kayerts standing alone.

'I can hardly believe it,' said Kayerts tearfully. 'We took care of them as if they had been our children.'

'They went with the coast people,' said Makola after a moment of hesitation.

'What do I care with whom they went – the ungrateful brutes!' exclaimed the other. Then with sudden suspicion, and looking hard at Makola, he added: 'What do you know about it?'

Makola moved his shoulders, looking down on the ground. 'What do I know? I think only. Will you come and look at the ivory I've got there? It is a fine lot. You never saw such.'

He moved towards the store. Kayerts followed him mechanically, thinking about the incredible desertion of the men. On the ground before the door of the fetish lay six splendid tusks.

'What did you give for it? 'asked Kayerts, after surveying the lot with satisfaction.

'No regular trade,' said Makola. 'They brought the ivory and gave it to me. I told them to take what they most wanted in the station. It is a beautiful lot. No station can show such tusks. Those traders wanted carriers badly, and our men were no good here. No trade, no entry in books; all correct.'

Kayerts nearly burst with indignation. Why!' he shouted, 'I believe you have sold our men for these tusks!' Makola stood impassive and silent. 'I – I – will – I,' stuttered Kayerts. 'You fiend! 'he yelled out.

'I did the best for you and the Company,' said Makola imperturbably. 'Why you shout so much? Look at this tusk.'

'I dismiss you! I will report you – I won't look at the tusk. I forbid you to touch them. I order you to throw them into the river. You – you!'

'You very red, Mr. Kayerts. If you are so irritable in the sun, you will get fever and die – like the first chief!' pronounced Makola impressively.

They stood still, contemplating one another with intense eyes, as if they had been looking with effort across immense distances. Kayerts shivered. Makola had meant no more than he said, but his words seemed to Kayerts full of ominous menace! He turned sharply and went away to the house. Makola retired into the bosom of his family; and the tusks, left lying before the store, looked very large and valuable in the sunshine.

Carlier came back on the verandah. 'They're all gone, hey?' asked Kayerts from the far end of the common room in a muffled voice. 'You did not find anybody?'

'Oh, yes,' said Carlier, 'I found one of Gobila's people lying dead before the huts – shot through the body. We heard that shot last night.'

Kayerts came out quickly. He found his companion staring grimly over the yard at the tusks, away by the store. They both sat in silence for a while. Then Kayerts related his conversation with Makola. Carlier said nothing. At the midday meal they ate very little. They hardly exchanged a word that day. A great silence seemed to lie heavily over the station and press on their lips.

Makola did not open the store; he spent the day playing with his children. He lay full-length on a mat outside his door, and the youngsters sat on his chest and clambered all over him. It was a touching picture. Mrs. Makola was busy cooking all day as usual. The white men made a somewhat better meal in the evening. Afterwards, Carlier smoking his pipe strolled over to the store; he stood for a long time over the tusks, touched one or two with his foot, even tried to lift the largest one by its small end. He came back to his chief, who had not stirred from the verandah, threw himself in the chair and said –

'I can see it! they were pounced upon while they slept heavily after drinking all that palm wine you've allowed Makola to give them. A put-up job! See? The worst is, some of Gobila's people were there, and got carried off too, no doubt. The least drunk woke up, and got shot for his sobriety. This is a funny country. What will you do now?'

'We can't touch it, of course,' said Kayerts.

'Of course not,' assented Carlier.

'Slavery is an awful thing,' stammered out Kayerts in an unsteady voice.

'Frightful – the sufferings,' grunted Carlier, with conviction.

They believed their words. Everybody shows a respectful deference to certain sounds that he and his fellows can make. But about feelings people really know nothing. We talk with indignation or enthusiasm; we talk about oppression, cruelty, crime, devotion, self-sacrifice, virtue, and we know nothing real beyond the words. Nobody knows what suffering or sacrifice mean – except, perhaps, the victims of the mysterious purpose of these illusions.

Next morning they saw Makola very busy setting up in the yard the big scales used for weighing ivory. By and by Carlier said: 'What's that filthy scoundrel up to?' and lounged out into the yard. Kayerts followed. They stood by watching. Makola took no notice. When the balance was swung true, he tried to lift a tusk into the scale. It was too heavy. He looked up helplessly without word, and for a minute they stood round that balance as mute and still as three statues. Suddenly Carlier said: 'Catch hold of the other end, Makola – you beast!' and together they swung the tusk up. Kayerts trembled every limb. He muttered, 'I say! O! say!' and putting his hand in his pocket found there a dirty bit of paper and the stump of a pencil. He turned his back on the other, as if about to do something tricky, and noted stealthily the weights which Carlier shout to him with unnecessary loudness. When all was over Makola whispered to himself 'The sun's very strong here for the tusks.' Carlier said to Kayerts in a careless tone: 'I say, chief, I might just as well give him a lift with this lot into the store

As they were going back to the house Kayerts observed with a sigh: 'It had to be done.' And Carlier said: 'It's deplorable, but, the men being Company's men, the ivory is Company's ivory. We must look after it.' 'I will report to the Director, of course,' said Kayerts. 'Of course; let him decide,' approved Carlier.

At mid-day they made a hearty meal. Kayerts sighed from time to time.

Whenever they mentioned Makola's name they always added to it an opprobrious epithet. It eased their conscience. Makola gave himself a half-holiday, and bathed his children in the river. No one from Gobila's villages came near the station that day. No one came the next day, and the next, nor for a whole week. Gobila's people might have all been dead and buried for any sign of life they gave. But they were only mourning for those they had lost by the witchcraft of white men, who had brought wicked people into their country. The wicked people were gone, but fear remained. Fear always remains. A man may destroy everything within himself, love and hate and belief, and even doubt; but as long as he clings to life he cannot destroy fear: the fear, subtle, indestructible, and terrible, that pervades his being; that tinges his thoughts; that lurks in his heart; that watches on his lips the struggle of his last breath. In his fear, the mild old Gobila offered extra human sacrifices to all the Evil Spirits that had taken possession of his white friends. His heart was heavy. Some warriors spoke about burning and killing, but the cautious old savage dissuaded them. Who could foresee the woe those mysterious creatures, if irritated, might bring? They should be left alone. Perhaps in time they would disappear into the earth as the first one had disappeared. His people must keep away from them, and hope for the best.

Kayerts and Carlier did not disappear, but remained above on this earth, that, somehow, they fancied had become bigger and very empty. It was not the absolute and dumb solitude of the post that impressed them so much as an inarticulate feeling that something from within them was gone, something that worked for their safety, and had kept the wilderness from interfering with their hearts. The images of home; the memory of people like them, of men that thought and felt as they used to think and feel, receded into distances made indistinct by the glare of unclouded sunshine. And out of the great silence of the surrounding wilderness, its very hopelessness and savagery seemed to approach them nearer, to draw them gently, to look upon them, to envelop them with a solicitude irresistible, familiar, and disgusting.

Days lengthened into weeks, then into months. Gobila's people drummed and yelled to every new moon, as of yore, but kept away from the station. Makola and Carlier tried once in a canoe to open communications, but were received with a shower of arrows, and had to fly back to the station for dear life. That attempt set the country up and down the river into an uproar that could be very distinctly heard for days. The steamer was late. At first they spoke of delay jauntily, then anxiously, then gloomily. The matter was becoming serious. Stores were running short. Carlier cast his lines off the bank, but the river was low, and the fish kept out in the stream. They dared not stroll far away from the station to shoot. Moreover, there was no game in the impenetrable forest. Once Carlier shot a hippo in the river. They had no boat to secure it, and it sank. When it floated up it drifted away, and Gobila's people secured the carcase. It was the occasion for a national holiday, but Carlier had a fit of rage over it, and talked about the necessity of exterminating all the niggers before the country could be made habitable. Kayerts mooned about silently; spent hours looking at the portrait of his Melie. It represented a

little girl with long bleached tresses and a rather sour face. His legs were much swollen, and he could hardly walk. Carlier, undermined by fever, could not swagger any more, but kept tottering about, still with a devil-may-care air, as became a man who remembered his crack regiment. He had become hoarse, sarcastic, and inclined to say unpleasant things. He called it 'being frank with you.' They had long ago reckoned their percentages on trade, including in them that last deal of 'this infamous Makola.' They had also concluded not to say anything about it. Kayerts hesitated at first – was afraid of the Director.

'He has seen worse things done on the quiet,' maintained Carlier, with a hoarse laugh. 'Trust him! He won't thank you if you blab. He is no better than you or me. Who will talk if we hold our tongues? There is nobody here.'

That was the root of the trouble! There was nobody there; and being left there alone with their weakness, they became daily more like a pair of accomplices than like a couple of devoted friends. They had heard nothing from home for eight months. Every evening they said, 'To-morrow we shall see the steamer.' But one of the Company's steamers had been wrecked, and the Director was busy with the other, relieving very distant and important stations on the main river. He thought that the useless station, and the useless men, could wait. Meantime Kayerts and Carlier lived on rice boiled without salt, and cursed the Company, all Africa, and the day they were born. One must have lived on such diet to discover what ghastly trouble the necessity of swallowing one's food may become. There was literally nothing else in the station but rice and coffee; they drank the coffee without sugar. The last fifteen lumps Kayerts had solemnly locked away in his box, together with a half-bottle of Cognac, 'in case of sickness,' he explained. Carlier approved. 'When one is sick,' he said, 'any little extra like that is cheering.'

They waited. Rank grass began to sprout over the courtyard. The bell never rang now. Days passed, silent, exasperating, and slow. When the two men spoke, they snarled; and their silences were bitter, as if tinged by the bitterness of their thoughts.

One day after a lunch of boiled rice, Carlier put down his cup untasted, and said: 'Hang it all! Let's have a decent cup of coffee for once. Bring out that sugar, Kayerts!'

'For the sick,' muttered Kayerts, without looking up.

'For the sick,' mocked Carlier. 'Bosh! ... Well! I am sick.'

'You are no more sick than I am, and I go without,' said Kayerts in a peaceful tone.

'Come! out with that sugar, you stingy old slave-dealer.'

Kayerts looked up quickly. Carlier was smiling with marked insolence. And suddenly it seemed to Kayerts that he had never seen that man before. Who was he? He knew nothing about him. What was he capable of? There was a surprising flash of violent emotion within him, as if in the presence of something undreamt-of, dangerous, and final. But he managed to pronounce with composure –

'That joke is in very bad taste. Don't repeat it.'

'Joke!' said Carlier, hitching himself forward on his seat. 'I am hungry – I am sick – I don't joke! I hate hypocrites. You are a hypocrite. You are a slave-dealer. I am a slave-dealer. There's nothing but slave-dealers in this cursed country. I mean to have sugar in my coffee to-day, anyhow!'

'I forbid you to speak to me in that way,' said Kayerts with a fair show of resolution.

'You! – What?' shouted Carlier, jumping up.

Kayerts stood up also. 'I am your chief,' he began, trying to master the shakiness of his voice.

'What?' yelled the other. 'Who's chief? There's no chief here. There's nothing here: there's nothing but you and I. Fetch the sugar – you pot-bellied ass.'

'Hold your tongue. Go out of this room,' screamed Kayerts. 'I dismiss you – you scoundrel!'

'Carlier swung a stool. All at once he looked dangerously in earnest. 'You flabby, good-for-nothing civilian – take that!' he howled.

Kayerts dropped under the table, and the stool struck the grass inner wall of the room. Then, as Carlier was trying to upset the table, Kayerts in desperation made a blind rush, head low, like a cornered pig would do, and overturning his friend, bolted along the verandah and into his room. He locked the door, snatched his revolver, and stood panting. In less than a minute Carlier was kicking at the door furiously, howling, 'If you don't bring out that sugar, I will shoot you at sight, like a dog. Now then – one – two – three. You won't? I will show you who's the master.'

Kayerts thought the door would fall in, and scrambled through the square hole that served for a window in his room. There was then the whole breadth of the house between them. But the other was apparently not strong enough to break in the door, and Kayerts heard him running round. Then he also began to run laboriously on his swollen legs. He ran as quickly as he could, grasping the revolver, and unable yet to understand what was happening to him. He saw in succession Makola's house, the store, the river, the ravine, and the low bushes; and he saw all those things again as he ran for the second time round the house. Then again they flashed past him. That morning he could not have walked a yard without a groan.

And now he ran. He ran fast enough to keep out of sight of the other man.

Then as, weak and desperate, he thought, 'Before I finish the next round I shall die,' he heard the other man stumble heavily, then stop. He stopped also. He had the back and Carlier the front of the house, as before. He heard him drop into a chair cursing, and suddenly his own legs gave way, and he slid down into a sitting posture with his back to the wall. His mouth was as dry as a cinder, and his face was wet with perspiration – and tears. What was it all about? He thought it must be a horrible illusion; he thought he was dreaming; he thought he was going mad! After a while he collected his senses. What did they quarrel about? That sugar! How absurd! He would give it to him – didn't want it himself. And he began scrambling to his feet with a sudden feel-

ing of security. But before he had fairly stood upright, a common-sense reflection occurred to him and drove him back into despair. He thought: If I give way now to that brute of a soldier, he will begin this horror again to-morrow – and the day after – every day – raise other pretensions, trample on me, torture me, make me his slave – and I will be lost! Lost! The steamer may not come for days – may never come. He shook so that he had to sit down on the floor again. He shivered forlornly. He felt he could not, would not move any more. He was completely distracted by the sudden perception that the position was without issue – that death and life had in a moment become equally difficult and terrible.

All at once he heard the other push his chair back; and he leaped to his feet with extreme facility. He listened and got confused. Must run again! Right or left? He heard footsteps. He darted to the left, grasping his revolver, and at the very same instant, as it seemed to him, they came into violent collision. Both shouted with surprise. A loud explosion took place between them; a roar of red fire, thick smoke; and Kayerts, deafened and blinded, rushed back thinking: I am hit – it's all over. He expected the other to come round – to gloat over his agony. He caught hold of an upright of the roof – 'All over!' Then he heard a crashing fall on the other side of the house, as if somebody had tumbled headlong over a chair – then silence. Nothing more happened. He did not die. Only his shoulder felt as if it had been badly wrenched, and he had lost his revolver. He was disarmed and helpless! He waited for his fate. The other man made no sound. It was a stratagem. He was stalking him now! Along what side? Perhaps he was taking aim this very minute!

After a few moments of an agony frightful and absurd, he decided to go and meet his doom. He was prepared for every surrender. He turned the corner, steadying himself with one hand on the wall; made a few paces, and nearly swooned. He had seen on the floor, protruding past the other corner, a pair of turned-up feet. A pair of white naked feet in red slippers. He felt deadly sick, and stood for a time in profound darkness. Then Makola appeared before him, saying quietly: 'Come along, Mr. Kayerts. He is dead.' He burst into tears of gratitude; a loud, sobbing fit of crying. After a time he found himself sitting in a chair and looking at Carlier, who lay stretched on his back. Makola was kneeling over the body.

'Is this your revolver?' asked Makola, getting up.

'Yes,' said Kayerts; then he added very quickly, 'He ran after me to shoot me – you saw!'

'Yes, I saw,' said Makola. 'There is only one revolver; where's his?'

'Don't know,' whispered Kayerts in a voice that had become suddenly very faint.

'I will go and look for it,' said the other gently. He made the round along the verandah, while Kayerts sat still and looked at the corpse. Makola came back empty-handed, stood in deep thought, then stepped quietly into the dead man's room, and came out directly with a revolver, which he held up before Kayerts. Kayerts shut his eyes. Everything was going round. He found life more terrible and difficult than death.

He had shot an unarmed man.

After meditating for a while, Makola said softly, pointing at the dead man who lay there with his right eye blown out –

'He died of fever.' Kayerts looked at him with a stony stare. 'Yes,' repeated Makola thoughtfully, stepping over the corpse, 'I think he died of fever. Bury him tomorrow.'

And he went away slowly to his expectant wife, leaving the two white men alone on the verandah. Night came, and Kayerts sat unmoving on his chair. He sat quiet as if he had taken a dose of opium. The violence of the emotions he had passed through produced a feeling of exhausted serenity. He had plumbed in one short afternoon the depths of horror and despair, and now found repose in the conviction that life had no more secrets for him: neither had death! He sat by the corpse thinking; thinking very actively, thinking very new thoughts. He seemed to have broken loose from himself altogether. His old thoughts, convictions, likes and dislikes, things he respected and things he abhorred, appeared in their true light at last! Appeared contemptible and childish, false and ridiculous. He revelled in his new wisdom while he sat by the man he had killed. He argued with himself about all things under heaven with that kind of wrong-headed lucidity which may be observed in some lunatics. Incidentally he reflected that the fellow dead there had been a noxious beast anyway; that men died every day in thousands; perhaps in hundreds of thousands – who could tell? – and that in the number, that one death could not possibly make any difference; couldn't have any importance, at least to a thinking creature. He, Kayerts, was a thinking creature. He had been all his life, till that moment, a believer in a lot of nonsense like the rest of mankind – who are fools; but now he thought! He knew! He was at peace; he was familiar with the highest wisdom! Then he tried to imagine himself dead, and Carlier sitting in his chair watching him; and his attempt met with such unexpected success, that in a very few moments he became not at all sure who was dead and who was alive. This extraordinary achievement of his fancy startled him, however, and by a clever and timely effort of mind he saved himself just in time from becoming Carlier. His heart thumped, and he felt hot all over at the thought of that danger. Carlier! What a beastly thing! To compose his now disturbed nerves – and no wonder! – he tried to whistle a little. Then, suddenly, he fell asleep, or thought he had slept; but at any rate there was a fog, and somebody had whistled in the fog.

He stood up. The day had come, and a heavy mist had descended upon the land: the mist penetrating, enveloping, and silent; the morning mist of tropical lands; the mist that clings and kills; the mist white and deadly, immaculate and poisonous. He stood up, saw the body, and threw his arms above his head with a cry like that of a man who, waking from a trance, finds himself immured for ever in a tomb. *'Help! ... My God!'*

A shriek inhuman, vibrating and sudden, pierced like a sharp dart the white shroud of that land of sorrow. Three short, impatient screeches followed, and then, for a time, the fog-wreaths rolled on, undisturbed, through a formidable silence. Then many more shrieks, rapid and piercing, like the yells of some exasperated and ruthless creature, rent the air. Progress was calling to Kayerts from the river. Progress and civilisation and all the virtues. Society was calling to its accomplished child to come, to be taken care of, to be instructed, to be judged, to be condemned; it called him to return to that rubbish heap from which he had wandered away, so that justice could be done.

Kayerts heard and understood. He stumbled out of the verandah, leaving the other man quite alone for the first time since they had been thrown there together. He groped his way through the fog, calling in his ignorance upon the invisible heaven to undo its work. Makola flitted by in the mist, shouting as he ran –

'Steamer! Steamer! They can't see. They whistle for the station. I go ring the bell. Go down to the landing, sir. I ring.'

He disappeared. Kayerts stood still. He looked upwards; the fog rolled low over his head. He looked round like a man who has lost his way; and he saw a dark smudge, a cross-shaped stain, upon the shifting purity of the mist. As he began to stumble towards it, the station bell rang in a tumultuous peal its answer to the impatient clamour of the steamer.

The Managing Director of the Great Civilising Company (since we know that civilisation follows trade) landed first, and incontinently lost sight of the steamer. The fog down by the river was exceedingly dense; above, at the station, the bell rang unceasing and brazen.

The Director shouted loudly to the steamer. 'There is nobody down to meet us; there may be something wrong, though they are ringing. You had better come, too!'

And he began to toil up the steep bank. The captain and the engine-driver of the boat followed behind. As they scrambled up the fog thinned, and they could see their Director a good way ahead. Suddenly they saw him start forward, calling to them over his shoulder:– 'Run! Run to the house! I've found one of them. Run, look for the other!'

He had found one of them! And even he, the man of varied and startling experience, was somewhat discomposed by the manner of this finding. He stood and fumbled in his pockets (for a knife) while he faced Kayerts, who was hanging by a leather strap from the cross. He had evidently climbed the grave, which was high and narrow, and after tying the end of the strap to the arm, had swung himself off. His toes were only a couple of inches above the ground; his arms hung stiffly down; he seemed to be standing rigidly at attention, but with one purple cheek playfully posed on the shoulder. And, irreverently, he was putting out a swollen tongue at his Managing Director.

137

3 Understanding the story

You will probably agree that there is a great deal of *substance* in this story – that is, a number of characters, a number of important issues, plenty of action, moral complexity, and quite a heavy sense of atmosphere. There are certainly more issues than we shall be able to deal with in just this one chapter. What I want to do is go through the basic elements of the story in the form of a series of questions – as usual graded from ones which are simple and straightforward and then later to ones which are more complex. I would urge you to make brief notes for yourself in response to the questions. Don't read the question then pass straight on to my own 'answers' to it. Give yourself the satisfaction of thinking through your own response then noting it down before you check it against mine.

Do not imagine that these questions are a test of your memory. If you are not sure of an answer, consult the text to make sure – and you will sometimes need to quote briefly to 'prove' that you are –right.

   1 Who are the two central characters in this story?

   2 What were their original occupations?

   3 What are their individual reasons for being in Africa?

   4 How would you describe their characters?

   5 What happens to them (briefly) in the story?

—⊰•◉•⊱—

These are my own responses. As we go on you will see that there are sometimes answers which are not simply 'right' or 'wrong' but are a matter of degree or emphasis.

1. Kayerts and Carlier.

2. Kayerts worked as a government clerk in the Administration of the Telegraphs. Carlier is 'an ex-non-commissioned officer of cavalry'.

3. Kayerts is in Africa to earn a dowry for his daughter. Carlier has had to accept the job of a 'second class agent' because he has no money of his own and cannot squeeze any more out of his relations.

4. They are lazy and incompetent, full of self-aggrandisement, and stupidly incurious about their surroundings. They have racist attitudes of superiority towards the Africans. They are improvident, greedy, self-seeking, and self-deluding. And they are both cowards.

5. Because of these weaknesses in their characters, they rapidly degenerate morally. They accommodate themselves to the acquisition of ivory by slave-trading, then when through their own negligence their supplies run low they quarrel. Kayerts kills Carlier and then hangs himself in fear of the consequences.

6 Who are the most important secondary characters?

7 What function do they have in the story: that is, what do they do that is important?

6. There are a number to choose from, but my selection would be Makola, the Director, and Gobila

7. Makola is in many senses the most active person in the story. He runs the station and decides how things will be done there. He trades the local workers to the slave traders in exchange for ivory. And he colludes with Kayerts to cover up the murder of Carlier. He is running the station after the death of the first agent, when Kayerts and Carlier arrive, and he is still in change at the end of the story when they are both dead.

The Director is important because he represents the greed and the cynicism of the Company in sending out ill-equipped and incompetent agents With no regard for what happens to them. He represents the forces of imperialism which are engaged in the economic exploitation of Africa. He is in a certain sense responsible for what happens – though of course behind *him* there is the Company back home which is even more cynical than him. 'They must be mad at home to send me such specimens' he curses.

Gobila is important in that he and his fellow villagers supply the station with food. He has quite positive feelings towards Europeans, and when some of his men are sold off to the slave traders he withdraws his support. Following this, Kayerts and Carlier run out of provisions and are precipitated into their moral crises.

On the issue of race in the story:

8 What are the attitudes of Kayerts and Carlier towards the Africans?

9 What are the attitudes of Makola and Gobila towards Europeans?

10 What attitude does Joseph Conrad himself seem to have towards racism and the Africans in the story?

8. The two principals are quite clearly overtly racist in their attitude to the Africans. They use terms like 'funny brute' and 'fine animals': even the positive commendation is couched in an offensive comparison with 'lower' species. They treat Gobila like a child, striking matches for his amusement and allowing him 'a sniff of the ammonia bottle': that is, they dangle their European technology before him in a patronising manner. And they call the language of the traders 'gibberish' because they don't understand it. Their racism fits perfectly well with their general stupidity and lack of imagination.

9. Makola and Gobila are a more complex matter and their responses to the Europeans are different. Makola, in pretending that his name is Henry Price, quite clearly aspires to some of the characteristics (or the advantages) of being European. But on the other hand, we are told that he 'despised' the two white men – though we might think that he has every reason to do so since they are so incompetent. But there doesn't seem to be any evidence that his attitude is *racially* biased. Gobila, on the other hand, is positively *benevolent* towards Europeans. We are told that 'he seemed really to love all white men'. And he proves this by supplying the station with food – until he is betrayed when some of his men are sold off. But notice that there is just a tinge of racism in his naive view that Europeans appear 'indistinguishably alike'. This is rather like the old racist notion of the British that all Chinese people look the same.

10. This is a much more difficult question to answer because Conrad does not make his opinions known by direct statement as the author (though you may note that he gives us his opinions on other matters). What we have to do therefore is judge by looking carefully at the manner in which he presents this issue via his characters.

To begin with, it should be quite obvious that he disapproves of Kayert's and Carlier's overt racism: he puts bigoted opinions into the mouths of two fools. Does that mean therefore that Conrad's sympathies lie with the Africans? Well – yes and no. He portrays Gobila fairly sympathetically yet you will notice that he offers '*human* sacrifices' (my emphasis) following the loss of his villagers, and Conrad has no hesitation in calling him a 'savage'. Similarly with Makola we have a complex characterisation: his skill and efficiency are obviously offered in positive contrast to the stupidity of his two white bosses. Yet he cherishes "in his innermost heart the worship of evil spirits' and worse than that he betrays his fellow men to the slave traders, who we should note, are themselves *also* Africans.

So the answer is not as clear cut as we might hope. Conrad is obviously aware of bad in the Europeans and good in the Africans – although in this particular story *none* of the Europeans is shown in a positive light. The main thrust of his message seems to be pointing to the moral weakness of these urban Europeans when confronted with a different environment and culture in the pursuit of what purports to be 'progress' but is in fact organised greed.

Don't worry if your responses to these questions were not exactly the same as mine. You may have drawn your evidence from elsewhere in the text for instance. But if your answers were generally similar this means that you have understood what was going on in quite a complex piece of work. This is the first part of our task – to grasp what is going on in the story. Next we will pass on to consider *how* it is being told.

4 Close reading

Before going any further I would strongly urge you to make sure that you have read 'An Outpost of Progress' not just once, but twice. The reason for this is that we will be making a special study of Conrad's use of *irony* in the story, and to fully appreciate some of it you need to approach the story already fully aware of what is going to happen in it. You will then be able to concentrate your attention on Conrad's *manner* of dealing with his material. So if you haven't already done so, undertake a second reading and make a note of those points where you think he is being ironic. This will be useful for our discussion in Section 5.

But our first exercise and discussion will be on close reading. This time, however, I don't want you to concentrate on points of vocabulary, grammar, and figures of speech, but on the *meaning* of what we are told and how it relates to the rest of the story. In other words, what each statement contributes to the story as a whole. For this exercise, therefore, you should consider each *sentence* and say what information it gives us that is significant for what comes later. The purpose of this exercise is to demonstrate the very subtle and complex manner in which a story is told and its meanings are transmitted to us. We assemble these meanings in our mind, and that too is a subtle and complex process of which we are not normally conscious. *Making* ourselves more conscious of it will help us appreciate more fully what literature has to offer. We will then be able to enjoy it at a deeper level.

Once again I suggest that you write down your observations. You can do it in rough note form. This will help you develop the discipline of articulating your thoughts and being specific in your responses. And don't forget to note any key words or expressions just as we have been doing in earlier chapters. So, STOP here and make this close reading on the first half of the opening paragraph – up to the sentence which ends 'away from the buildings'.

⟶⊶⟵

These are my own observations with which you can compare your own. My numbering system refers to the sequence of the sentences.

1. 'White men' is significant because the story is about the exploitation of black African by white Europeans. And 'in charge' is mildly ironic because we rapidly learn that they are only nominally in charge: it is Makola who really determines what goes on, whilst they are hopelessly incompetent.

2. The names 'Kayerts' and Carlier' tell us that the setting of the story is the *Belgian* Congo: Carlier is a French name, Kayerts is Flemish, and these are the two linguistic groups which compose Belgium. The physical descriptions *contrast* the two men in a way which makes them slightly ridiculous, and the term 'perched' reinforces this.

3. 'Maintained' suggests just the opposite – that Makola has given himself the name Henry Price because he wants to identify his interests with those of his employers. (Just, by the way, note Conrad's use of the racist term 'nigger' which would be in common use in 1897 when he wrote the story.)

4. The natives call him 'Makola' – and so does Conrad, which reinforces our reading of the previous sentence. His 'wanderings' suggest that he is experienced.

5. Makola speaks two European languages in addition to his own African language and his wife's (which would be different). He is also a skilled clerk. Thus he has absorbed European culture, in contrast to the two Europeans who are completely incapable of absorbing his. Yet he still worships evil spirits. He has a foot in both cultures.

6. Loanda is on the coast of Angola, close to what was once called the 'Slave Coast'. This is why it is 'Mrs Price' Who understands what the slave traders are saying later in the story.

7. 'Rolled about' suggests that the children are at ease in their natural environment. 'Shed-like' tells us how poor their accommodation is.

8. 'Impenetrable' (a typically Conradian term) suggests that he keeps his feelings and his motivation well hidden. It is a similar term to those which Conrad uses later to describe the topographical surroundings – 'hopeless' and 'irresistable'. Such details contribute to the reason why Africa in a moral sense defeats Europe in the story. 'Despised', however, is a key insight into Makola's judgement and feelings: this points to the element of racial conflict in the story.

9. We notice that the 'trade goods' are an assortment of cheap rubbish: they are being traded for ivory – therefore the Europeans are cheating the Africans (in general). But 'pretended' tells us that Makola may be engaged in a

little cooking-of-the-books on his own account.

10. 'Only one large building': this is a very *undeveloped* trading station and its isolation is emphasised.

11. 'Neatly' and 'verandah' contrast sharply with Makola's 'shed-like' dwelling: the Europeans have the better accommodation.

12-14. The furnishing is sparse, but the two men have a room each.

15. The mosquito net would be very important: they are close to the equator, and therefore a long way away from their European homeland.

16. Notice how the two men do not know how to look after themselves: the floor is 'littered' with their 'broken' and 'dirty' goods. And how inappropriate some of those goods are: they have brought 'town wearing apparel' when they are in the tropics.

17. 'Dwelling-place' is another irony of Conrad's: what he is referring to is the grave of the first station chief who has died of fever. So Africa has already killed off one representative of Europe when the story opens.

These are the sorts of details which it is possible to observe in a text. Don't worry if you didn't note as many as I have done. This type of exercise becomes easier as you gain more experience of literary analysis. You might even have been vaguely aware of some of these details but might not have thought of noting them down. This is part of the purpose of the exercise – to encourage you to become more *conscious* of exactly what is written on the page and what it means.

What I hope you will have grasped is the point that some of these details *could* not have been grasped at first reading, because their significance is only accessible to us if we know what happens in the rest of the story.

5 Irony

I want to turn now to a literary feature for which Conrad is justly renowned – the use of irony. But first of all, as ever, let's be quite sure what it means. There are, in fact, three types of irony. The first is a simple figure of speech where the intended meaning is the opposite of what is said. For instance, 'So you have lost the book I lent you. That's *fine!*' The second type (called Socratic irony after Socrates, who used it to ridicule his rivals) occurs when a speaker pretends to adopt another person's viewpoint in order to exaggerate it and thus reveal its weaknesses. The third, taken from the world of the stage, is called dramatic irony: this occurs when the spectator (or reader) is allowed to be aware of something when the actors (or fictional characters) are not. We will be dealing here with the first and the third of these types. In fact we have already touched on a couple of mild examples in close reading of the opening page of the story. What I am going to do next is illustrate one or more from the beginning of the story.

We left off our close reading at the point where Conrad mentions 'another dwelling place' in which '*slept* the man who had seen the beginning of all this' (my emphasis). The use of this term 'slept' is grim irony on Conrad's part because the man is *dead* (and we note that this is also a use of *euphemism*). Then later on in the same long opening paragraph, the director tells the two men that the appointment he is offering them is an 'exceptional opportunity' and 'a favour done to beginners'. At this 'Kayerts was moved almost to tears by his director's kindness'. But we learn on the next page that the director is lying. He thinks the two men are 'imbeciles' and this particular station on the river is 'useless'. There is thus a double irony of the dramatic kind: *we* know that the director is deceiving the two men, his act is not a 'kindness' at all, and Kayerts's reaction is therefore made ridiculous to us.

Shortly after the director has left, Kayerts and Carlier take stock of each other. On the surface they talk about who is boss and what an easy time they will have of it, but Conrad lets us into their inner thoughts and we are thus presented with another dramatic irony: they are both speculating about the other's possible death. Kayerts thinks 'the idea that he would, perhaps, have to bury Carlier and remain alone, gave him an inward shiver'. Carlier, in his turn, thinks 'that poor Kayerts: he is so fat and unhealthy. It would be awful if I had to bury him here'. This is one layer of dramatic irony: we know something which they do not – their secret thoughts about each other. But there is another layer on top of that created by the fact that whilst the two men are at this very moment calling each other 'my dear fellow' we know that before long they will be locked in a grotesque fight, trying to kill each other, and that by the end of the story both of them *will* be dead, one shot by the other, who then commits suicide.

You can perhaps appreciate now if you didn't before why one single reading of a text is not enough for a *full* appreciation of what it has to offer. We would not be aware of the dramatic irony Conrad was offering here if we didn't know what was going to happen later in the story. And if you are still not quite sure about this concept of irony, re-read the passage I have just discussed keeping my commments in mind. Then consider the following two examples.

Once he has established their presence at the station, Conrad refers to Kayerts and Carlier as 'the two pioneers of trade and progress'. Now this is fairly clearly irony of the first type I described: Conrad must mean the opposite of what he is saying here because all the other information he gives us about the two men contradicts this description. They hardly know what they are doing, and they have come out to Africa simply because they need the money. Similarly, any 'trade' that takes place is done by other people, not them, and there is not the slightest sign of any 'progress' in anything they do.

I hope I do not seem to spoil the effect of the irony by analysing it in such detail. These are artistic devices which many readers pick up quite easily; but I think it is important to know *how* and *why* they work as they do. Now for our second example of dramatic irony.

The two men discover at their station an old newspaper from home which carries an article on 'Our Colonial Expansion'. This speaks of 'the sacredness of the civilizing work and ... the merits of those who went about bringing light, and faith and commerce to the dark places of the earth'. It is quite obvious to the reader that this is not true of Kayerts and Carlier at all, and it is dramatically ironic because *we* can see this whilst both the newspaper editor and the two men themselves can *not*. There is what the American literary critic Wayne Booth calls a sort of 'secret collusion' between the author (Conrad) and the reader behind the backs of his characters. The two men are so self-deluding they even believe what they read in the newspaper (ignoring the immediate example of their own hopeless existence) and begin to congratulate themselves for great works which they have not yet performed, nor ever will.

6 Conrad's prose style

It is not uncommon for some readers to complain about the difficulties they feel in grappling With Conrad's style when they encounter his writing for the first time. I'm not going to pretend that his prose is the clearest and the easiest to understand of all the writers in our anthology: in fact I would say that a *liking* for his style is something of an acquired taste. But it is possible to come to terms with those difficulties with concentration, thoughtful reflection, and practice. I also believe that it is useful to be able to analyse a writer's style whether you like it or not. This is simply one of those literary skills which the casual reader does not think about particularly, but should be acquired by the serious student or those who want to get more out of literature.

What I propose to do is another close reading on a selected passage. We will not be exhaustive this time: in fact I am going to *tell* you what to look for. The passage is the third main paragraph of the story starting 'The two men watched the steamer round the bend'. Use the list of literary terms if you need to, and try to say something about each of the following stylistic features: sentence length; narrative mode; language; and rhythm. As usual, you should try to give a name to anything you identify, but even if you cannot do this, still make a note of anything which strikes you as significant, unusual, or even 'difficult'.

<hr />

In offering you my own response I am going to deal with those features which most commonly cause problems for newcomers to Conrad.

Sentence length. Some of the sentences here (particularly the last) are quite long. This is because he is often expressing quite complex ideas or generating a very charged atmosphere. But they are not *all* long; the first, for instance, dealing with an action by characters, is much shorter.

Narrative mode. He adopts the common third person omniscient mode: that is, Conrad tells us what his characters do, how they feel, and what they think. But you may have noticed that statements such as the one beginning 'Few men realize' is of a different kind than, say, 'The two men watched'. Conrad has stopped telling the story for a moment and is offering us his opinion. In fact everything else up to the end of the paragraph is Conrad's general opinion. Conrad is being what is called an 'intrusive narrator' at this point. He intrudes into his own narrative to comment on the story and offer his philosophic reflections on life in general.

Language. You will probably have notcied that he uses a number of terms which cause us to think 'Now what exactly does he mean by that?'. Terms such as 'irresistible force', 'unmitigated savagery', 'perception', 'negation of the habitual', and 'discomposing intrusion'; there are many other such examples. What makes this difficult to grasp at first is that he is switching from the very concrete and specific descriptions of the two men and the trading station to an *abstract* and very *general* consideration of their condition. This is almost the language of philosophy. The terms 'force', 'savagery', 'habitual', and 'intrusion' are all *abstract nouns*. We are not necessarily conscious of this whilst reading the text, but they take us away from the 'story' and force us to consider rather large scale social reflections on life. In fact the combination of a rather unusual and powerful adjective qualifying an abstract noun – 'unmitigated savagery', 'profound trouble' – is a sort of trade-mark of Conrad's style. You will see many other examples in this story and throughout his work in general.

Rhythm. In prose writing rhythm is easier to feel than to define. You do not need to go into all the detail of stress analysis as you might with poetry, but it should be possible to sense that Conrad puts a lot of rhythmic emphasis into what he writes by his use of alliteration, repetition, and what are called balanced clauses and parallel constructions. For instance you might have noticed that 'The courage, the composure, the confidence' was a fairly obvious example of *alliteration*, with an insistent stress falling on the initial letter 'c' in each of those words (and note too that they are all abstract nouns). Then, 'with primitive nature and primitive man' combines both alliteration (the initial 'p') with *repetition* of the word 'primitive' itself. You might also note that his use of the second 'primitive' here throws the emphasis onto the word which follows it – 'man'. There are plenty of other examples of the same thing in this one paragraph: 'more strange, more incomprehensible' and 'every great and every insignificant' are just two. There is a different kind of repetition in the last sentence, which begins 'to the sentiment of being'. This is a long sentence as we have already noted, and in order to 'tug' us through it he repeats the initial 'to' and the construction of the clause of which it is part, so that we have 'To the sentiment of being ... to the clear perception ... to the negation of the habitual' (and notice yet again how many of those terms are abstractions). Finally, look at the *construction* of the sentence which begins 'Few men realize that their life'. Conrad immediately wants to explain what he means by 'life', so he inserts two-clauses which expand the notion. But in doing so, and whilst we are, so to speak, waiting for the end of the sentence, his expansion is nicely balanced: 'the very essence of their character', with its emphasis falling on 'essence' and character', is paralleled by the following clause: 'their capabilities and their audacities' with emphasis falling again on the two (abstract!) nouns. All these devices – alliteration, repetition, and parallel construction – help to create a very strong sense of rhythm in his prose.

<hr>

Now you might have found this exercise fairly difficult. You may not have been sure what to say about the features I selected, or you may have been aware of the complexities in Conrad's prose style but not able to find the right terms to express yourself. The solution to this problem is quite simple. Don't worry! Just read my analyses and get used to the technical vocabulary as we go along. Prose analysis is not something which can be mastered at one attempt. You need to familiarise yourself with a number of quite subtle concepts and the terms in which they are expressed.. Even if the examples offered here still seem difficult to understand you can always come back to them and read them again later.

I am including such advanced material here for two reasons. To give a challenge to more advanced readers and to show the less advanced what is possible – something of a taste of what lies ahead and an opportunity to become familiar with the language of literary-analysis.

For those who *did* find it difficult and those who may think that we have strayed a long way away from the story, you will be glad to hear that we now go back to some simpler and more straightforward comprehension exercises in our self-assessment questions.

7 Self-assessment questions

LANGUAGE

1 What is an 'opprobrious epithet'?

2 'Immense forests, holding fateful complications of fantastic life, lay in the eloquent silence of mute greatness'

(a) What literary device is most obviously being used here?

(b) How is the rhythm of the sentence created?

(c) What parts of speech are 'mute greatness'?

3 Comment on the syntax in the statement 'The director was a man ruthless and efficient'.

4 What is meant by 'the old stager'?

5 What figure of speech is being used in 'They lived like blind men in a large room'?

COMPREHENSION

1 Which country does Makola come from?

2 What goods are traded in exchange for ivory?

3 What position does Gobila hold?

4 Over what household item do Kayerts and Carlier quarrel?

5 (This is an extra difficult question. You are already very well read if you get any part of this correct.) Name the three *authors* of the novels Carlier and Kayerts read in the story.

ANALYSIS

1 What is meant by 'a wilderness rendered more strange by ... the mysterious glimpses of the vigorous life it contained'?

2 Over approximately what length of time do the events of the story unfold?

3 Why does Makola seem to forget how to speak French when the traders arrive?

4 'Kayerts was moved almost to tears by his director's kindness. He would, he said, by doing his best, try to justify the flattering confidence, etc., etc.' What does Conrad mean by this 'etc., etc.'?

5 The final paragraph of the story describes the director confronting Kayerts, who has hanged himself. Which details in the paragraph would you say are most ironic?

8 Course work

1 Choose a substantial paragraph from the story (which does not contain conversation) and, using the checklist of literary terms (Chapter One, Section 5) produce a close reading of the passage. Try to say as much as possible about its constituent parts and any relation they might have to the story as a whole.

2 Write a general appreciation of 'An Outpost of Progress' using the guidance notes in Chapter Four, Section 8.

3 Give an account of the various characters in the story and their relationship to the setting – that is, the physical environment in which the story takes place.

4 Discuss Conrad's use of irony in 'An Outpost of Progress'. (Try to avoid using the examples discussed in this chapter.)

5 Discuss the *structure* of 'An Outpost of Progress'.

6 Compare and contrast 'An Outpost of Progress' with 'The Voyage'

9 Further reading

STORIES

Conrad's greatest stories or tales are generally considered to be 'Heart of Darkness', 'The Secret Sharer', 'Youth', 'Il Conde', 'An Outpost of Progress', and 'The Lagoon'. There are many more, but they vary a great deal in quality. They often turn around dramatic or even melodramatic incidents; they all feature his vivid and muscular prose style; and even the weakest are worth reading – though some of them reveal a startling misogyny which has gone largely unnoticed in Conrad criticism.

NOVELS

His greatest novels are, by general consent:

Lord Jim, London: Dent, 1900.

Nostromo: A Tale of the Seaboard, London: Dent, 1904.

The Secret Agent, London: Dent, 1907.

Under Western Eyes, London: Dent, 1911.

If you have not read any of his novels before, start with *The Secret Agent*: the others are longer and much more complex.

BIOGRAPHY

Two easily available biographies of Conrad are worth recommending:

Jocelyn Baines, *Joseph Conrad: A Critical Biography*, London: Weidenfeld and Nicolson, 1960.

Frederick R. Karl, *Joseph Conrad: The Three Lives*, London: Faber, 1975.

Both offer criticism of the stories and novels, as well as a detailed life history.

CRITICISM

Most criticism of Conrad focuses attention on his novels. The following are amongst the more accessible:

Edward Crankshaw, *Joseph Conrad: Some Aspects of the Art of the Novel*, London: John Lane, 1936.

Douglas Hewitt, *Conrad: A Reassessment*, Cambridge, England: Bowes and Bowes, 1952.

F. R. Leavis, *The Great Tradition*, London: Chatto and Windus, 1936.

Frederick Karl, *A Reader's Guide to Joseph Conrad*, New York: Farrar, Straus and Giroux, 1960.

Norman Sherry, *Conrad: The Critical Heritage*, London: Routledge and Kegan Paul, 1973.

CHAPTER SIX

Close reading and social class

1 Introduction

We come now to a writer whose work has often aroused strong feelings – both of enthusiasm and of antipathy. D. H. Lawrence himself had very passionate views on literature, ideas and life in general, and he gave full expression to them in his writing. He also changed his mind from time to time, held contradictory views, and believed in going to extremes if necessary. He is therefore quite a complex phenomenon to discuss. Fortunately for us, 'Fanny and Annie' is one of his more straightforward stories.

He is the first writer in English with a truly international reputation to have come from the working class, and this is reflected in his work both in terms of his subject matter and some of his attitudes. Many of his stories, for instance, deal with elemental conflicts between men and women but are set amongst ordinary working people rather in the same manner as Thomas Hardy, a writer Lawrence admired a great deal.

He is typically a writer of what is called the 'modernist' period (1900–30) in that he wanted, as the American poet Ezra Pound put it, to 'make it new'. That is, he felt that the new feelings and perceptions of the twentieth century needed fresh and vigorous expression to sweep away all that was old and stale. But he believed that fiction could be made new both in content *and* form. In this respect he is of course famous for his courageous and forthright discussion of sexual relations in *Lady Chatterley's Lover*, but he also brought issues of social class, politics, and individual psychology to the forefront; and in doing so he broke many of the rules or conventions of what was considered 'good writing'.

Even in so short a piece as 'Fanny and Annie' you will see that his manner of writing changes from one scene to the next. Sometimes in his work he is plain and direct, sometimes lush and florid, and sometimes he intrudes into his narrative to deliver lectures in a style which is flagrantly rhetorical and often incantatory. It is this aspect of Lawrence – the seer, the prophet – which most irritates his detractors.

What nobody can deny is his prodigious energy and the range of his output. He is one of the few writers (along with Hardy) considered to be equally accomplished in the writing of stories, novels, and poetry – but in addition to this he also wrote travel books, plays, essays on moral and social issues, literary criticism, and philosophic works on psychology and the unconscious. He even produced a series of interesting paintings too – which got him into a lot of trouble.

After the fairly complex issues we considered in the last chapter, we will be going back in this one to the relatively straightforward approach we made earlier under the heading 'Understanding the Story'. This is both to rehearse some basic critical categories again and to give you a breather before we tackle Dickens's story – possibly the most complex in the programme. Then following the basics we will look at just one aspect of the subject matter – Lawrence's presentation of social class, before undertaking our last exercise in close reading.

2 Biographical note

Lawrence was born in 1885, the fourth of five children, in a mining village near Nottingham. His father was a miner and his mother a cultivated and artistic woman with whom Lawrence had a very close relationship. He attended Nottingham High School and then Nottingham University College, and for a few years worked as a teacher in Croydon. The early part of his adult life was dominated by his relationship with two women, Jessie Chambers and Louise Burrows, and with his mother, who died in 1910. All these experiences form the subject material for his first important novel, *Sons and Lovers* which was published in 1913.

The year before this Lawrence met Frieda von Richthofen (sister of the famous German flying ace – the 'Red Baron') who was married to a professor at Nottingham University. They ran away together to Germany and began a problematic relationship which, despite its tempests and occasional separations, lasted for the rest of Lawrence's

F

life. His early publications included poetry, plays which were unsuccessful but have since become very popular (like *A Collier's Friday Night*), novels which were written then re-written several times over, book reviews, and the stories which some critics argue are his most accomplished work.

He met the famous Bloomsbury group (Bertrand Russell, E. M. Forster, Lady Ottoline Morrell and others) but disliked them because of their social class and because he thought they were spiritually dead. For a while he and Frieda lived in Cornwall with Katherine Mansfield and Middleton Murry but he ended up quarrelling with them as he did with most other people. He was eventually expelled from Cornwall by the police because his reading lamp, left on late at night, was thought to be a signal to German submarines in the English Channel. This was the England of the Edwardian and Georgian eras against which Lawrence protested so much.

For the rest of his life he moved restlessly between England, Italy, France, Sicily, Ceylon, Australia and New Mexico – constantly on the move, in general searching for an environment to suit the tuberculosis from which he was suffering. He became famous as someone with controversial views and in particular, because of his portrayal of *female* sexuality he was thought of as a prophet of 'free love'. This was quite a mistaken view of his beliefs, because although he was frank about sexuality he was, in fact, quite puritanical and reactionary in many of his views and attitudes.

Many of Lawrence's polemical essays seek to justify these views, and his arguments are conducted with great vigour and panache. But his ideas, particularly later on in his life, are shot through with misogyny and proto-fascism which are a great embarrassment to his supporters.

He had produced what most people regard as his greatest work (*The Rainbow, Women in Love*) by 1920 and after that pushed most of his political, psychological, and fictional ideas to the limits for which they are famous but which some critics argue spoilt their artistic merit. Martin Seymour Smith puts his finger on these problems when he says of Lawrence 'Much in his writing is loveable and irresistible on any terms but his tiresomeness as a man also intrudes damagingly into it. He is full of insights, but as full of neurotic and unpleasant idiocies.'

But he went on producing an astonishing range of work right up to his death in 1930. It is typical that one of his last conflicts with the

Establishment should be over the exhibition of his paintings which was closed by the police in 1929 because, amongst other things, the works depicted *male* nudes.

FANNY AND ANNIE
D. H. LAWRENCE

Flame-lurid his face as he turned among the throng of flame-lit and dark faces upon the platform. In the light of the furnace she caught sight of his drifting countenance, like a piece of floating fire. And the nostalgia, the doom of homecoming went through her veins like a drug. His eternal face, flame-lit now! The pulse and darkness of red fire from the furnace towers in the sky, lighting the desultory, industrial crowd on the wayside station, lit him and went out.

Of course he did not see her. Flame-lit and unseeing ! Always the same, with his meeting eyebrows, his common cap, and his red-and-black scarf knotted round his throat. Not even a collar to meet her! The flames had sunk, there was shadow.

She opened the door of her grimy, branch-line carriage, and began to get down her bags. The porter was nowhere, of course, but there was Harry, obscure, on the outer edge of the little crowd, missing her, of course.

'Here! Harry!' she called, waving her umbrella in the twilight. He hurried forward.

'Tha's come, has ter?' he said, in a sort of cheerful welcome. She got down, rather flustered, and gave him a peck of a kiss.

'Two suit-cases !' she said.

Her soul groaned within her, as he clambered into the carriage after her bags. Up shot the fire in the twilight sky, from the great furnace behind the station. She felt the red flame go across her face. She had come back, she had come back for good. And her spirit groaned dismally. She doubted if she could bear it.

There, on the sordid little station under the furnaces, she stood, tall and distinguished, in her well-made coat and skirt and her broad grey velour hat. She held her umbrella, her bead chatelaine, and a little leather case in her grey-gloved hands, while Harry staggered out of the ugly little train with her bags.

'There's a trunk at the back,' she said in her bright voice. But she was not feeling bright. The twin black cones of the iron foundry blasted their sky-high fires into the night. The whole scene was lurid. The train waited cheerfully. It would wait another ten minutes. She knew it. It was all so deadly familiar.

Let us confess it at once. She was a lady's maid, thirty years old, come back to marry her first-love, a foundry worker: after having kept him dangling, off and on, for a dozen years. Why had she come back? Did she love him? No. She didn't pretend to. She had loved her brilliant and ambitious cousin, who had jilted her, and who had died. She had had other affairs which had come to nothing. So here she was, come back suddenly to marry her first-love, who had waited – or remained single – all these years.

'Won't a porter carry those?' she said, as Harry strode with his workman's stride down the platform towards the guard's van.

'I can manage,' he said.

And with her umbrella, her chatelaine, and her little leather case, she followed him.

The trunk was there.

'We'll get Heather's greengrocer's cart to fetch it up,' he said.

'Isn't there a cab?' said Fanny, knowing dismally enough that there wasn't.

'I'll just put it aside o' the penny-in-the-slot, and Heather's greengrocers'll fetch it about half past eight,' he said.

He seized the box by its two handles and staggered with it across the level-crossing, bumping his legs against it as he waddled. Then he dropped it by the red sweet-meats machine.

'Will it be safe there?' she said.

'Ay – safe as houses,' he answered. He returned for the two bags. Thus laden, they started to plod up the hill, under the great long black building of the foundry. She walked beside him – workman of workmen he was, trudging with that luggage. The red lights flared over the deepening darkness. From the foundry came the horrible, slow clang, clang, clang of iron, a great noise, with an interval just long enough to make it unendurable.

Compare this with the arrival at Gloucester: the carriage for her mistress, the dog-cart for herself with the luggage; the drive out past the river, the pleasant trees of the carriage approach; and herself sitting beside Arthur, everybody so polite to her.

She had come home – for good! Her heart nearly stopped beating as she trudged up that hideous and interminable hill, beside the laden hgure. What a come-downl What a come-downl She could not take it with her usual bright cheerfulness. She knew it all too well. It is easy to bear up against the unusual, but the deadly familiarity of an old stale past!

He dumped the bags down under a lamp-post, for a rest. There they stood, the two of them, in the lamplight. Passers-by stared at her, and gave good-night to Harry. Her they hardly knew, she had become a stranger.

'They're too heavy for you, let me carry one,' she said.

'They begin to weigh a bit by the time you've gone a mile,' he answered.

'Let me carry the little one,' she insisted.

'Tha can ha'e it for a minute, if ter's a mind,' he said, handing over the valise.

And thus they arrived in the streets of shops of the little ugly town on top of the hill. How everybody stared at her; my word, how they stared! And the cinema was just going in, and the queues were tailing down the road to the corner. And everybody took full stock of her. 'Night, Harry!' shouted the fellows, in an interested voice.

However, they arrived at her aunt's – a little sweet-shop in a side street. They 'pinged' the door-bell, and her aunt came running forward out of the kitchen.

'There you are, child! Dying for a cup of tea, I'm sure. How are you?' Fanny's aunt kissed her, and it was all Fanny could do to refrain from bursting into tears, she felt so low. Perhaps it was her tea she wanted.

'You've had a drag with that luggage,' said Fanny's aunt to Harry.

'Ay – I'm not sorry to put it down,' he said, looking at his hand which was crushed and cramped by the bag handle.

Then he departed to see about Heather's greengrocery cart.

When Fanny sat at tea, her aunt, a grey-haired, fair-faced little woman, looked at her with an admiring heart, feeling bitterly sore for her. For Fanny was beautiful: tall, erect, finely coloured, with her delicately arched nose, her rich brown hair, her large lustrous grey eyes. A passionate woman – a woman to be afraid of. So proud, so inwardly violent! She came of a violent race.

It needed a woman to sympathize with her. Men had not the courage. Poor Fanny! She was such a lady, and so straight and magnificent. And yet everything seemed to do her down. Every time she seemed to be doomed to humiliation and disappointment, this handsome, brilliantly sensitive woman, with her nervous, overwrought laugh.

'So you've really come back, child?' said her aunt.

'I really have, Aunt,' said Fanny.

'Poor Harry! I'm not sure, you know, Fanny, that you're not taking a bit of an advantage of him.'

'Oh, Aunt, he's waited so long, he may as well have what he's waited for. 'Fanny laughed grimly.

'Yes, child, he's waited so long, that I'm not sure it isn't a bit hard on him. You know, I *like* him, Fanny – though as you know quite well, I don't think he's good enough for you. And I think he thinks so himself, poor fellow.'

'Don't you be so sure of that, Aunt. Harry is common, but he's not humble. He wouldn't think the Queen was any too good for him, if he'd a mind to her.'

'Well – It's as well if he has a proper opinion of himself.'

'It depends what you call proper,' said Fanny. 'But he's got his good points –'

'Oh, he's a nice fellow, and I like him, I do like him. Only, as I tell you, he's not good enough for you.'

'I've made up my mind, Aunt,' said Fanny, grimly.

'Yes,' mused the aunt.' They say all things come to him who waits –'

'More than he's bargained for, eh, Aunt?' laughed Fanny rather bitterly.

The poor aunt, this bitterness grieved her for her niece.

They were interrupted by the ping of the shop-bell, and Harry's call of 'Right!' But as he did not come in at once, Fanny, feeling solicitous for him presumably at the moment, rose and went into the shop. She saw a cart outside, and went to the door.

And the moment she stood in the doorway, she heard a woman's common vituperative voice crying from the darkness of the opposite side of the road:

'Tha'rt theer, ar ter? I'll shame thee, Mester. I'll shame thee, see if I dunna.'

Startled, Fanny stared across the darkness, and saw a woman in a black bonnet go under one of the lamps up the side street.

Harry and Bill Heather had dragged the trunk off the little dray, and she retreated before them as they came up the shop step with it.

'Wheer shalt ha'e it ? ' asked Harry.

'Best take it upstairs,' said Fanny.

She went up first to light the gas.

When Heather had gone, and Harry was sitting down having tea and pork pie, Fanny asked:

'Who was that woman shouting?'

'Nay, I canna tell thee. To somebody, Is'd think,' replied Harry. Fanny looked at him, but asked no more.

He was a fair-haired fellow of thirty-two, with a fair moustache. He was broad in his speech, and looked like a foundry-hand, which he was. But women always liked him. There was something of a mother's lad about him – something warm and playful and really sensitive.

He had his attractions even for Fanny. What she rebelled against so bitterly was that he had no sort of ambition. He was a moulder, but of very commonplace skill. He was thirty-two years old, and hadn't saved twenty pounds. She would have to provide the money for the home. He didn't care. He just didn't care. He had no initiative at all. He had no vices – no obvious ones. But he was just indifferent, spending as he went, and not caring. Yet he did not look happy. She remembered his face in the fire-glow: something haunted, abstracted about it. As he sat there eating his pork pie, bulging his cheek out, she felt he was like a doom to her. And she raged against the doom of him. It wasn't that he was gross. His *way* was common, almost on purpose. But he himself wasn't really common. For instance, his food was not particularly important to him, he was not greedy. He had a charm, too, particularly for women, with his blondness and his sensitiveness and his way of making a woman feel that she was a higher being. But Fanny knew him, knew the peculiar obstinate limitedness of him, that would nearly send her mad.

He stayed till about half past nine. She went to the door with him.

'When are you coming up?' he said, jerking his head in the direction, presumably, of his own home.

'I'll come tomorrow afternoon,' she said brightly. Between Fanny and Mrs Goodall, his mother, there was naturaliy no love lost.

Again she gave him an awkward little kiss, and said goodnight.

'You can't wonder, you know, child, if he doesn't seem so very keen,' said her aunt. 'It's your own fault.'

'Oh, Aunt, I couldn't stand him when he was keen. I can do with him a lot better as he is.'

The two women sat and talked far into the night. They understood each other. The aunt, too, had married as Fanny was marrying: a man who was no companion to her, a violent man, brother of Fanny's father. He was dead, Fanny's father was dead.

Poor Aunt Lizzie, she cried woefully over her bright niece, when she had gone to bed.

Fanny paid the promised visit to his people the next afternoon. Mrs Goodall was a large woman with smooth-parted hair, a common, obstinate woman, who had spoiled her four lads and her one vixen of a married daughter. She was one of those old-fashioned powerful natures that couldn't do with looks or education or any form of showing off. She fairly hated the sound of correct Engiish. She *thee'd* and *tha'd* her prospective daughter-in-law, and said:

'I'm none as ormin' as I look, seest ta.'

Fanny did not think her prospective mother-in-law looked at all orming, so the speech was unnecessary.

'I towd him mysen,' said Mrs Goodall, ''Er's held back all this long, let 'er stop as 'er is. 'E'd none ha' had thee for *my* tellin' – tha hears. No, 'e's a fool, an' I know it. I says to him, 'Tha looks a man, doesn't ter, at thy age, goin' an' openin' to her when ter hears her scrat' at th' gate, after she's done gallivantin' round wherever she'd a mind. That looks rare an' soft.' But it's no use o' any talking: he answered that letter o' thine and made his own bad bargain.'

But in spite of the old woman's anger, she was also flattered at Fanny's coming back to Harry. For Mrs Goodall was impressed by Fanny – a woman of her own match. And more than this, everybody knew that Fanny's Aunt Kate had left her two hundred pounds: this apart from the girl's savings.

So there was high tea in Princes Street when Harry came home black from work, and a rather acrid odour of cordiality, the vixen Jinny darting in to say vulgar things. Of course Jinny lived in a house whose garden end joined the paternal garden. They were a clan who stuck together, these Goodalls.

It was arranged that Fanny should come to tea again on the Sunday, and the wedding was discussed. It should take place in a fortnight's time at Morley Chapel. Morley was a hamlet on the edge of the real country, and in its little Congregational Chapel Fanny and Harry had first met.

What a creature of habit he was! He was still in the choir of Morley

Chapel – not very regular. He belonged just because he had a tenor voice, and enjoyed singing. Indeed his solos were only spoilt to local fame because when he sang he handled his aitches so hopelessly.

'And I saw 'eaven hopened
And be'old, a wite 'orse –'

This was one of Harry's classics, only surpassed by the fine outburst of his heaving:

'Hangels – hever bright an' fair-'

It was a pity, but it was inalterable. He had a good voice, and he sang with a certain lacerating fire, but his pronunciation made it all funny. And *nothing* could alter him.

So he was never heard save at cheap concerts and in the little, poorer chapels. The others scoffed.

Now the month was September, and Sunday was Harvest Festival at Morley Chapel, and Harry was singing solos. So that Fanny was to go to afternoon service, and come home to a grand spread of Sunday tea with him. Poor Fanny! One of the most wonderful afternoons had been a Sunday afternoon service, with her cousin Luther at her side, Harvest Festival in Morley Chapel. Harry had sung solos then – ten years ago. She remembered his pale blue tie, and the purple asters and the great vegetable marrows in which he was framed, and her cousin Luther at her side, young, clever, come down from London, where he was getting on well, learning his Latin and his French and German so brilliantly.

However, once again it was Harvest Festival at Morley Chapel, and once again, as ten years before, a soft, exquisite September day, with the last roses pink in the cottage gardens, the last dahlias crimson, the last sunflowers yellow. And again the little old chapel was a bower, with its famous sheaves of corn and corn-plaited pillars, its great bunches of grapes, dangling like tassels from the pulpit corners, its marrows and potatoes and pears and apples and damsons, its purple asters and yellow Japanese sunflowers. Just as before, the red dahlias round the pillars were dropping, weak-headed among the oats. The place was crowded and hot, the plates of tomatoes seemed balanced perilously on the gallery front, the Rev. Enderby was weirder than ever to look at, so long and emaciated and hairless.

The Rev. Enderby, probably forewarned, came and shook hands with her and welcomed her, in his broad northern, melancholy singsong before he mounted the pulpit. Fanny was handsome in a gauzy dress and a beautiful lace hat. Being a little late, she sat in a chair in the side-aisle wedged in, right in front of the chapel. Harry was in the gallery above, and she could only see him from the eyes upwards. She noticed again how his eyebrows met, blond and not very marked, over his nose. He was attractive too: physically lovable, very. If only – if only her *pride* had not suffered! She felt he dragged her down.

'Come, ye thankful people come,
Raise the song of harvest-home.
All is safely gathered in
Ere the winter storms begin –'

Even the hymn was a falsehood, as the season had been wet, and half the crops were still out, and in a poor way.

Poor Fanny! She sang little, and looked beautiful through that inappropriate hymn. Above her stood Harry – mercifully in a dark suit and dark tie, looking almost handsome. And his lacerating, pure tenor sounded well, when the words were drowned in the general commotion. Brilliant she looked, and brilliant she felt, for she was hot and angrily miserable and inflamed with a sort of fatal despair. Because there was about him a physical attraction which she really hated, but which she could not escape from. He was the first man who had ever kissed her. And his kisses, even while she rebelled from them, had lived in her blood and sent roots down into her soul. After all this time she had come back to them. And her soul groaned, for she felt dragged down, dragged down to earth, as a bird which some dog has got down in the dust. She knew her life would be unhappy. She knew that what she was doing was fatal. Yet it was her doom. She had to come back to him.

He had to sing two solos this afternoon: one before the 'address' from the pulpit and one after. Fanny looked at him, and wondered he was not too shy to stand up there in front of all the people. But no, he was not shy. He had even a kind of assurance on his face as he looked down from the choir gallery at her: the assurance of a common man deliberately entrenched in his commonness. Oh, such a rage went through her veins as she saw the air of triumph, laconic, indifferent triumph which sat so obstinately and recklessly on his eyelids as he looked down at her. Ah, she despised him! But there he stood up in that choir gallery like Balaam's ass in front of her, and she could not get beyond him. A certain winsomeness also about him. A certain physical winsomeness, and as if his flesh were new and lovely to touch. The thorn of desire rankled bitterly in her heart.

He, it goes without saying, sang like a canary this particular afternoon, with a certain defiant passion which pleasantly crisped the blood of the congregation. Fanny felt the crisp flames go through her veins as she listened. Even the curious loud-mouthed vernacular had a certain fascination. But, oh, also, it was so repugnant. He would triumph over her, obstinately he would drag her right back into the common people: a doom, a vulgar doom.

The second performance was an anthem, in which Harry sang the solo parts. It was clumsy, but beautiful, with lovely words.

'They that sow in tears shall reap in joy,
He that goeth forth and weepeth, bearing precious seed
Shall doubtless come again with rejoicing, bringing his sheaves with him –'

'Shall doubtless come, Shall doubtless come – ' softly intoned the altos – 'Bringing his she-e-eaves with him,' the trebles flourished brightly, and then again began the half-wistful solo:

'They that sow in tears shall reap in joy –'

Yes, it was effective and moving.

But at the moment when Harry's voice sank carelessly down to his close, and the choir, standing behind him, were opening their mouths for the final triumphant outburst, a shouting female voice rose up from the body of the congregation. The organ gave one startled trump, and went silent; the choir stood transfixed.

'You look well standing there, singing in God's holy house,' came the loud, angry female shout. Everybody turned electrified. A stoutish, red-faced woman in a black bonnet was standing up denouncing the soloist. Almost fainting with shock, the congregation realized it. 'You look well, don't you, standing there singing solos in God's holy house, you, Goodall. But I said I'd shame you. You look well, bringing your young woman here with you, don't you? I'll let her know who she's dealing with. A scamp as won't take the consequences of what he's done.' The hard-faced, frenzied woman turned in the direction of Fanny. 'That's what Harry Goodall is, if you want to know.'

And she sat down again in her seat. Fanny, startled like all the rest, had turned to look. She had gone white, and then a burning red, under the attack. She knew the woman: a Mrs Nixon, a devil of a woman, who beat her pathetic, drunken, red-nosed second husband, Bob, and her two lanky daughters, grown-up as they were. A notorious character. Fanny turned round again, and sat motionless as eternity in her seat.

There was a minute of perfect silence and suspense. The audience was open-mouthed and dumb; the choir stood like Lot's wife; and Harry, with his music-sheet, stood there uplifted, looking down with a dumb sort of indifference on Mrs Nixon, his face naïve and faintly mocking. Mrs Nixon sat defiant in her seat, braving them all.

Then a rustle, like a wood when the wind suddenly catches the leaves. And then the tall, weird minister got to his feet, and in his strong, bell-like, beautiful voice – the only beautiful thing about him – he said with infinite mournful pathos:

'Let us unite in singing the last hymn on the hymn-sheet; the last hymn on the hymn-sheet, number eleven.

"Fair waved the golden corn,
In Canaan's pleasant land."'

The organ tuned up promptly. During the hymn the offertory was taken. And after the hymn, the prayer.

Mr Enderby came from Northumberland. Like Harry, he had never been able to conquer his accent, which was very broad. He was a little simple, one

162

of God's fools, perhaps, an odd bachelor soul, emotional, ugly, but very gentle.

'And if, O our dear Lord, beloved Jesus, there should fall a shadow of sin upon our harvest, we leave it to Thee to judge, for Thou art judge. We lift our spirits and our sorrow, Jesus, to Thee, and our mouths are dumb. o, Lord, keep us from froward speech, restrain us from foolish words and thoughts, we pray Thee, Lord Jesus, who knowest all and judgest all.'

Thus the minister said in his sad, resonant voice, washed his hands before the Lord. Fanny bent forward open-eyed during the prayer. She could see the roundish head of Harry, also bent forward. His face was inscrutable and expressionless. The shock left her bewildered. Anger perhaps was her dominating emotion.

The audience began to rustle to its feet, to ooze slowly and excitedly out of the chapel, looking with wildly-interested eyes at Fanny, at Mrs Nixon, and at Harry. Mrs Nixon, shortish, stood defiant in her pew, facing the aisle, as if announcing that, without rolling her sleeves up, she was ready for anybody. Fanny sat quite still. Luckily the people did not have to pass her. And Harry, with red ears, was making his way sheepishly out of the gallery. The loud noise of the organ covered all the downstairs commotion of exit.

The minister sat silent and inscrutable in his pulpit, rather like a death's-head, while the congregation filed out. When the last lingerers had unwillingly departed, craning their necks to stare at the still seated Fanny, he rose, stalked in his hooked fashion down the little country chapel and fastened the door. Then he returned and sat down by the silent young woman.

'This is most unfortunate, most unfortunate!' he moaned. 'I am so sorry, I am so sorry, indeed, indeed, ah, indeed!' he sighed himself to a close.

'It's a sudden surprise, that's one thing,' said Fanny brightly.

'Yes – yes – indeed. Yes, a surprise, yes. I don't know the woman, I don't know her.'

'I know her,' said Fanny. 'She's a bad one.'

'Well! Well!' said the minister. 'I don't know her. I don't understand. I don't understand at all. But it is to be regretted, it is very much to be regretted. I am very sorry.'

Fanny was watching the vestry door. The gallery stairs communicated with the vestry, not with the body of the chapel. She knew the choir members had been peeping for information.

At last Harry came – rather sheepishly – with his hat in his hand.

'Well!' said Fanny, rising to her feet.

'We've had a bit of an extra,' said Harry.

'I should think so,' said Fanny.

'A most unfortunate circumstance – a most *unfortunate* circumstance. Do you understand it, Harry? I don't understand it at all.'

'Ah, I understand it. The daughter's goin' to have a childt, an' 'er lays it on to me.'

'And has she no occasion to?' asked Fanny, rather censorious.

'It's no more mine than it is some other chap's,' said Harry, looking aside.

There was a moment of pause.

'Which girl is it?' asked Fanny.

'Annie – the young one –'

There followed another silence.

'I don't think I know them, do I?' asked the minister.

'I shouldn't think so. Their name's Nixon – mother married old Bob for her second husband. She's a tanger—'s driven the gel to what she is. They live in Manners Road.'

'Why, what's amiss with the girl?' asked Fanny sharply. 'She was all right when I knew her.'

'Ay – she's all right. But she's always in an' out o' th' pubs, wi' th' fellows,' said Harry.

'A nice thing!' said Fanny.

Harry glanced towards the door. He wanted to get out.

'Most distressing, indeed!' The minister slowly shook his head.

'What about tonight, Mr Enderby?' asked Harry, in rather a small voice. 'Shall you want me?'

Mr Enderby looked up painedly, and put his hand to his brow. He studied Harry for some time, vacantly. There was the faintest sort of a resemblance between the two men.

'Yes,' he said. 'Yes, I think. I think we must take no notice, and cause as little remark as possible.'

Fanny hesitated. Then she said to Harry.

'But *will* you come?'

He looked at her.

'Ay, I s'll come,' he said.

Then he turned to Mr Enderby.

'Well, good-afternoon, Mr Enderby,' he said.

'Good-afternoon, Harry, good-afternoon,' replied the mournful minister. Fanny followed Harry to the door, and for some time they walked in silence through the late afternoon.

'And it's yours as much as anybody else's?' she said.

'Ay,' he answered shortly.

And they went without another word, for the long mile or so, till they came to the corner of the street where Harry lived. Fanny hesitated. Should she go on to her aunt's? Should she? It would mean leaving all this, for ever. Harry stood silent.

Some obstinacy made her turn with him along the road to his own home. When they entered the house-place, the whole family was there, mother and father and Jinny, with Jinny's husband and children and Harry's two brothers.

'You've been having yours ears warmed, they tell me,' said Mrs Goodall grimly.

'Who told thee?' asked Harry shortly.

'Maggie and Luke's both been in.'

'You look well, don't you!' said interfering Jinny.

Harry went and hung his hat up, without replying.

'Come upstairs and take your hat off,' said Mrs Goodall to Fanny, almost kindly. It would have annoyed her very much if Fanny had dropped her son at this moment.

'What's 'er say, then?' asked the father secretly of Harry, jerking his head in the direction of the stairs whence Fanny had disappeared.

'Nowt yet,' said Harry.

'Serve you right if she chucks you now,' said Jinny. 'I'll bet it's right about Annie Nixon an' you.'

'Tha bets so much,' said Harry.

'Yi – but you can't deny it,' said Jinny.

'I can if I've a mind.'

His father looked at him inquiringly.

'It's no more mine than it is Bill Bower's, or Ted Slaney's, or six or seven on 'em,' said Harry to his father.

And the father nodded silently.

'That'll not get you out of it, in court,' said Jinny.

Upstairs Fanny evaded all the thrusts made by his mother, and did not declare her hand. She tidied her hair, washed her hands, and put the tiniest bit of powder on her face, for coolness, there in front of Mrs Goodall's indignant gaze. It was like a declaration of independence. But the old woman said nothing.

They came down to Sunday tea, with sardines and tinned salmon and tinned peaches, besides tarts and cakes. The chatter was general. It concerned the Nixon family and the scandal.

'Oh, she's a foulmouthed woman,' said Jinny of Mrs Nixon. 'She may well talk about God's holy house, *she* had. It's first time she's set foot in it, ever since she dropped off from being converted. She's a devil and she always was one. Can't you remember how she treated Bob's children, mother, when we lived down in the Buildings? I can remember when I was a little girl she used to bathe them in the yard, in the cold, so that they shouldn't splash the house. She'd half kill them if they made a mark on the floor, and the language she'd use! And one Saturday I can remember Garry, that was Bob's own girl, she ran off when her stepmother was going to bathe her – ran off without a rag of clothes on – can you remember, mother? And she hid in Smedley's closes – it was the time of mowing grass – and nobody could fnd her. She hid out there all night, didn't she, mother? Nobody could find her. My word, there was a talk. They found her on Sunday morning – '

'Fred Coutts threatened to break every bone in the woman's body, if she touched the children again,' put in the father.

'Anyhow, they frightened her,' said Jinny. 'But she was nearly as bad with her own two. And anybody can see that she's driven old Bob till he's gone soft.'

'Ah, soft as mush,' said Jack Goodall. ''E'd never addle a week's wage, nor yet a day's if th' chaps didn't make it up to him.'

'My word, if he didn't bring her a week's wage, she'd pull his head off,' said Jinny.

'But a clean woman, and respectable, except for her foul mouth,' said Mrs Goodall. 'Keeps to herself like a bull-dog. Never lets anybody come near the house, and neighbours with nobody.'

'Wanted it thrashed out of her,' said Mr Goodall, a silent, evasive sort of man.

'Where Bob gets the money for his drink from is a mystery,' said Jinny.

'Chaps treats him,' said Harry.

'Well, he's got the pair of frightenedest rabbit-eyes you'd wish to see,' said Jinny.

'Ay, with a drunken man's murder in them, I think,' said Mrs Goodall.

So the talk went on after tea, till it was practically time to start off to chapel again.

'You'll have to be getting ready, Fanny,' said Mrs Goodall.

'I'm not going tonight,' said Fanny abruptly. And there was a sudden halt in the family. 'I'll stop with *you* tonight, Mother,' she added.

'Best you had, my gel,' said Mrs Goodall, flattered and assured.

3 Understanding the story

Let me remind you of the categories which were offered earlier as being common to most stories. If you are still not sure what these terms mean, re-read Section 3 in Chapter Four.

☆ construction

☆ dramatisation

☆ characterisation

☆ setting

☆ subject

☆ treatment

Your task now is to re-read 'Fanny and Annie' keeping these terms in mind and then to make notes on your own observations for comparison with my own which will follow. As usual I urge you to be self-disciplined: do *not* look ahead to my responses until you have noted your own.

You may be able to say a lot more under some of these headings than others. Don't worry about this: the purpose of the exercise is to get you used to *thinking* about these aspects of fiction and offering your *considered* observations – for as I have said before these are not aspects of fiction that you can spot or look up: you must be able to both read closely and attentively *and* hold the overall story in your head at the same time. Reading and understanding fiction is a more complex issue than it might seem at first. But once again do not imagine that any of this is a test of memory: you should become used to working with the text, looking through it and checking to see that your observations and claims can be substantiated. And make notes for your answers. Don't forget to be an active reader.

━━━◁◦◉◦▷━━━

CONSTRUCTION

Actually, construction was not one of Lawrence's strong points as a writer, and it is not immediately apparent that there is any particular shape or form to this story. But if you look more closely you will see that it is composed of three separate episodes. In the first Fanny arrives back in her native town to meet Harry and her Aunt. In the second she visits Harry's home and meets his family – in particular his mother. And in the third she witnesses the incident in the chapel then goes back to his home again, where she decides to stay.

You might think that these scenes are quite an arbitrary choice on which to base the notion of 'construction' or the shape of a story. After all, the second scene is fairly brief and the third much longer. But I would defend this choice by pointing to two underlying issues which seem to me to strengthen this claim.

In the first scene Fanny is coming back into contact with two *individuals* – Harry and her Aunt. In the second she meets Harry's *family*. And in the third she mixes amongst other people in the *community*. The scenes therefore reflect the stages of Fanny's re-absorption into the working-class society from which she originally came, which is one of the most important subjects of the story.

My second point is that each of these three episodes involves a scene of *eating*. In the first Fanny has tea with her Aunt. In the second she has high tea with the Goodall clan. And in the third she has 'Sunday tea' with the whole family. The meals become more formal and elaborate at each stage.

So there is a construction or a shaping of the narrative, but its elements are buried deeply below the surface of events in the story.

DRAMATISATION

We are plunged straight into the action of the story – Fanny meets Harry – and only later told why she has come back. We are presented with the clash of two cultures, largely from Fanny's point of view. And many readers may wonder what qualities Harry possesses that have brought Fanny back to him. These are only gradually revealed as we see Harry in action. Then Fanny's love-hate feelings about both Harry and the family into which she will marry are put to the test with Annie's public denunciation. She could use this as an excuse to break off the engagement. We are uncertain of her decision until the very last words she speaks – 'I'll stop with *you* tonight, Mother'.

The essential dramatic conflict and interest of the story is therefore one of psychological tensions and motivation played out in the three episodes which become increasingly dramatic in the original theatrical sense of that term. The obvious climax occurs in the church, and the resolution of the drama follows in the Sunday tea scene which follows.

CHARACTERISATION

Lawrence's characterisation combines both a presentation of their external or physical appearance and their internal or psychological life with a dramatic presentation of their characters. That is, we are told what they *look* like, what they *think* and *feel*, and how they *behave* as the drama unfolds. I shall take just one example – Fanny – to illustrate the point.

We are introduced to Fanny first of all via her emotional or psychological reactions on meeting Harry at the station. She finds his appearance ('his common cap ... not even a collar to meet her!') very irritating. She is even unenthusiastic about returning to her native town: 'the doom of homecoming went through her veins like a drug'. It is of course only later that we learn why this is the case, but the important point is that we are *inside* Fanny's mind.

Then we are presented with her external appearance: 'tall and distinguished in her well-made coat and skirt'. Now we have a physical description to fill her out as a credible fictional character.

We are presented with plenty more information of both kinds, but I will not bother listing it all here. The important thing to recognise is that Lawrence is creating Fanny both as a physical and a psychological being. Now, how does he complete the characterisation with the third element of *behaviour*?

In fact she does not *act* a great deal in the unfolding of the drama. She is polite, proper, and well behaved. We see her stillness and calmness very much in contrast with the bustle of others around her. But we know that she must eventually 'act' by choosing to stay or to leave following the revelation of Harry's liaison with Annie. Partly because she is physically attracted to him ('his kisses ... had lived in her blood and sent roots down into her soul') and partly because she wants the status of being a married woman, she decides to stay. We thus see her character 'tested' in action.

Lawrence does not portray all his other characters in such a fully rounded

168

manner, but in the case of Fanny we can see that his method of characterisation results in what is often referred to as a 'three-dimensional character': that is, one depicted in a physical, psychological, and moral sense.

SETTING

This feature of his work should have been easier to put your finger on. His story is set in a very credible or realistic working class community. The railway station, iron foundry, shops, cinema, and the Congregational Chapel of what Fanny perceives as 'the little ugly town' are presented in a perfectly straightforward manner. Most readers will probably feel confident that Lawrence is being honest and accurate in his creation of this northern setting. And all the smaller details reinforce this effect of 'truthful realism' (if that isn't tautology!): the greengrocer's coat, Harry's tea of a pork pie, even Mrs Nixon who beats her 'pathetic, drunken, red-nosed second husband' help to create a no-nonsense world of work, tough-living, and close relationships which forms the 'setting' for the 'subject' of the story.

SUBJECT

This will depend upon your interpretation of the story as a whole. It is what you think the most important issue or element of the narrative. You can probably guess from what I have said above that in my reading of the story the subject is Fanny's mixed feelings about returning to and fitting in with a group of people amongst whom she feels herself to be an outsider. It is precisely the world of working-class life, tough-living and close family relationships which threaten Fanny. She *wanted* to be independent and live closer to the middle class. But she feels that these options are closed off to her and she has come back to marry her first love. It is a physical attraction to Harry which has kept her interest alive – even though she resents this attraction. She is repelled by much of what she perceives around her, and yet in the end she gives in and resigns herself to it. *This* is what I read as being the subject of the story.

TREATMENT

This is not an easy feature to describe unless you are used to analysing fiction: it is rather like discussing the question of *tone* in a piece of work and requires a fair degree of experience and sensitivity. It becomes a lot easier if you are well acquainted with the writer's other work: you will then be used to the particular approach which the writer brings to his or her subjects.

Here, I would describe Lawrence's treatment as a combination of seriousness and wry amusement. He obviously takes Fanny's predicament seriously and clearly presents the limitations in Harry as a potential husband. And yet Harry is given a fairly honourable sense of self: *he* is quite clear about who he is and what he is capable of. There is a sensitive discrimination made by Lawrence between the thoughtful yet critical comments of Fanny's aunt to the proposed marriage and the objections made by Mrs Goodall. And the scene in the church is clearly presented as a mildly amusing piece of public embarrassment. What is particularly noteworthy is the fact that Lawrence quite obviously doesn't take sides: he is neither for nor against either Fanny or Harry. He takes a morally neutral stance to his subject and lets it speak for itself. (I must warn you that he does *not* do this in the majority of his other tales and novels.) Perhaps his attitude could best be summed up in the terms amused, detached, and realistic.

4 Social class

I am sure you probably had no difficulty understanding the story in a general sense, so in this section we are going to concentrate on just one aspect of it – social class. The purpose of this exercise is twofold: first, to practise the skill of focusing attention on one particular topic, and second, to see how Lawrence deals with this topic at a number of different levels in the story

If you have not read the story for at least a second time, I suggest you do so right away. I hope that by now you can see that a first reading of a piece of work just enables us to know what it is about: only on second and subsequent readings are we able to appreciate its subtleties and the connections between them. And if you wish you can keep our selected topic in mind. Ask yourself 'In what ways does Lawrence include the issue of class in his work?'

But for those who may not be altogether sure, here are a few words concerning the phenomenon of social class.

There are many theories about how an individual's exact position in the class structure of society is determined. These theories need not detain us here. All we need to be aware of is the fact that there are roughly speaking three classes in society:

UPPER CLASS — judges, aristocrats, landowners

MIDDLE CLASS — teachers, business people, journalists

WORKING CLASS — cleaners, bricklayers, miners

and that people in these different classes *tend* to have their own codes of belief, manners, attitudes, life-styles, and even dress. There is not space or time enough here to go into all the subtle distinctions belonging to these separate classes – what people eat, how they speak, how they spend their time – but you should try to keep the phenomenon of social class and its distinctions in mind as you consider the story. That is your task just for the moment.

For those who are not certain how to group or arrange their observations on such a wide issue as this, let me suggest the following headings (which I will be following myself): setting, family life, class mobility, attitudes, speech, clothes, and food.

Here are my own observations. They do not include every single instance in the story. What I have done is try to illustrate the *range* of different ways Lawrence includes the issue of class in his story.

SETTING

You will notice that the story is set in an emphatically working-class industrial environment. The foundry furnaces dominate the opening of the story, and Harry works there (as a moulder) – as, it appears, do his father and other males mentioned in the story. The harshness of this environment is emphasised by its being seen from Fanny's point of view – 'The twin black cones of the iron foundry blasted their sky-high fires into the night' – and she contrasts it with the more genteel nature of her arrival in (middle-class) Gloucester: 'the drive out past the river, the pleasant trees of the carriage-approach'.

FAMILY LIFE

Notice how closely interlocked the members of all the families are – even at a physical level. Harry's married sister lives in a house whose garden adjoins her father's. And when the family gathers for Sunday tea there are eight family members plus children in attendance – despite the fact that the house would have, if it was anything like typical, no more than two small downstairs rooms. This reflects very accurately typical working-class living conditions in the earlier years of this century (which in many areas have not changed much since).

CLASS MOBILITY

We are offered a sharp and sometimes amusing contrast between Harry's stubborn refusal to be ambitious and Fanny's disappointment following her attempts at what is called upward social mobility. She has left the town to become a lady's maid – a step upwards in class terms. But unmarried at thirty years of age she lacks social status: she will gain this by marrying Harry, but to do so she must take a step back and become downwardly socially mobile.

Harry knows that there is almost no escape from his class position at all – and so he accepts the fact and lives happily with it. This is what annoys Fanny: 'What she rebelled against so bitterly was that he had no sort of ambition'.

You might also note that Fanny seems to come from a slightly higher position in the class structure than Harry. Her aunt is a shopkeeper – technically what is called petit-bourgeois.

ATTITUDES

In addition to Fanny's notions of social ambition there are many other subtle class attitudes reflected in the story.

Harry, for instance, carries Fanny's bags even though they are obviously quite heavy. He is used to being self-reliant and independent, and certainly *not* used to such ideas as hiring a cab as Fanny suggests. His personal economic system would rate this as an extravagance. Instead, he calls on his social connections and arranges for a friend to collect the trunk later.

His mother, Mrs Goodall, is an even more exaggerated example of class consciousness verging on perverse defiance. She not only speaks in dialect and disparages education, but she even 'hate[s] the sound of correct English'. This is a good example of the sort of inverted snobbery sometimes found in the working class.

SPEECH

There are many obvious examples of working class speech patterns. Harry uses regional dialect – 'Tha's come, has ter' – with it's archaic employment of the second person pronoun 'thou'. This was very typical of working-class northerners, and in fact the habit has even now not completely disappeared in some areas.

You will note that Lawrence also draws our attention to the fact that Harry doesn't pronounce his aitches properly: 'Hangels – hever bright an' fair'. This is another detail which roots him firmly in his class.

And of course his mother, Mrs Goodall, uses fairly obscure working-class dialect terms like 'ormin' (simple-minded) and 'tanger' (sharp-tongued).

CLOTHES

When Harry meets Fanny at the station he is wearing, much to her annoyance, 'his common cap, and his red-and-black scarf knotted around his throat'. These are not only typical of the industrial working- class male in the earlier years of this century, but you may also note how the colours red and black form a contrast with the colour of Fanny's own clothes. She has a grey hat and grey gloves – a colour of understatement and restraint, more in keeping with the class from which she has come. And she carries an umbrella, which at that time was considered a very bourgeois accoutrement.

But notice too that for his appearance in the church choir Harry wears 'Sunday best' in the form of a 'dark suit and dark tie'. When free of the clothes necessary for his (dirty) job he dresses very formally for a public event.

FOOD

When Harry arrives with Fanny in the evening at her aunt's house, notice that he sits down to an evening 'meal' of 'tea and a pork pie'. This is very typically working class, and these class patterns in eating are also reflected in the menu for 'Sunday tea' at Mrs Goodall's – 'sardines and tinned salmon and tinned peaches, besides tarts and cakes'. Tinned food, not fresh, with salmon as a special treat for the weekend.

You may have noted quite different examples than the ones I have offered, but I hope you can see the main point of this section – that Lawrence includes aspects of class at just about every level in this story.

What we are doing in this type of exercise is to consider the text in the light of another non-literary subject or discipline (sociology). At more advanced levels of study this is quite common, and a great deal of contemporary literary criticism considers literature from points of view informed by the study of such diverse subjects as linguistics, politics, history, feminism, and psychoanalysis. Many of these other disciplines can provide interesting insight into literary texts, but the important thing to keep in mind is that before moving on to such advanced forms of interpretation we *must* have a full and disciplined grasp of the basics of literary criticism.

5 *Close reading*

I hope by now you have come to appreciate the full significance of close reading. As I have stressed before it is the most important skill you will need for the critical analysis and appreciation of literature, and along with essay writing a skill you will be able to bring to bear on most other subjects in the humanities you might go on to study.

Don't worry if you are still not quite sure of the technical vocabulary we use in close critical analysis. This is just a matter of practice. Get into the habit of using the lists of literary terms given in Chapter One and the glossary in Chapter Eight. Check anything you are not sure of, and take the trouble to look up the meaning of any new terms you come across.

This particular exercise should be relatively straightforward – if only because in the selected passage Lawrence's prose is so dense. You should, as usual, read the passage as many times as you wish and note as many of its linguistic features as you can. And I want you to concentrate in this exercise on elements of vocabulary, figures of speech, grammar, and syntax rather than on the kind of close reading in which we relate the meaning(s) of a passage to the rest of the work as a whole.

The passage I have chosen is the first two paragraphs of the story, and you should list your responses one sentence at a time.

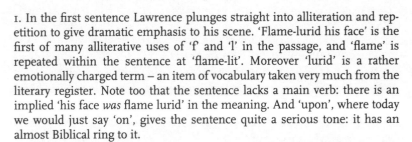

1. In the first sentence Lawrence plunges straight into alliteration and repetition to give dramatic emphasis to his scene. 'Flame-lurid his face' is the first of many alliterative uses of 'f' and 'l' in the passage, and 'flame' is repeated within the sentence at 'flame-lit'. Moreover 'lurid' is a rather emotionally charged term – an item of vocabulary taken very much from the literary register. Note too that the sentence lacks a main verb: there is an implied 'his face *was* flame lurid' in the meaning. And 'upon', where today we would just say 'on', gives the sentence quite a serious tone: it has an almost Biblical ring to it.

2. 'Furnace' and 'floating fire' continue the alliteration. A simile is used to compare his face ('his drifting countenance') to the piece of fire. And 'drifting' here seems to carry two meanings: both 'moving along the platform' and 'independent and untroubled' (we learn later that this is how Fanny views Harry). 'Countenance' is another literary and quasi-Biblical term. And 'a piece of floating fire' is a fairly striking image – but perfectly in keeping with the charged manner of Fanny's perceptions.

3. Following 'nostalgia', the term 'doom of homecoming' is almost a tautology, but Lawrence is obviously piling on emphasis here – as the onomatopoeic 'doom' illustrates. Note too that he is using the phenomenon of nostalgia in a very negative sense. The simile 'like a drug' is another very emotive comparison.

4. It is not altogether clear (to me) what 'eternal' means in this context. I take it to represent Fanny's feelings of annoyance: she does after all resent the fact that she is having to come back to Harry. And I support my reading by pointing to Lawrence's use of the exclamation mark to indicate that the sentence is a segment of narrative from Fanny's point of view.

5. 'The pulse and darkness of red fire' gives a strong impressionistic image in the sense that although very literally red fire cannot possess darkness we know that Lawrence means alternating periods of lightness and dark. And the terms 'pulse', 'darkness', 'red', and 'fire' are all charged with very

elemental connotations relating to life in a primitive sense.

6. 'Of course' is rather conversational in tone, and it is an expression which reinforces the impression that we are seeing events from Fanny's point of view.

7. 'Flame-lit' is the fifth occasion of the f/l alliteration in these two paragraphs: this is Lawrence being unashamedly rhetorical in his prose style. 'Unseeing' is another term which is not immediately clear: I take it to mean 'not paying attention'. The sentence, you may note, is another which is impressionistic — incomplete in the strict grammatical sense.

8. This sentence too omits an implied 'He was' at its beginning: (the technical term for this device is *elision*). 'Meeting' is being transferred from its use as a verb to be an adjective.

9. Another grammatically incomplete sentence in which, apart from the last word ('her') we are almost in Fanny's mind. Lawrence is almost using 'stream of consciousness' here to reflect the technical incompleteness and sometimes fragmentary nature of our thoughts. His third exclamation mark reinforces this impression.

10. The very absence of rhetorical devices in this sentence seems to me to indicate that Lawrence is preparing the reader for a transition to a less highly charged and impressionistic narrative manner.

By now I hope you will have realised that there are no right and wrong answers in a close reading exercise – just responses which are more (or less) sensitive, persuasive, and insightful. You may have noted different features than I have done, but your list in its totality should be something *like* mine. If you are still in any doubt about some of the finer details, use the Self-assessment exercises to check on your understanding.

6 Self-assessment questions

LANGUAGE

1 What figure of speech is used in the expression 'Dying for a cup of tea'?

2 What does 'vituperative' mean in 'a woman's common vituperative voice'?

3 What does 'Tha'rt theer, ar ter?' mean in conventional English?

4 What does 'laconic' mean in 'laconic, indifferent triumph'?

5 What figure of speech is used in 'like Lot's wife' – and what does this mean?

COMPREHENSION

1 What is meant when Fanny is described as 'inwardly violent'?

2 What is the name of Fanny's 'brilliant and ambitious cousin' with whom she was in love?

3 What does Lawrence mean when he says of Fanny in relation to Harry, 'she could not get beyond him'?

4 What does Lawrence mean by saying 'Fanny felt the crisp flames go through her veins as she listened'?

5 What is meant by '[Fanny] did not declare her hand'?

ANALYSIS

1 What significance does the church – Morley Chapel – have within the story? Try to think of any important ways in which it is connected with the events of the story.

2 What does Mrs Goodall think and feel about her son's renewed connexion with Fanny?

3 What is the possible significance of the three hymns sung in the chapel?

4 Which influences work on Fanny to bring about her final decision to accept Harry?

5 What crucial decisions of a moral and social nature are taken by the Reverend Enderby and Harry in the chapel following the public denunciation?

7 Course work

1 Consider 'Fanny and Annie' as a story concerned with what used to be called 'The Battle of the Sexes'.

2 Lawrence was a great admirer of Thomas Hardy. Compare 'Fanny and Annie' with 'The Withered Arm'. What, if anything, do you think Lawrence might have learned from the older novelist?

3 Write a character study of both Fanny and Harry. (Do not just

describe them, and try to avoid re–telling the story.)

4 Write an essay on 'Fanny and Annie' considering the characters in their relationship to the setting of the story.

5 In his essay 'Morality and the Novel', Lawrence says that 'The business of art is to reveal the relation between man and his circumambient universe, at the living moment'. Do you think he does this in 'Fanny and Annie'?

8 Further reading

Lawrence's output as a writer is so enormous and so varied that I have listed only a *selection* of the most widely admired works in each genre.

SHORT STORIES

These sometimes appear under the separate titles given to their first publication:

The Prussian Officer, London: Duckworth, 1914.

England, My England, London: Secker, 1922.

Love Among the Haystacks, London: Nonesuch, 1930.

But there is now an edition of his collected short stories:

The Collected Short Stories of D.H.Lawrence, London: Penguin, 1976.

NOVELLAS

These sometimes appear separately, but are often collected together and called 'short novels':

The Fox, London: Secker, 1923.

The Captain's Doll, London: Secker, 1923.

The Ladybird, London: Secker, 1923.

St Mawr, London: Secker, 1925.'

The Virgin and the Gypsy, London: Secker, 1930.

NOVELS

Sons and Lovers, London: Duckworth, 1913.

The Rainbow, London: Methuen, 1915.

Women in Love, London: Secker, 1921.
Lady Chatterley's Lover, London: Penguin, 1970.

LITERARY CRITICISM

Study of Thomas Hardy, 1914.
Studies in Classic American Literature, London: Secker, 1924.

TRAVEL WRITING

Twilight in Italy, London: Duckworth, 1916.
Sea and Sardinia, London: Secker, 1921.
Etruscan Places, London: Secker, 1932.

PSYCHOLOGICAL THEORY

Psychoanalysis and the Unconscious, London: Secker, 1923.
Fantasia of the Unconscious, London: Secker, 1922.

BIOGRAPHY

Emile Delavenay, *D.H.Lawrence: The Man and His Work*, London: Heinemann, 1972.
Harry T. Moore, *The Priest of Love*, London: Heinemann, 1974.
Keith Sagar, *The Life of D.H.Lawrence*, London: Methuen, 1980.

CRITICISM

Ronald Draper, *D. H. Lawrence: The Critical Heritage*, London: Routledge, 1970.
Philip Hobsbaum, *A Reader's Guide to D. H. Lawrence*, London: Thames and Hudson, 1981.
Graham Hough, *The Dark Sun*, London: Duckworth, 1956.
F. R. Leavis, *D. H. Lawrence: Novelist*, London: Chatto and Windus, 1955.
F. B. Pinion, *A D. H. Lawrence Companion*, London: Macmillan, 1978.
Keith Sagar, *The Art of D. H. Lawrence*, London: Cambridge University Press, 1966.

CHAPTER SEVEN

Narrators and interpretation

1 Introduction

You may be wondering why this story by Dickens has been placed at the end of the study programme. After all, it is the oldest story in our collection: why didn't we begin with it? The answer – and I'm sure you will agree with me if you have read the story – is that it is so profoundly, complex and enigmatic. Even if we read it as a straightforward ghost story or tale of the supernatural there are many puzzling features in it which have been sending literary commentators into critical spins even since it was published in Dickens's own magazine *All the Year Round* in 1866. I have saved it until this point so that we can take for granted all the groundwork we have done on the course and concentrate instead on different *interpretations* of a story – which is a fairly advanced critical approach.

'Interpretation' is one of the last stages of literary analysis and criticism. It takes place when you have all the elements of a piece of work in your intellectual grasp and you feel that by looking at them in a certain manner or from a particular point of view you can make sense of the work or explain its deeper meanings. I will be demonstrating this by offering what are called two different 'readings' of the story later on – but of course I want you to have the pleasure of tackling it yourself first.

You might be interested to know that it is one of a group of stories with the railway as settings which Dickens wrote for the Christmas edition of his magazine. One other is called 'The Boy at Mugby' – a hilariously funny dramatic monologue of a boy who works in the Refreshment room at Mugby Junction, and whose proudest boast is that he 'never yet refreshed a mortal being'. I mention this to underline the amazing fecundity of Dickens's imagination – a feature for which he is quite rightly celebrated.

You will know by now that I consider more than one reading and close attention to the details of a story necessary for a good understanding of it. And in the case of 'The Signalman' this is even more than usually the case. I hope it will not spoil or prejudice your reading of it if I urge you now to be attentive to all those finer points which echo, reinforce, and repeat each other throughout the story. Without my saying exactly which ones I mean, it should be fairly obvious to you after your first reading that lots of the small details are connected with each other in ways which are sometimes baffling and even contradictory. Even if in the end the story will baffle us (as it has most other people for the last hundred years) we will make more sense of it if we have noticed those details and can bring them to bear upon our interpretation of it.

The structure of this chapter will be to offer, after the usual biographical note, a guide to understanding the story and then an opportunity to consider two different interpretations of it. For one of these I have added a note on narrators to provide you with some further ideas on what is quite an important topic in literary studies – how stories are told, and who tells them.

2 Biographical note

Charles Dickens was born in Portsmouth in 1812, the second of eight children in his family. His father was a clerk in the Naval Pay Office, and although he was hard-working he was rarely able to manage his finances properly and the family lived in a state of insecurity. They moved to London in 1823, shortly after which his father was arrested for debt and the whole family was imprisoned in Marshalsea Debtor's Prison. Charles escaped this ignominy – but only by being sent at the age of twelve to work in a factory which made shoe-blacking. These two events made a profound effect on him and haunted his imagination for the rest of his life, and many of his later masterpieces feature images of imprisonment as well as children threatened by hardship and injustice.

When the family was released he was sent to school where he did well. At fifteen he began work in an office of Gray's Inn attorneys, but stifled by the drudgery of being a clerk he taught himself shorthand and eighteen months later began work as a freelance reporter in the Courts of Law. Next he moved on to report parliamentary debates and was highly praised for his speed and accuracy. His first creative writing began to appear in magazines around the time he was twenty-one, and when his reputation grew the publishers Chapman and Hall commissioned him to write stories which would accompany a series of sporting prints to be published in monthly instalments. For these he devised the character Mr Pickwick, and the whole enterprise was an enormous success.

On the strength of this he married Catherine Hogarth in 1836. They had ten children in all and Dickens was an enthusiastic family man, very fond of any sort of games and jollification. He was as vigorous in his recreation as he was in his work – his typical idea of relaxation being a long walk of anything up to twenty miles taken at high speed. He was also a great enthusiast for the theatre and amateur dramatics, and he both devised and participated with great relish in home entertainments.

Quite apart from his enormous talent for creating memorable characters and devising riveting stories, his success as a novelist rested on the fact that he captured the public imagination at all levels. Pathos, drama, comedy, and suspense all operate in his work at the same time. He also had the good business sense and the energy to exploit the method of publishing his novels in the form of cheap monthly or weekly magazines. All his early successes appeared in this way, and he even went on to publish his own weekly magazines, *Household Words* and *All the Year Round,* which combined entertainment with a sort of reforming social purpose.

For in addition to being an immensely energetic creative writer, Dickens also took a great deal of interest in social causes. He was very critical of the institutions of society and a tireless defender of the underdog. Many of his novels feature criticisms of the law, bureaucracy, authoritarianism, industrialisation, and class privilege in society.

Following his early success he travelled to the United States hoping to find more egalitarianism in the young republic, but he came back rather disillusioned, even though he was very well received there. He also travelled widely in Europe – yet all the time managing to maintain an enormous rate of production in both his novels and his journalism.

His marriage, however, was not happy. His wife, a somewhat shadowy person, was not in harmony with his exuberant disposition, and they separated in 1858. He later took up with a young actress, Ellen Ternan, with whom he probably had an affair. And it should be said that despite his great concern for and love of children, his relationship with his own was problematic. As Angus Wilson once pointed out, 'finally, he was too much for his children, as he had been for his wife'.

His later novels took a more serious turn and were more carefully constructed, and it is in this period that he created what are now considered his masterpieces – *Dombey and Son, Bleak House,* and *Little Dorrit.* He continued working at a frantic pace even when his health started to deteriorate in the 1860s, and it is generally considered that the lecture tour and public readings (fully rendered with great dramatic vigour) that he gave in America speeded his decline. He collapsed during a reading on his return, suffered a stroke in 1870, and died the following day. He was buried in the Poets' Corner of Westminster Abbey and given full public honours.

THE SIGNALMAN
CHARLES DICKENS

'Halloa! Below there!'
  When he heard a voice thus calling to him, he was standing at the door of his box, with a flag in his hand, furled round its short pole. One would have thought, considering the nature of the ground, that he could not have doubted from what quarter the voice came; but, instead of looking up to where I stood on the top of the steep cutting nearly over his head, he turned himself about and looked down the Line. There was something remarkable in his manner of doing so, though I could not have said for my life, what. But, I know it was remarkable enough to attract my notice, even though his figure was foreshortened and shadowed, down in the deep trench, and mine was high above him, so steeped in the glow of an angry sunset that I had shaded my eyes with my hand before I saw him at all.
  'Halloa! Below!'
  From looking down the Line, he turned himself about again, and, raising his eyes, saw my figure high above him.
  'Is there any path by which I can come down and speak to you?'

He looked up at me without replying, and I looked down at him without pressing him too soon with a repetition of my idle question. Just then, there came a vague

vibration in the earth and air, quickly changing into a violent pulsation, and an oncoming rush that caused me to start back, as though it had force to draw me down. When such vapour as rose to my height from this rapid train, had passed me and was skimming away over the landscape, I looked down again, and saw him re-furling the flag he had shown while the train went by.

I repeated my inquiry. After a pause, during which he seemed to regard me with fixed attention, he motioned with his rolled-up flag towards a point on my level, some two or three hundred yards distant. I called down to him, 'All right!' and made for that point. There, by dint of looking closely about me, I found a rough zigzag descending path notched out, which I followed.

The cutting was extremely deep, and unusually precipitate. It was made through a clammy stone that became oozier and wetter as I went down. For these reasons, I found the way long enough to give me time to recall a singular air of reluctance or compulsion with which he had pointed out the path.

When I came down low enough upon the zig-zag descent, to see him again, I saw that he was standing between the rails on the way by which the train had lately passed, in an attitude as if he were waiting for me to appear. He had his left hand at his chin, and that left elbow rested on his right hand crossed over his breast. His attitude was one of such expectation and watchfulness, that I stopped a moment, wondering at it.

I resumed my downward way, and, stepping out upon the level of the railroad and drawing nearer to him, saw that he was a dark sallow man, with a dark beard and rather heavy eyebrows. His post was in as solitary and dismal a place as ever I saw. On either side, a dripping-wet wall of jagged stone, excluding all view but a strip of sky; the perspective one way only a crooked prolongation of this great dungeon; the shorter perspective in the other direction, terminating in a gloomy red light, and the gloomier entrance to a black tunnel, in whose massive architecture there was a barbarous, depressing, and forbidding air. So little sunlight ever found its way to this spot, that it had an earthy deadly smell; and so much cold wind rushed through it, that it struck chill to me, as if I had left the natural world.

Before he stirred, I was near enough to him to have touched him. Not even then removing his eyes from mine, he stepped back one step, and lifted his hand.

This was a lonesome post to occupy (I said), and it had riveted my attention when I looked down from up yonder. A visitor was a rarity, I should suppose; not an unwelcome rarity, I hoped? In me, he merely saw a man who had been shut up within narrow limits all his life, and who, being at last set free, had a newly-awakened interest in these great works. To such purpose I spoke to him; but I am far from sure of the terms I used, for, besides that I am not happy in opening any conversation, there was something in the man that daunted me.

He directed a most curious look towards the red light near the tunnel's mouth, and looked all about it, as if something were missing from it, and then looked at me.

That light was part of his charge? Was it not?

He answered in a low voice: 'Don't you know it is?'

The monstrous thought came into my mind as I perused the fixed eyes and the saturnine face, that this was a spirit, not a man. I have speculated since, whether there may have been infection in his mind.

In my turn, I stepped back. But in making the action, I detected in his eyes some latent fear of me. This put the monstrous thought to flight.

'You look at me,' I said, forcing a smile, 'as if you had a dread of me.'

'I was doubtful,' he returned, 'whether I had seen you before.'

'Where?'

He pointed to the red light he had looked at.

'There?' I said.

Intently watchful of me, he replied (but without sound), Yes.

'My good fellow, what should I do there? However, be that as it may, I never was there, you may swear.'

'I think I may,' he rejoined. 'Yes. I am sure I may.'

His manner cleared, like my own. He replied to my remarks with readiness, and in well-chosen words. Had he much to do there? Yes; that was to say, he had enough responsibility to bear; but exactness and watchfulness were what was required of him, and of actual work – manual labour – he had next to none. To change that signal, to trim those lights, and to turn this iron handle now and then, was all he had to do under that head. Regarding those many long and lonely hours of which I seemed to make so much, he could only say that the routine of his life had shaped itself into that form, and he had grown used to it. He had taught himself a language down here – if only to know it by sight, and to have formed his own crude ideas of its pronunciation, could be called learning it. He had also worked at fractions and decimals, and tried a little algebra; but he was, and had been as a boy, a poor hand at figures. Was it necessary for him when on duty, always to remain in that channel of damp air, and could he never rise into the sunshine from between those high stone walls? Why, that depended upon times and circumstances. Under some conditions there would be less upon the Line than under others, and the same held good as to certain hours of the day and night. In bright weather, he did choose occasions for getting a little above these lower shadows; but, being at all times liable to be called by his electric bell, and at such times listening for it with redoubled anxiety, the relief was less than I would suppose.

He took me into his box, where there was a fire, a desk for an official book in which he had to make certain entries, a telegraphic instrument with its dial face and needles, and the little bell of which he had spoken. On my trusting that he would excuse the remark that he had been well educated, and (I hoped I might say without offence), perhaps educated above that station, he observed that instances of slight incongruity in such-wise would rarely be found wanting among large bodies of men; that he had heard it was so in workhouses, in the police force, even in that last desperate resource, the army; and that he knew it was so, more or less, in any great railway staff. He had been, when young (if I could believe it, sitting in that hut; he scarcely could), a student of natural philosophy, and had attended lectures; but he had run wild, misused his opportunities, gone down, and never risen again. He had no complaint to offer about that. He had made his bed, and he lay upon it. It was far too late to make another.

All that I have here condensed, he said in a quiet manner, with his grave dark regards divided between me and the fire. He threw in the word 'Sir', from time to time, and especially when he referred to his youth: as though to request me to understand that he claimed to be nothing but what I found him. He was several times interrupted by the little bell, and had to read off messages, and send replies. Once, he had to stand without the door, and display a flag as a train passed, and make some verbal communication to the driver. In the discharge of his duties I observed him to be remarkably exact and vigilant, breaking off his discourse at a syllable, and remaining silent until what he had to do was done.

In a word, I should have set this man down as one of the safest of men to be employed in that capacity, but for the circumstance that while he was speaking to me he twice broke off with a fallen colour, turned his face towards the little bell when it did NOT ring, opened the door of the hut (which was kept shut to exclude the unhealthy damp), and looked out towards the red light near the mouth of the tunnel. On both of those occasions, he came back to the fire with the inexplicable air upon him which I had remarked, without being able to define, when we were so far asunder.

Said I when I rose to leave him: 'You almost make me think that I have met with a contented man.'

(I am afraid I must acknowledge that I said it to lead him on.)

'I believe I used to be so,' he rejoined, in the low voice in which he had first spoken; 'but I am troubled, sir, I am troubled.'

He would have recalled the words if he could. He had said them, however, and I took them up quickly.

'With what? What is your trouble?'

'It is very difficult to impart, sir. It is very, very difficult to speak of. If ever you make me another visit, I will try to tell you.'

'But I expressly intend to make you another visit. Say, when shall it be?'

'I go off early in the morning, and I shall be on again at ten tomorrow night, sir.'

'I will come at eleven.'

He thanked me, and went out at the door with me. 'I'll show my white light, sir,' he said, in his peculiar low voice, 'till you have found the way up. When you have found it, don't call out! And when you are at the top, don't call out!'

G

His manner seemed to make the place strike colder to me, but I said no more than 'Very well.'

'And when you come down to-morrow night, don't call out! Let me ask you a parting question. What made you cry "Halloa! Below there!" to-night?'

'Heaven knows,' said I 'I cried something to that effect –'

'Not to that effect, sir. Those were the very words. I know them well.'

'Admit those were the very words. I said them, no doubt, because I saw you below.'

'For no other reason?'

'What other reason could I possibly have!'

'You have no feeling that they were conveyed to you in any supernatural way?'

'No.'

He wished me good night, and held up his light. I walked by the side of the down Line of rails (with a very disagreeable sensation of a train coming behind me), until I found the path. It was easier to mount than to descend, and I got back to my inn without any adventure.

Punctual to my appointment, I placed my foot on the first notch of the zig-zag next night, as the distant clocks were striking eleven. He was waiting for me at the bottom, with his white light on. 'I have not called out,' I said, when we came close together; 'may I speak now?' 'By all means, sir.' 'Good night then, and here's my hand.' 'Good night, sir, and here's mine.' With that, we walked side by side to his box, entered it, closed the door, and sat down by the fire.

'I have made up my mind, sir,' he began, bending forward as soon as we were seated, and speaking in a tone but a little above a whisper, 'that you shall not have to ask me twice what troubles me. I took you for some one else yesterday evening. That troubles me.'

'That mistake?'

'No. That some one else.'

'Who is it?'

'I don't know.'

'Like me?'

'I don't know. I never saw the face. The left arm is across the face, and the right arm is waved. Violently waved. This way.'

I followed his action with my eyes, and it was the action of an arm gesticulating with the utmost passion and vehemence: 'For God's sake clear the way!'

'One moonlight night,' said the man, 'I was sitting here, when I heard a voice cry "Halloa! Below there!" I started up, looked from that door, and saw this Someone else standing by the red light near the tunnel, waving as I just now showed you. The voice seemed hoarse with shouting, and it cried, "Look out! Look out!" And then again "Halloa! Below there! Look out!" I caught up my lamp, turned it on red, and ran towards the figure, calling, "What's wrong? What has happened? Where?" It stood just outside the blackness of the tunnel. I advanced so close upon it that I wondered at its keeping the sleeve across its eyes. I ran right up at it, and had my hand stretched out to pull the sleeve away, when it was gone.'

'Into the tunnel,' said I.

'No. I ran on into the tunnel, five hundred yards. I stopped and held my lamp above my head, and saw the figures of the measured distance, and saw the wet stains stealing down the walls and trickling through the arch. I ran out again, faster than I had run in (for I had a mortal abhorrence of the place upon me), and I looked all round the red light with my own red light, and I went up the iron ladder to the gallery atop of it, and I came down again, and ran back here. I telegraphed both ways: "An alarm has been given. Is anything wrong?" The answer came back, both ways: "All well."'

Resisting the slow touch of a frozen finger tracing out my spine, I showed him how that this figure must be a deception of his sense of sight, and how that figures, originating in disease of the delicate nerves that minister to the functions of the eye, were known to have often troubled patients, some of whom had become conscious of the nature of their afflic-tion, and had even proved it by experiments upon themselves. 'As to an imaginary cry,' said I, 'do but listen for a moment to the wind in this unnatural valley while we speak so low, and to the wild harp it makes of the telegraph wires!'

That was all very well, he returned, after we had sat listening for a while, and he ought to know something of the wind and the wires, he who so often passed long winter nights there, alone and watching. But he would beg to remark that he had not finished.

I asked his pardon, and he slowly added these words, touching my arm:

'Within six hours after the Appearance, the memorable accident on this Line happened, and within ten hours the dead and wounded were brought along through the tunnel over the spot where the figure had stood.'

A disagreeable shudder crept over me, but I did my best against it. It was not to be denied, I rejoined, that this was a remarkable coincidence, calcu-lated deeply to impress his mind. But, it was unquestionable that remark-able coincidences did continually occur, and they must be taken into ac-count in dealing with such a subject.

Though to be sure I must admit, I added (for I thought I saw that he was going to bring the objection to bear upon me), men of common sense did not allow much for coincidences in making the ordinary calculations of life.

He again begged to remark that he had not finished.

I again begged his pardon for being betrayed into interruptions.

'This,' he said, again laying his hand upon my arm, and glancing over his shoulder with hollow eyes, 'was just a year ago. Six or seven months passed, and I had recovered from the surprise and shock, when one morning, as the day was breaking, I, standing at that door, looked towards the red light, and saw the spectre again.' He stopped, with a fixed look at me.

'Did it cry out?'

'No. It was silent.'

'Did it wave its arm?'

'No. It leaned against the shaft of the light, with both hands before the face. Like this.'

Once more, I followed his action with my eyes. It was an action of mourning. I have seen such an attitude in stone figures on tombs.

'Did you go up to it?'

'I came in and sat down, partly to collect my thoughts, partly because it had turned me faint. When I went to the door again, daylight was above me, and the ghost was gone.'

'But nothing followed? Nothing came of this?'

He touched me on the arm with his forefinger twice or thrice, giving a ghastly nod each time:

'That very day, as a train came out of the tunnel, I noticed, at a carriage window on my side, what looked like a confusion of hands and heads, and something waved. I saw it, just in time to signal the driver, Stop! He shut off, and put his brake on, but the train drifted past here a hundred and fifty yards or more. I ran after it, and, as I went along, heard terrible screams and cries. A beautiful young lady had died instantaneously in one of the compartments, and was brought in here, and laid down on this floor between us.'

Involuntarily, I pushed my chair back, as I looked from the boards at which he pointed, to himself.

'True, sir. True. Precisely as it happened, so I tell it you.'

I could think of nothing to say, to any purpose, and my mouth was very dry. The wind and the wires took up the story with a long lamenting wail.

He resumed. 'Now, sir, mark this, and judge how my mind is troubled. The spectre came back, a week ago. Ever since, it has been there, now and again, by fits and starts.'

'At the light?'

'At the Danger-light.'

'What does it seem to do?'

He repeated, if possible with increased passion and vehemence, that former gesticulation of 'For God's sake clear the way!'

Then, he went on. 'I have no peace or rest for it. It calls to me, for many minutes together, in an agonized manner, "Below there! Look out! Look out!" It stands waving to me. It rings my little bell —'

I caught at that. 'Did it ring your bell yesterday evening when I was here, and you went to the door?'

'Twice.'

'Why, see,' said I, 'how your imagination misleads you. My eyes were on the bell, and my ears were open to the bell, and if I am a living man, it did not ring at those times. No, nor at any other time, except when it was rung in the natural course of physical things by the station communicating with you.'

He shook his head. 'I have never made a mistake as to that, yet, sir. I have never confused the spectre's ring with the man's. The ghost's ring is a strange vibration in the bell that it derives from nothing else, and I have not asserted that the bell stirs to the eye. I don't wonder that you failed to hear it. But *I* heard it.'

'And did the spectre seem to be there, when you looked out?'

'It WAS there.'

'Both times?'

He repeated firmly: 'Both times.'

'Will you come to the door with me, and look for it now?'

He bit his under-lip as though he were somewhat unwilling, but arose. I opened the door, and stood on the step, while he stood in the doorway. There, was the Danger-light. There, was the dismal mouth of the tunnel. There, were the high wet stone walls of the cutting. There, were the stars above them.

'Do you see it?' I asked him, taking particular note of his face. His eyes were prominent and strained; but not very much more so, perhaps, than my own had been when I had directed them earnestly towards the same spot.

'No,' he answered. 'It is not there.'

'Agreed,' said I.

We went in again, shut the door, and resumed our seats. I was thinking how best to improve this advantage, if it might be called one, when he took up the conversation in such a matter of course way, so assuming that there could be no serious question of fact between us, that I felt myself in the weakest of positions.

'By this time you will fully understand, sir,' he said, 'that what troubles me so dreadfully, is the question, What does the spectre mean?'

I was not sure, I told him, that I did fully understand.

'What is its warning against?' he said, ruminating, with his eyes on the fire, and only by times turning them on me. 'What is the danger? Where is the danger? There is danger overhanging, somewhere on the Line. Some dreadful calamity will happen. It is not to be doubted this third time, after what has gone before. But surely this is a cruel haunting of *me*. What can *I* do!'

He pulled out his handkerchief, and wiped the drops from his heated forehead.

'If I telegraph Danger, on either side of me, or on both, I can give no reason for it,' he went on, wiping the palms of his hands. 'I should get into trouble, and do no good. They would think I was mad. This is the way it would work: Message: "Danger! Take care!" Answer: "What Danger? Where?" Message: "Don't know. But for God's sake take care!" They would displace me. What else could they do?'

His pain of mind was most pitiable to see. It was the mental torture of a conscientious man, oppressed beyond endurance by an unintelligible responsibility involving life.

'When it first stood under the Danger-light,' he went on, putting his dark hair back from his head, and drawing his hands outward across and across his temples in an extremity of feverish distress, 'why not tell me where that accident was to happen – if it must happen? Why not tell me how it could be averted – if it could have been averted? When on its second coming it hid its face, why not tell me instead: "She is going to die. Let them keep her at home"? If it came, on those two occasions, only to show me that its warnings were true, and so to prepare me for the third, why not warn me plainly now? And I, Lord help me! A mere poor signalman on this solitary station! Why not go to somebody with credit to be believed, and power to act!'

When I saw him in this state, I saw that for the poor man's sake, as well as for the public safety, what I had to do for the time was, to compose his mind. Therefore, setting aside all question of reality or unreality between us, I represented to him that whoever thoroughly discharged his duty, must do well, and that at least it was his comfort that he understood his duty, though he did not understand these confounding Appearances. In this effort I succeeded far better than in the attempt to reason him out of his conviction. He became calm; the occupations incidental to his post as the night advanced, began to make larger demands on his attention; and I left him at two in the morning. I had offered to stay through the night, but he would not hear of it.

That I more than once looked back at the red light as I ascended the pathway, that I did not like the red light, and that I should have slept but poorly if my bed had been under it, I see no reason to conceal. Nor, did I like the two sequences of the accident and the dead girl. I see no reason to conceal that, either.

But, what ran most in my thoughts was the consideration how ought I to act, having become the recipient of this disclosure? I had proved the man to be intelligent, vigilant, painstaking, and exact; but how long might he remain so, in his state of mind? Though in a subordinate position, still he held a most important trust, and would I (for instance) like to stake my own life on the chances of his continuing to execute it with precision?

Unable to overcome a feeling that there would be something treacherous in my communicating what he had told me to his superiors in the Company, without first being plain with himself and proposing a middle course to him, I ultimately resolved to offer to accompany him (otherwise keeping his secret for the present) to the wisest medical practitioner we could hear of in those parts, and to take his opinion. A change in his time of duty would come round next night, he had apprised me, and he would be off an hour or two after sunrise, and on again soon after sunset. I had appointed to return accordingly.

Next evening was a lovely evening, and I walked out early to enjoy it. The sun was not yet quite down when I traversed the fieldpath near the top of the deep cutting. I would extend my walk for an hour, I said to myself, half an hour on and half an hour back, and it would then be time to go to my signalman's box.

Before pursuing my stroll, I stepped to the brink, and mechanically looked down, from the point from which I had first seen him. I cannot describe the thrill that seized upon me, when, close at the mouth of the tunnel, I saw the appearance of a man, with his left sleeve across his eyes, passionately waving his right arm.

The nameless horror that oppressed me, passed in a moment, for in a moment I saw that this appearance of a man was a man indeed, and that there was a little group of other men standing at a short distance, to whom he seemed to be rehearsing the gesture he made. The Danger-light was not yet lighted. Against its shaft, a little low hut, entirely new to me, had been made of some wooden supports and tarpaulin. It looked no bigger than a bed.

With an irresistible sense that something was wrong – with a flashing self-reproachful fear that fatal mischief had come of my leaving the man there, and causing no one to be sent to overlook or correct what he did – I descended the notched path with all the speed I could make.

'What is the matter?' I asked the men.

'Signalman killed this morning, sir.'

'Not the man belonging to that box?'

'Yes, sir.'

'Not the man I know?'

'You will recognize him, sir, if you knew him,' said the man who spoke for the others, solemnly uncovering his own head and raising an end of the tarpaulin, 'for his face is quite composed.'

'O! how did this happen, how did this happen?' I asked, turning from one to another as the hut closed in again.

'He was cut down by an engine, sir. No man in England knew his work better. But somehow he was not clear of the outer rail. It was just at broad day. He had struck the light, and had the lamp in his hand. As the engine came out of the tunnel, his back was towards her, and she cut him down. That man drove her, and was showing how it happened. Show the gentleman, Tom.'

The man, who wore a rough dark dress, stepped back to his former place at the mouth of the tunnel:

'Coming round the curve in the tunnel, sir,' he said, 'I saw him at the end, like as if I saw him down a perspective-glass. There was no time to check speed, and I knew him to be very careful. As he didn't seem to take heed of the whistle, I shut it off when we were running down upon him, and called to him as loud as I could call.'

'What did you say?'

'I said, Below there! Look out! Look out! For God's sake clear the way!'

I started.

'Ah! it was a dreadful time, sir. I never left off calling to him. I put this arm before my eyes, not to see, and I waved this arm to the last; but it was no use.'

Without prolonging the narrative to dwell on any one of its curious circumstances more than on any other, I may, in closing it, point out the coincidence that the warning of the Engine-Driver included, not only the words which the unfortunate Signalman had repeated to me as haunting him, but also the words which I myself – not he – had attached, and that only in my own mind, to the gesticulation he had imitated.

3 Understanding the story

It should be obvious from even one reading that 'The Signalman' presents us with a number of puzzles and mysteries. Quite apart from first of all being short of information (Why is the Signalman so troubled? And how could he recognise the Narrator if he had never met him before?) we are even at the end left with several conundrums to consider. How do the very same gestures and words – 'Halloa! Below there!' – come to be used by the Narrator, the engine driver and the Spectre? Does the Spectre really exist, or is it a figment of the Signalman's fevered imagination? Is there a supernatural force at work, or are we just being presented with a set of coincidences?

I will say quite frankly now that I do not know the answers to all these questions, and no single interpretation of the story that I have read explains away all the problems it poses. But I do think it is possible to formulate a reading of the story which takes most of these problems into account and offers a reasoned explanation of the tale. For just as was the case in Hardy's 'The Withered Arm' most people will somehow seek an explanation of the story which rests on more than just a belief in the supernatural.

You might wish to argue however that many people do actually believe in ghosts. The Signalman was being given warnings by a spectre, but was frightened by the fact – so much so that he eventually lost control of himself and was killed. This is a one-sentence 'reading' of the story which takes its details at face value. But it doesn't seem very satisfactory, does it? The detail of the coincidence of the engine driver's and the Spectre's gestures being identical is left unexplained; but even if we ignore this as just a coincidence or a means of creating mystery and tension in fiction, we are still left with an explanation which is only going to be persuasive if we believe in ghosts (though I must admit that Dickens himself was certainly *prepared* to believe in such things).

I also have to admit that it would be possible to strengthen this reading with more evidence from the text. The Signalman is quite well educated and so has reason to doubt the existence of spectres. He is also encouraged to do so by the Narrator. And the end result? He is killed. Perhaps the story is a warning against doubting the existence of that which cannot be proved?

I hope you can understand from these argument outlines what I mean by a reading of the story – that is, an interpretation of it. A fuller explanation would draw on more details from the text of course as evidence in support of the case being made. What I am going to do next is offer a 'common sense' reading then ask you to elaborate it. After that I shall pose a more radical reading in Section 5.

When the story opens its setting is particularly unpleasant. The Narrator descends into a cutting which is 'extremely deep and unusually precipitous': it is oozily wet and at the bottom described as a 'dungeon'. Everything the Narrator tells us about it emphasises its oppressiveness. This is the Signal-man's working environment. No wonder the Narrator thinks of him as a 'spirit' who may have had 'infection in his mind'. He has been put under so much stress by his job that he has become ill. Just look at his conditions of work. He works alone – so he is removed from the humanising effect of company. And he is working on what used to be called 'permanent nights'. Moreover he feels under threat by the fear of losing his job. He has 'come down in the world' after having 'misused his opportunities' and feels it is too late to change. The detailed responsibilities of the job put him under stress too. He must be constantly vigilant listening for the bell signal, and he must transmit his messages accurately and promptly. Consequently he is put under even more stress by the warnings he receives. If he transmits a warning of the danger which he cannot explain his employers will sack him. And presumably if he fails to give any warnings for what is becoming a series of accidents he will be under suspicion of being negligent. He is thus in what is called a 'double bind': whatever he does, he will be thought wrong. And he is an intelligent man, note. The Narrator calls him 'well educated' and adds later that he is 'intelligent, vigilant, painstaking, and exact'.

Isn't it possible – taking this common sense line on the story – that Dickens is offering us a comment on the de-humanising effects of industrial progress? As a matter of fact Dickens was very sceptical about the benefits of the railways (as were many other people at that time) – but even if we did *not* know that it would be possible to argue from the story alone that it quite obviously puts the railway as a system into a very negative light. The Signal-man is a prisoner of automation: he is isolated, put under stress, given appalling working conditions – and eventually the system kills him.

I'm not sure how convinced you will be by this 'reading' of the story, but I hope you will agree that it is at least more satisfying than the first one I offered which was rather like a one sentence précis. What I have done is concentrate on the system (the railway) and the individual (the Signalman) that is, on the actual social developments which were taking place in the mid-to-late nineteenth century. In this reading Dickens is issuing a warning against the bad effects of industrialisation, just as he did in his novels against the legal system and the abuse of children

But – you may well be protesting – this reading doesn't take account of one very important feature of the story – the Spectre. How do I account for this in my reading, my interpretation of the story? And my explanation would be as follows. I would argue that Dickens had merely used the convention of a ghost story and that what he most essentially had to say about the railways as a system didn't *rely upon* a belief in the supernatural. I would say that we as readers could regard the spectre and its warnings as something like metaphors for the Signalman's intuitive sense that something might go wrong with the over-mechanistic and de-humanising aspects of industrial progress.

For those who are still not satisfied with my explanation I will first of all admit that as a rationalist I find it difficult to believe in the supernatural, and then I will invite you to give *your* reading of the story, taking into account this element, by answering Question 3 in the course work assignment.

Now it is time for you to do some work. I want to push this reading a little further by asking you to consider the remark I just made concerning the Signalman's 'intuition'. What if we were to regard the story not just as Dickens's warning against railways but against the dangers of being over-rational and not paying attention to those 'signals' we sometimes receive from sources or in a manner we cannot rationally explain? And at this point we will be able to introduce another significant element from the story – the Narrator. One last clue concerning him: notice how very reasonable and rational *he* seems to be. So, STOP here and make notes for a reading of the story based on the contrast between rationality and intuition in these two characters. What evidence is there in the text to support such a reading?

I think you should have had little difficulty in demonstrating that for instance the Signalman is certainly a *sensitive* man. He is very alert to everything going on around him. You could even point to the Narrator's words – 'this was a spirit, not a man' – and interpret them to mean that Dickens is giving us a clue that he is the embodiment of a temperament – intuition, perception, call it what you will. He also has a 'latent fear' of the Narrator: that is, Instinct is distrustful of Reason. To this we can add the detail that he hears the bell ringing even when the Narrator does not. And he has an explanation for this puzzling detail: 'the ghost's ring is a strange vibration in the bell that it derives from nothing else, and I have not asserted that the bell stirs to the eye'. That is, he has something akin to extra-sensory perception or he is picking up 'signals' beyond the range of an average person's ability. This reading of him is perfectly compatible with that of him as an oppressed employee of the railway.

But the Narrator on the other hand seems like rationality itself. He is making a dispassionate inspection of 'these great works' – that is, the railway system. And when confronted by the puzzling tales of the ghostly warnings. he seeks a rational explanation: 'I showed him how that this figure must be a deception of his sense of sight'. That is, he is trying to talk the Signalman out of fears which, it turns out, are very well founded. Indeed you might have noticed that he represses his own instinctive fear in doing so: he makes his remarks 'Resisting the slow touch of a frozen finger tracing out my spine'. So here we have the grounds for a reading of Intuition versus Reason, and what happens subsequently in the story supports this view.

When the Signalman tells the Narrator of the accident which followed the warning, the Narrator again represses an instinctive shudder and explains away the occurrence by suggesting that it is mere coincidence. But the Signalman has another example to relate, which squashes that explanation.

The Narrator can then see that the Signalman is in a desperate condition, and he uses his *reason* to decide what to do. First of all he sets out to 'compose his mind' that is, to calm him temporarily. This *seems* reasonable to us, and yet looked at in another way we could say that it allowed him to get away from the situation with an easier mind than he might otherwise have had. And he *does* suspect that the Signalman could crack up at any time.

He *might* have reported everything to the railway company, but he persuades himself that this might be disloyal to the Signalman. And he *intends* to propose taking him to see a doctor some time in the future. What this adds up to is that he actually *does nothing*. The Signalman is killed the following morning, and the Narrator's conscience pricks him with 'a flashing self-reproachful fear that total mischief had come of my leaving the man there, and causing no one to be sent to overlook or correct what he did'.

In other words, this reading posits the story as a warning that we should not neglect the signals transmitted to us by our intuition by overriding them or explaining them away with rational but superficial arguments. You may have found other evidence in the story: there are other details which might have been brought in to support such a reading. But I hope you can see that such an interpretation of the story rests on a case being made which is based on what might be regarded as a submerged meaning to the story – but which must be justified by details from the text itself.

You may wish to object that I *still* have not taken into account the Spectre. Does it exist or not? My answer is that it can be taken as a symbol of the Signalman's intuitive fears that no matter how vigilant he is at work, railway accidents may still be likely to occur. So, if we convert it to a symbolic figure – say like an angel announcing the virgin birth – it fits with the interpretation I have just given. Are you still not convinced? Well, as I said before, this story is resistant to a water-tight interpretation. If you wish to include the spectre, explain how we do so in an account of your own.

Another question or objection might arise at this point. 'Did Dickens *intend* us to interpret the story in this way?' And the answer is – we don't know, and it doesn't matter anyway. The question of 'intention' in works of art is very complex, but in general even knowing an author's conscious intention doesn't necessarily help us, because it not the same thing as what that author eventually *produces*. All we can do is try to persuade other people of our interpretation by proving our case with evidence from the text. And if we take a perverse or remote interpretation ('The Signalman' as a plea for more cheerfulness or courage in dealing with ghosts, for instance, or for a better signalling system on the railways) then other people will not be persuaded by us. Our interpretations must make sense, they must arise from the content of the story, and they must be capable of being 'proven' with evidence from the text.

And still one further objection might be in your mind. Did you think I had been too hard on the Narrator? After all, he seems such a reasonable and well-intentioned man, doesn't he? Did I appear to drag up negative views of him which had not occurred to you or which seemed unjustified. If this is so then you are going to be even more horrified by the last 'reading' I shall offer, which casts him as the 'villain' of the piece. But before I do so, I want to offer you a few observations on the narrators of stories. They are not always the honest and innocent people they may seem to be.

The majority of the fiction we read is narrated in the 'third person omniscient' mode or voice. That is, the *author* sits down and writes 'Mr X was a tall man. He was also ...'. In other words the author is also the *narrator*. He or she is telling the story. We learn various things about Mr X, and in the vast majority of cases we are given every reason to concentrate our attention on him and the events of the story, and we quite rightly forget all about the author.

On the other hand, sometimes a story might be told in the 'first person' mode. In this case the author sits down and writes 'I am about to tell you the story of ...'. And this is where we as readers need to be attentive and careful because we have been conditioned by so much of what we read to automatically assume that the 'I' in this opening sentence is the author. But it need not be. It *could* be the author, or it could be a character the author is creating, like Dr Watson in 'A Scandal in Bohemia'.

Dickens's *Great Expectations* for instance is narrated by its hero, Pip. He is relating his own life history, and so the novel begins:

My father's family name being Pirrip, and my christian name Phillip, my infant tongue could make of both names nothing longer or more explicit than Pip. So, I called myself Pip, and came to be called Pip.

This is a typical first person narrative, and we quite reasonably forget that Dickens is *creating* this character. We attend instead to what Pip is telling us about himself and his adventures.

But Dostoyevski's novella *Notes from Underground* begins 'I am a sick man ... I am an angry man'. Is this Dostoyevski speaking to us directly, or is it some fictional character he is creating? It is extremely difficult to tell, because the narrator is never named and the story he tells is more or less an account of ideas we know to be identical to those held by Dostoyevski himself.

At this point the relationship between author and narrator *can* become a very complex issue, and I don't want to burden you with more problems than are necessary at this stage. Those who are at a fairly advanced level or who are particularly interested in this phenomenon can go on to read Wayne Booth's very influential book on the topic, *The Rhetoric of Fiction*. But even if you don't do this you should try to keep the issue in mind, because many writers exploit the ambiguities inherent in the use of the first person mode to lay traps for us or give us extra problems to deal with. Let me give you a couple of examples to show you what I mean.

Emily Bronte's *Wuthering Heights* begins '1801. – I have just returned from a visit to my landlord – the solitary neighbour that I shall be troubled with'. The story is being told by a man called Lockwood, and we see the opening events of the novel from his point of view. And so strong is the tendency in us as readers to give full credence to everything we are being told by a story's narrator that it is quite some time before we begin to realise that Lockwood is rather limited in his understanding of what is going on around him. We therefore have the problem of trying to work out what the *truth* of the story is when the person telling it to us doesn't understand it himself. How do we do this? Emily Bronte helps us by having Lockwood introduce other characters who then take over the story and give us another point of view. We then check the information they give us against Lockwood's and realise how *limited* he is. What he tells us is true as far as he is concerned, but he has not enough intelligence to recognise his own limitations.

This approach to the creation of what are called 'unreliable narrators' is pushed even further by a writer like Vladimir Nabokov whose novel *Pale Fire* is narrated by a professor of languages who has escaped from eastern Europe and now teaches in an American University. His first person account of his life is very witty and entertaining, but the further we read in the novel the more doubts we begin to have about his story. What Nabokov does is create a first person narrator who is actually a *liar*! His story is an intricate web of fabrications – but he gives us just enough information to be able to work out the truth for ourselves.

I have oversimplified both these examples in order to highlight the fact that we should always pay close attention to what we are told, and when the information comes to us from a fictional narrator we should keep in mind the fact that there may be bias, there may be a *lack* of insight, or we may even be misinformed. This isn't always the case but it *can* be. So watch out. Don't take everything at face value, and be prepared to be sceptical about everything you are told, and *not* told.

5 Interpretation

What I want to propose to you now is probably the most advanced exercise we have attempted so far – so if you find it too difficult, don't worry, leave it and come back to it again later. What I shall do is give you a particular reading of the story to consider, ask you to look at it in the manner I propose and try to find evidence to support this view, after which I shall offer my own evidence.

My reading, in brief, is as follows. It is in fact the Narrator who is the villain of the story and he is instrumental in bringing about the death of the Signalman. I might even go so far as to argue that the Narrator and the Spectre are one and the same person. This might seem an extreme or even ridiculous view to take, but I would like you to consider it and see what evidence you could find in the text to support it. To do so you will need to take into account all the warnings I have just given about narrators. Just because they are telling us the story doesn't mean that they are revealing the whole truth. You will need to overcome a reader's natural tendency to be well-disposed towards narrators.

Your task therefore is to see what evidence there is in the story to support this idea that the Narrator *is* the Spectre. So, STOP here and make notes for your answers. Then I will give you my own.

————◦•◉•◦————

There are a number of small points of detail you may have produced in support of this reading, plus a number of arguments drawn from your own interpretation of what we are told by the narrator. I will now offer a list which combines these – in no particular order of importance.

1. The most immediately striking similarity between the Narrator and the Spectre is the fact that the narrator uses the same words of warning as the spectre – 'Halloa! Below there!'. Moreover, he also repeats the Spectre's gesture – 'I had shaded my eyes with my hand'.

2. We notice that the Signalman thinks he recognises the Narrator, and has a 'latent fear' of him – because he thinks he is the Spectre. If my proposal is 'correct' he has every reason to be afraid.

3. The Narrator tries to prove to the Signalman that he is imagining things by showing that the Spectre is *not* at the tunnel on his second visit (p. 189). But if the two are one and the same person of course he *is* there speaking to the Signalman.

4. We note that both Narrator and Spectre appear at *night'* – and both have been visiting 'by fits and starts' quite recently. And if we were to take the Narrator at face value – why should anyone go inspecting railways at *night*?

5. As I argued in Section 3, the Narrator *claims* that he wants to help the Signalman, but in fact he talks him out of his reasonable fears, doesn't help him when he might have done, and *conceals* the danger from the Signalman's employers. Even when the Signalman appeals to him – 'why not go to somebody with credit to be believed and power to act?' – he ignores the plea.

6. There a number of verbal ambiguities which we might interpret as clues to the true identity of the Narrator. In presenting his account he uses phrase like '*if* I am a living man' (my emphasis) and 'setting aside all question of reality or unreality between us' which might be taken as little 'slips' behind which we can perceive the Spectre 'speaking'.

So, what is my general argument? That if we think of the Narrator *as* the Spectre some of the baffling features of the story can be 'explained'. And what happens at the end of the story? Well, we could argue that the Signalman, poor chap, is terrified by yet another set of identical warning gestures and shouts (the driver's) and is held in thrall like a rabbit in a car's headlights and killed by the oncoming train.

Now you may think that such an explanation is stretching a point or not very convincing. And I am not committed to it one hundred per cent myself. But I am offering it just as one way in which the story *might* be considered. It still leaves one or two questions unanswered, but we need to be at a more advanced level of literary analysis to deal with these. If you feel that my argument is inadequate you can always provide one of your own which you feel explains the story. I invite you to do this as one of the Course work assignments.

This brings us to the end of the study programme. We have now covered the most important basic skills and intellectual tools required for making a study of fiction – from description, through analysis, to interpretation. But beyond this, at a more advanced level which is outside the scope of this book, there exist a number of different theories of literary criticism. These assume that you have acquired all the basic skills of comprehension and analysis, and they then go on to look at literature from a number of different perspectives. These are often informed by the critical skills of other disciplines (say, linguistics or psycho-analysis) by some political theory such as Marxism or feminism, or by some branch of what has come to be called Critical Theory – that is, theoretical ideas about exactly what constitutes 'literary criticism'. These approaches can provide fresh insights into a text by forcing us to look at it from a particular point of view or in a fresh context. If you wish to follow up your introductory studies with a view of what such criticism offers, then the lists of Further reading offered in the next chapter will provide you with a starting point.

I hope you have enjoyed our exploration of the six stories and the skills their authors have demonstrated in creating them. I also wish you well in pursuing any further literary studies and sign off with the suggestion that if you have any comments on the usefulness of this study programme or suggestions for improving the book in your hands – then the author would be pleased to hear from you.

6 Self-assessment questions

LANGUAGE

1 What does 'by dint of' mean in 'by dint of looking closely about me'?

2 What parts of speech are the following (given emphasis): 'It was made through a *clammy* stone, that became *oozier* and *wetter* as I went down'?

3 What is meant by the Signalman's '*saturnine* face'?

4 What is 'natural philosophy'?

5 What is meant by 'I saw him at the end [of the tunnel] like as if I saw him down a perspective glass'?

COMPREHENSION

1 What does the narrator mean when he speaks of his 'newly awakened interest in these great works'?

2 Which subjects has the Signalman taught himself during his long hours of work?

3 Who was killed in the second accident?

4 What reason does the narrator give for *not* reporting his concerns to the railway company?

5 At what time of day is the Signalman killed?

H

6. What does the narrator mean by describing the army as 'that last desperate resource'?

ANALYSIS

1 When the narrator first introduces himself to the Signalman there is one phrase he uses which draws a parallel between them. What is the phrase – and what are the parallels?

2 When they first meet, why does the Signalman think he has met the narrator before?

3 Mention of a 'bed' occurs four times in the story. Do these references have anything in common?

4 How does Dickens create the impression of the Signalman's workplace as a kind of prison or hellish nether–world?

7 Course work

1 Write a general appreciation of 'The Signalman' using the guidance notes in Chapter Four, Section 8.

2 Discuss the manner in which Dickens creates the mystery in 'The Signalman'.

3 Give your *own* explanation of what happens in 'The Signalman' – in a way which includes an account of the Narrator, the Signalman, the Spectre, and the relationships between them.

4 Compare Dickens's treatment of the supernatural in 'The Signalman' with Hardy's in 'The Withered Arm'.

5 Discuss the *construction* of 'The Signalman'.

8 Further reading

If you have not read any of Dickens's stories or novels before, then you have a great deal of pleasure in store for you. He has sometimes been criticised for being too sentimental in some of his scenes and for using too much contrivance in the arrangement of his plots – but these occasional weaknesses are vastly outweighed by his narrative drive, his vivid characterisation, comic sense, dramatic flair, linguistic verve, and tremendously fertile imagination. You could begin your further reading almost anywhere in his *oeuvre*. As I mentioned in the biographical note, the later novels are the longest and most complex, but also the greatest.

FICTION

Pickwick Papers, 1836.

Oliver Twist, 1837.

Nicholas Nickleby, 1838.

The Old Curiosity Shop, 1840.

Barnaby Rudge, 1841.

Martin Chuzzlewit, 1844.

Dombey and Son, 1848.

David Copperfield, 1850.

Bleak House, 1853.

Hard Times, 1854

Little Dorrit, 1857.

A Tale of Two Cities, 1859.

Great Expectations, 1860.

Our Mutual Friend, 1865.

BIOGRAPHY

There are two 'standard' biographies.

John Forster, *The Life of Charles Dickens*, Chapman and Hall, 1872.

This was written by a close friend of Dickens, and draws heavily on personal reminiscence and the details of their relationship. It has both the advantages and the drawbacks of this proximity.

Edgar Johnson, *Charles Dickens: Tragedy and Triumph*, London: Gollancz, 1953.

This is exhaustive in detail, embodies material either neglected or suppressed by Forster, and gives criticism of each of the novels.

CRITICISM

G. L. Brook, *The Language of Dickens*, London: Methuen, 1970.

J. Butt and K. Tillotson, *Dickens at Work*, London: Methuen, 1957.

Philip Collins, *Dickens: The Critical Heritage*, London: Routledge, 1971

Kate Flint, *Dickens*, London: Brighton: Harvester, 1985.

Humphrey House, *The Dickens World*, London: Oxford University Press, 1941.

F. R. and Q. D. Leavis, *Dickens the Novelist*, London: Chatto and Windus, 1970.

Steven Marcus, *Dickens: from Pickwick to Dombey*, London: Chatto and Windus, 1965.

CHAPTER EIGHT

Further reading
Glossary of literary terms

1 Further reading   2 Glossary of literary terms

1 Further reading

These suggestions for further reading are arranged in four sections. The first lists some recently published books dealing with *theories* of literary criticism; the second, books which offer examples of criticism shown in practice; the third, books from a variety of sources which offer essays on general literary topics and commentary on well known texts and writers. The fourth is a brief list of studies devoted to criticism of the short story form, since that is what we have been studying in this programme. Many of the titles listed are currently available in cheap paperback editions.

CRITICAL THEORY

M. H. Abrams, *A Glossary of Literary Terms*, London: Holt, Rinehart and Winston, 1986.

Richard Dutton, *An Introduction to Literary Criticism*, London: Longman, 1984.

Terry Eagleton, *Literary Theory: An Introduction*, Oxford: Blackwell, 1983.

Roger Fowler, *Linguistics and the Novel*, London: Methuen, 1977.

Jeremy Hawthorn, *Unlocking the Text*, London: Arnold, 1988.

— (ed), *Criticism and Critical Theory*, London: Arnold, 1984.

Ann Jefferson and David Robey (eds), *Modern Literary Theory*, London: Batsford, 1986.

David Lodge (ed), *Twentieth-Century Literary Criticism*, London: Longman, 1972.

— (ed), *Modern Criticism and Theory: A Reader*, London: Longman, 1988.

Raman Selden, *A Reader's Guide to Contemporary Literary Theory*, Brighton: Harvester, 1985

Dale Spender, *Man Made Language*, London: Routledge, 1980.

Jeremy Tambling, *What is Literary Language?*, Milton Keynes: Open University Press, 1988.

Roger Webster, *Studying Literary Theory: An Introduction*, London: Arnold, 1990.

PRACTICAL CRITICISM

Wayne Booth, *The Rhetoric of Fiction*, Chicago: University of Chicago Press, 1961.

Marjorie Boulton, *An Anatomy of Literary Studies*, London: Routledge, 1980.

—, *The Anatomy of Prose*, London: Routledge, 1954.

R. L. Brett, *An Introduction to English Studies*, London: Arnold, 1965.

S. H. Burton, *The Criticism of Prose*, London: Longman, 1975.

Christopher Butler and Alastair Fowler (eds), *Topics in Criticism*, London: Longman, 1971.

Raymond Chapman, *Linguistics and Literature*, London: Arnold, 1973.

H. L. Coombes, *Literature and Criticism*, London: Chatto and Windus, 1953.

Alan Durant and Nigel Fabb, *Literary Studies in Action*, London: Routledge, 1988.

E. M. Forster, *Aspects of the Novel*, London: Arnold, 1927.

Tom Gibbons, *Literature and Awareness*, London: Arnold, 1979.

Richard Gill, *Mastering English Literature*, London: Macmillan, 1985.

Jeremy Hawthorn, *Studying the Novel*, London: Arnold, 1985.

Malcolm Hicks and Bill Hutchings, *Literary Criticism: A Practical Guide for Students*, London: Arnold, 1989.

Jonathan Raban, *The Technique of Modern Fiction*, London: Arnold, 1968.

LITERARY ESSAYS

Roland Barthes, *Writing Degree Zero*, London: Cape, 1967.

Walter Benjamin, *Illuminations*, Trans. Harry Zohn, New York: Schocken, 1969.

Malcolm Bradbury (ed), *The Novel Today*, London: Collins, 1977.

Richard Hoggart, *Speaking to Each Other*, London: Chatto and Windus, 1970.

Henry James, *Selected Literary Criticism*, London: Heinemann, 1963.

—, *The House of Fiction*, London: Rupert Hart-Davis, 1957.

F. R. Leavis, *'Anna Karenina' and Other Essays*, London: Chatto and Windus, 1967.

George Lukacs, *Studies in European Realism*, New York: Grosset & Dunlap, 1964.

George Steiner, *Language and Silence*, London: Faber, 1967.

—, *Extraterritorial*, London: Faber, 1972.

Tony Tanner, *City of Words*, London: Cape, 1971.

Edmund Wilson, *The Triple Thinkers*, London: John Lehmann, 1952.

—, *The Shores of Light*, London: W. H. Allen, 1952.

Virginia Woolf, *Collected Essays*, London: Hogarth, 1966.

THE SHORT STORY

Walter Allen, *The Short Story in English*, London: Oxford University Press, 1981.

T. O. Beachcroft, *The Modest Art*, London: Oxford University Press, 1968.

Sean O'Faolain, *The Short Story*, London: Collins, 1948.

Ian Reid, *The Short Story*, London: Methuen, 1977.

Valerie Shaw, *The Short Story: A Critical Introduction*, London: Longman, 1983.

2 Glossary of literary terms

This glossary is a reference list offering definitions and explanations of some of the more common terms you may come across or be required to use in the study of literature. You will see that it combines terms from a number of different aspects of literary studies: Linguistics ('semantics'); figures of speech ('euphemism'); literary criticism ('narrator'); literary categories ('novella'); and some of the semi-philosophical notions which are often employed in the discussion of art ('romantic'). I have left out some of the simpler and more straightforward terms like 'character' or 'comedy' as well as more difficult ones such as 'Weltanschauung' or 'Zeugma'.

Do not attempt to memorise these terms or learn their meanings off by heart. They can only be properly understood in some context. But do get into the habit of looking up terms whose meanings you are not sure of. On the other hand, if you are going to use one of these terms in your writing, check that you are using it correctly if you are not absolutely sure.

AFFECTIVE FALLACY A critical term used to describe the error of judging a work of art in terms of its results, especially its emotional effect upon a reader. (The converse is the INTENTIONAL FALLACY.)

ALLEGORY A description of one thing under the guise of another suggestively similar. An extended metaphor, e.g.: Bunyan's *Pilgrim's Progress*.

ALLITERATION Repetition of consonants. e.g.: 'she sells sea shells along the sea shore'.

ALLUSION A reference, explicit or indirect, to a person, place or event, or to another literary work or passage.

AMBIGUITY Double meaning, or an expression capable of more than one meaning. (In literary studies, can be used as a term of approval.)

ANACHRONISM A mistake in dating or time: placing a detail in the wrong historical period, e.g.: Shakespeare mentions doublets in *Julius Caesar*.

ANALOGY A likeness or comparison of a non-figurative kind – that is, not based on a simile or metaphor, e.g.: 'There is an analogy between our present age and the last days of the Roman Empire.'

ANTHROPOMORPHISM Attributing a human personality to anything impersonal or inanimate, e.g.: 'The man in the moon'.

APHORISM A concise observation or statement, distinguished from an epigram by being more solemn and less witty, e.g.: 'the life so short, the craft so long to learn' (Chaucer).

ASSONANCE The repetition of vowel sounds, e.g.: 'The rain in Spain falls mainly on the plain.'

BAROQUE Originally a florid or extravagant style of architecture developed in the seventeenth and eighteenth centuries, now applied to other arts, especially music. Characterised by exuberant ornamentation.

BOMBAST Pompous, inflated language.

CIRCUMLOCUTION A roundabout method of expression, often used (like euphemism) to avoid direct discussion of an embarassing topic.

CLASSIC(AL) This can have two general meanings: (i) A work which, like that of Greek or Roman classics, lays emphasis on form, decorum, and tradition, e.g.: Milton's *Paradise Lost*; (ii) A work which has come to be regarded as outstandingly important in literary history, e.g.: Cervantes' *Don Quixote*.

DIDACTIC Used of a work which expounds some moral, political, or religous teaching. Can also be used to describe the tone of a work which has a teaching or instructional accent, e.g. *The Bible*; Aesop's *Fables*.

DRAMATIC IRONGY This is a situational device where the audience in a theatre or the reader of a book perceives a crux or significance of which the fictional characters are unaware.

EMPATHY The power of entering into the experience of or understanding objects or emotions outside ourselves. The power to project oneself into the object of contemplation.

EPIC A very long narrative poem presenting adventures on a grand scale and organically united through a central figure of heroic proportions, e.g.: *The Odyssey; Beowulf; Paradise Lost.*

EPIGRAM Short poem or statement, concisely written, and ending on a witty or ingenious turn of thought. Coleridge's definition is itself an epigram: 'What is an epigram? A dwarfish whole:/Its body brevity, and wit its soul.'

EUPHEMISM Mild or evasive description used to avoid painful, distasteful, or embarrassing topic, e.g.: 'eliminate' for 'kill'; 'passed on' for 'dead'.

FABLE story in which animals and birds behave like human beings, illustrating some moral truth e.g.: Aesop's *Fables*; Orwell's *Animal Farm.*

FANTASY Used to designate a conscious breaking-free from reality. The term is often applied to a work which takes place in a non-existent and unreal world such as a fairyland, or concerns incredible and unreal characters.

GENRE A literary kind or type, e.g.: epic; tragedy; comic.

HYPERBOLE figure of speech consisting of exaggerated or extravagant statement, used to express strong feeling or to create a striking effect, and not intended to be understood literally, e.g.: 'He is dying of love for her.'

IDEALISM This can have two general meanings: (i) One of the philosphical systems, deriving from Plato, which claims that the world is composed of ideas, rather than objects (the opposite of materialism); (ii) Popularly, the aspiration towards lofty moral objectives. In literature this term is used to describe a tendency to depict the world as the author thinks it should be, rather than as it is.

IMAGERY A term used to suggest the creation of a striking picture in words, e.g.: 'O my love is like a red, red rose!' Although it was originally used to suggest visual 'pictures' conjured up in the mind, it is today taken to mean that part of a literary work which appeals to the senses – sight, hearing, taste and smell – as well as the kinaesthetic sense which relates to our sense of movement or awareness of bodily effort.

INTENTIONAL FALLACY A critical term used to describe the error of judging a work of art by the author's intention in producing it.

INTERIOR MONOLOGUE This records the internal emotional experience of a character 'thinking'.

IRONY A figure of speech where the speaker says one thing but intends the opposite to be understood. Often used for humorous or satirical purposes e.g.: 'You've lost my money? That's *fine!*'

JARGON A manner of speech or writing full of specialist and therefore unfamiliar terms. The vocabulary of a science, profession, or art.

LEITMOTIV A phrase, image, or even word consistently reappearing with the reappearance of a given character, problem, action, or thought in order to underline it.

LYRICAL Expressed in poetically emotional terms (From 'song-like').

MATERIALISM This can have two general meanings: (i) the philosophic doctrine that matter is the primary substance of all things, including human beings; (ii) an overriding concern with the acquisition of goods and money. It is worth noting that these two meanings have no necessary connection with each other.

METAPHOR One thing described in terms of another, e.g.: 'He is a tower of strength'; 'You are a donkey!'

METONYMY This means 'change of name', used when the name of an attribute or something closely related is substituted for the thing itself, e.g.: 'Whitehall' is used to describe the Civil Service.

MORAL This can have two general meanings: (i) the moral of a story is its overt or implied lesson for the reader; (ii) 'moral' is used to describe systems or rules of ethics or behaviour, and notions of right or wrong. Linguistically, it can be used as a noun ('the moral of a story') or as an adjective ('a morally dubious activity').

MYTH Anonymous stories having their roots in the primitive folk beliefs of races or nations, often presenting supernatural episodes to make concrete a particular perception of man or a cosmic view, e.g.: the Greek, Roman, or Norse myths.

NARRATIVE The recounting of a series of facts or events and the establishing of some connection between them. Also, how these facts are related to a reader.

NARRATOR The person who is telling the story . This can be either (i) the author, using the third person narrative – mode ('John felt angry. He left the room'), or the first person narrative mode ('I am going to tell you this tale'), or (ii) a fictional character recounting events in either the first or third person narrative mode

NOVELLA A prose fiction whose length is somewhere between the long short story and the novel, e.g.: Thomas Mann's *Death in Venice*; Joseph Conrad's *Heart of Darkness* .

OMNISCIENT NARRATOR ('all-knowing'). A narrator (usually the author, using the third person narrative mode) who claims to know the innermost thoughts and feelings of the characters, as well as the events of the fiction .

ONOMATOPOEIA Words which sound like the thing they describe, e.g.: 'pop'; 'bang'; 'Swish'; 'murmur'.

OXYMORON The combining in one phrase of two terms with opposite meanings, e.g. 'an open secret'; ''bitter-sweet''.

PARABLE A brief story serving as an example of some general prinicple, usually ethical, which gives the story its significance. Most parables are miniature allegories, e.g.: Christ's parable of The Good Samaritan.

PARADOX A statement which, though it seems to be self-contradicting, contains an element of truth. It often provokes the reader to consider a particular point afresh, e.g.: 'The child is father to the man.'

PARAPHRASE To put a piece of writing into other words. Usually, to render more complex writing into simple contemporary English.

PARODY A composition which mimics the characteristic features of a writer's style and thought for the purpose of ridicule.

PATHETIC FALLACY Accrediting nature with the emotions of human beings. Carrying over into inanimate objects the moods and passions of humans, e.g.: 'the weeping willow'.

PERSONA In a poem like Eliot's 'Prufrock' or a novel like Dostoyevsky's *Notes from Underground*, the 'I' telling the story is not (necessarily) the author, but his projection into another person.

PERSONIFICATION A figure of speech in which some object, place, or abstract idea is turned into a person with human attributes, e.g.: 'England's concern for the poor', or 'Charity seeketh not its own.'

PLOT In *Aspects of the Novel* E. M. Forster says 'A story is a narrative of events arranged in time sequence ... A plot is also a narrative of events, the emphasis falling on causality. "The King died and then the Queen died" is a story. "The King died and then the Queen died of grief" is a plot.'

POINT OF VIEW The relationship of either the author, or a particular character, to the events of the narrative.

PRÉCIS An abstract or summary of a piece of work.

PUN A play on words for humorous or serious purposes, usually involving either (i) one word used in two different senses, e.g.: 'Ask for me tomorrow and you shall find me a grave man', or (ii) two words which sound the same but have different meanings, e.g.: 'Rose of Castille ... rows of cast steel'.

ROMANCE Originally a fictitious tale, often in verse, in which scenes and incidents were remote from real life, e.g.: Sydney's *Arcadia*. Today used to describe tale of improbable events.

ROMANTIC Late eighteenth-century movement which emphasised the imagination and emotions over reason and intellect, e.g.: the poetry of Wordsworth and Keats, Emily Bronte's *Wuthering Heights*. NB The use of romance and romantic as literary terms should not be confused with the popular use of 'romantic' to describe fiction concerning love.

SEMANTICS That branch of linguistics which deals with the meanings of words and especially with historical changes in those meanings.

SIMILE An imaginative and direct comparison of two things for the purpose of explanation, allusion, or ornament, e.g.: 'My heart is like a singing bird'.

STREAM OF CONSCIOUSNESS Similar to INTERIOR MONOLOGUE, but with the addition that the 'thinking' is often depicted as fragmentary, associational, uncensored, and sometimes illogical.

STRUCTURE The planned framework of a piece of literature. This may relate to the story or plot, or to the arrangements of underlying elements such as themes. The shape or arrangement of a piece of work. Usually refers to the organisation of elements other than words.

STYLE Those aspects of a writer's work which concern the form and manner of expression rather than the content. Though the distinction between style and content is sometimes rather artificial it is often necessary in literary criticism.

SYMBOL An object or phenomenon which is generally regarded as typifying or representing something else, e.g.: the cross is a symbol of Christianity.

SYNTAX The arrangement and grammatical relation of words within a sentence. Words may often be shifted to unexpected positions to give emphasis, e.g.: 'Things were not lastly as firstly well / With us twain, you tell?' (Hardy).

TEXT The piece of work under consideration, which may be a part (a page, a chapter) or the whole work (a story, a novel).

THEME The central or dominating idea in a literary work, often an abstract concept which is made concrete through characters and action, e.g.: Imprisonment is a theme in Dickens's *Little Dorrit*.

TONE The author's attitude or moral outlook, shown in the work by his choice of subject, literary devices, and language in general.

TRAGEDY Originally, a work which represents the downfall of a great person, expressed in a serious manner, using elevated and poetic language, e.g.: Sophocles' *Oedipus Rex*. A serious work in which the chief figures, by some peculiarity of character, pass through a series of misfortunes leading to the final catastrophe, e.g.: Shakespeare's *King Lear*. Because of this element of 'peculiarity of character' (often expressed as idealism, excessive ambition, or lack of self-knowledge) the term tragedy should not be used to describe a work whose outcome is accidentally unfortunate.

TRANSFERRED EPITHET Figure of speech in which an adjective or adverb is separated from the word to which it belongs grammatically and transferred to some other word in the sentence, e.g.: 'The prisoner entered the condemned cell.'

Guidance notes

Chapter One

1 A simile ('*like* a slender shaving').

2 A metaphor ('Night' is described as a 'black bat').

3 (a) A simile ('*like* a ... rose').

   (b) Alliteration ('*r*ed, *r*ed *r*ose').

   (c) An image ('red rose').

4 (a) Repetition ('fog').

   (b) Bonus points if you spotted that there was also repetition in the construction of phrases. ('fog up the river/fog down the river', 'Fog on the Essex marshes / fog on the Kentish heights').

5 (a) Repetition of the 'd', which is called *alliteration*, in 'During' / 'dull' / 'dark ' / 'day'.

   (b) 'dull '/ 'dark' / 'soundless' / 'autumn' / 'oppressively' / 'dreary' / 'melancholy'.

   (c) Adjectives.

   (d) Adverb.

   (e) It is a very 'literary' term, with Biblical overtones, and is being used to denote 'the sky'.

Chapter Two

LANGUAGE

1 *Incognito* means 'with one's name or identity kept secret'.

2 'go into harness' is a metaphor.

3 Watson returning to his profession is being compared to a horse which is put into harness when it is going to work.

4 '*Carte blanche*' means that the King gives Holmes 'full discretionary power' in using the money.

5 The verb is at the end of the sentence – which is normal practice in German. The sentence in English would more naturally be 'we have received this account of you from all quarters'.

6 Adverb / adjective / adjective / noun.

7 A simile.

1 Because Watson smells of iodoform (an antiseptic) and has 'a black mark of silver nitrate upon his right finger'.

2 James Boswell is famous for his biography of his friend Samuel Johnson. Watson's stories purport to be a record of Holmes's cases.

3 The King's flamboyant manner of dressing – in particular his astrakhan covered coat, cloak lined with flame coloured silk, and fur topped boots.

4 A 'drunken-looking groom, ill kempt and side-whiskered with an inflamed face and disreputable clothes'.

5 To extract information from them about Irene Adler.

6 'Some cold beef and a glass of beer'.

7 He thinks it would be 'the blackest treachery' to break his promise to help Holmes, and he reasons that they are not injuring Irene Adler but 'preventing her from injuring another'.

8 To panic Irene Adler into revealing where she keeps her most valuable (and hidden) possessions.

1 The implication is that Holmes is scrupulously honest and rigorously business-like – but I think it is also slightly insulting to the King. He is refusing to allow himself to be patronised by an aristocrat. Notice that he is loftily critical of him elsewhere: ('If your majesty would condescend to state your case').

2 They are both admirers of Irene Adler, both tall, and both 'Bohemian'. The King is a native of that state, and Holmes is bohemian in its sense of denoting 'unconventional in behaviour, attitudes, and even morals'.

3 They all put on disguise. The King wears his vizard mask; Holmes the clothes of a groom and then a clergyman; and Irene Adler the 'male costume' of a 'slim youth in an ulster' to follow Holmes.

4 Since Watson is the narrator of the stories he needs to be present at a scene if at all possible so as to render his description of it later. Holmes is aware that Watson writes accounts of the 'cases' they work on together. But the remark is principally a sort of sly wink from Conan Doyle to the reader, putting into the mouth of his fictional character (Holmes) the observation that he could not *exist* without a narrator – who is of course also created by the author.

5 We learn that Watson used to share rooms with Holmes at Baker Street, has since married and has resumed his practice as a doctor. He obviously admires and knows Holmes very well, and he is loyal to him even when his conscience is troubled. He is prepared to be brave and even break the law, is articulate and of moderate intelligence. I say 'moderate' because he

214

is obviously created by Conan Doyle to be a foil to Holmes's sharp intelligence. Watson poses the questions the man–in–the–street would ask. He sometimes seems to speak for us, the readers – especially on the phenomenon of Holmes's 'deductions' (which technically speaking are 'inductions'): 'When I hear you give your reasons ... the thing always appears to me to be so ridiculously simple that I could easily do it myself, though at each successive instance of your reasoning I am baffled until you explain your process.' Most readers of the Sherlock Holmes stories feel the same way – and this is one of the reasons which makes them so attractive. Watson as character and narrator is so very *un*obtrusive that he allows us to feel that we are there in his place – asking the same basic question: 'How does he do it?''

Chapter Three

1 (a) It is a porthole.

   (b) Anthropomorphism: (the porthole is given life to 'gleam').

2 A simile: (the hair is being directly compared to silk).

3 (a) Repetition (of 'cold pale').

   (b) Adjective ('cold') adjective ('pale') noun ('sea').

4 (a) 'drummed' is onomatopoeia: (the word sounds like the action it describes).

   (b) 'sank softly into the sandy road' is alliteration: (the repeated 's' emphasises the action described).

5 Metaphor (the form of the smoke is likened to that of a feather.

6 Simile (cat and camel are being directly compared).

7 'Picotees' are a type of carnation, and 'bluchers' are high shoes or low boots.

COMPREHENSION

1 Presumably because of the emotional strain caused by recent events in his life. His wife has just died, and now he is being separated from both his mother and his daughter.

2 If Fenella's mother has been ill for some time, the grandmother may have been making repeated visits to see her. The stewardess says that it's 'not often' she has a cabin, and the grandmother explains that her son has provided for it '*this* time (my emphasis). Both these remarks suggest that she has made a number of crossings – enough for the stewardess to know that she is called Mrs Crane.

3 Some sort of alcoholic drink.

4 The umbrella.

5 Katherine Mansfield is describing the ship's arrival in port from Fenella's point of view. Fenella perceives the ship as being stationary, and the landing stage moving towards them.

ANALYSIS

1 We know from physical description that Fenella's grandmother is a white-haired old lady. She wears stays and is relieved when she takes them off – from which we could reasonably conclude that she is plump. And she must be small, because her taking the top bunk is the subject of comment, and she reaches it with 'little spider-like steps'. From her behaviour we can see that she is obviously brisk and efficient. She has the foresight to take some items of food for the trip, and we know that she is religious because she prays more than once on the journey and encourages Fenella to do so too.

All her interaction with other characters in the story cast her in a positive light. She is clearly cherished by her son, she takes good care of Fenella, and she is treated in a friendly and engaging manner by the stewardess. Obviously she embodies traditional and slightly strict moral values. She is shocked by the price of the ready-made sandwiches, the stewardess knows that she would not accept an alcoholic pick-me-up, and the motto she has painted expresses a slightly puritanical sentiment.

2 The motto is framed in black, which links it to the mourning clothes in which Fenella and her grandmother are both dressed. And the sentiment of its message, apart from being touchingly naive – rather like a birthday card motto – is concerned with the transience of life and the fact that time can never be recovered. The object for both these reasons therefore has a symbolic link with the element of death which hovers in the background of the story as a *leitmotiv*. Fenella's mother has died, and her grandparents are old people who will one day in the near rather than the distant future, die in their turn.

3 No – the whole point here is that although the stewardess and her grandmother *think* that Fenella is asleep, she is not, and she therefore overhears their conversation. This includes the mention of her as a 'Poor little motherless mite'. She in fact falls asleep immediately after this, and the story continues without a break as she wakes up in the morning. There is thus a continuity in the narrative perspective.

4 You could say that the story is composed of three roughly equal parts:

> PART I   Taking leave in the late evening
>
> PART II The journey at night
>
> PART III Arrival in the early morning

This pattern is strengthened if we think of other elements which are 'arranged' in a similar fashion:

> PART I   The departure is from *land* and one source of security – Fenella's father

You may have found other patterns based on different elements of the story, but this one seems attractive to me in combining such basic elements.

5 You might have listed any of the following. The small boy who Fenella notices being 'jerked along angrily between his mother and father'. The emotional scene between Fenella's grandmother and her father which she finds 'awful'. The flight of stairs she has to climb down and finds 'terribly steep'. The odour in the saloon, which is like 'paint and burnt chop bones and india-rubber'. Conditions in the cabin, which has soap which will not produce a lather, water 'like a kind of blue jelly', and bed-sheets which are difficult to turn down because they are so stiff. The coldness in the cabin and on deck in the early morning. Withered trees on land which are likened to skeletons. And of course the black framed motto above Mr Crane's bed.

Chapter Four

LANGUAGE

1 A 'yeoman' is a landowner who is qualified for jury service. It is not a common working man as is often mistakenly supposed.

2 (a) Personification: (the heath is given a 'face')

(b) Simile ('like')

(c) Onomatopoeia and alliteration ('whewed and whistled')

3 Although this attractive maid had put it out of the question that Lodge may have compensated Rhoda for his actions in the past, all indignation against the unknowing displacement had disappeared from the thoughts of the older woman.

4 The depressingly dull greyish-brown colours of the countryside's vegetation.

5 Dramatic irony. Her feeling is more tragically accurate than she can know. Her destiny is entwined with her husband's son, and both of them will be dead within four days.

COMPREHENSION

1 Lodge is forty; Rhoda is thirty; Gertrude is nineteen, and the boy is twelve.

2 We take it that she sees Rhoda's face – though the only 'proof' of this comes later, after six years have passed: "the indistinct form he had raised in the glass had undoubtedly resembled the only woman in the world who – as she now knew – could have a reason for bearing her ill-will'.

3 The boy is executed as a precautionary example to others – just because he happened to be present when a hayrick was set on fire.

4 Lodge leaves his money to a reformatory for boys – with an annuity to Rhoda (which she does not claim).

5 Lodge is uncommunicative about the coming assizes because he knows that they are being held for the sole purpose of executing his only son.

ANALYSIS

1 Rhoda has mixed or even contradictory feelings about Gertrude because whilst one part of her feels friendly towards the younger woman, another feels guilty that she has been 'responsible' for inflicting the injury to Gertrude's arm. Rhoda also suspects that she might possess the mystical powers of a witch that enable her to 'exercise a malignant power over people against [her] own will'. The *conscious* part of her mind therefore feels uneasy about these matters, and the 'something in her own individuality' which she thinks is convicting her of a crime we might take to be one of two things. Either it is her conscience holding her responsible for the exercise of her mystic powers – even if done against her own will. Or it may be that Rhoda is vaguely aware of her own possible *sub*-conscious wish to overthrow and displace her rival.

Notice how the first of these two possibilities fits the 'supernatural' reading of the story, and the second the psychological.

2 We learn at the outset that the boy is Farmer Lodge's illegitimate son and that he thus carries the stigma of that illegitimacy which sets him apart from others in society. He obviously feels bad about this, because he does not like being exposed socially: 'he hated going afield on the farms'. His origins therefore victimise him and set him apart from the beginning of his life. He lives with his mother, set apart from others and in some poverty – and they rely upon his *poaching* in order to eat. 'The hare you wired is very tender', Rhoda tells him, but her warning which follows – 'mind that nobody catches you' – alerts us to the fact that he is straying over the boundary of what is legal – and he is therefore in danger.

His mother decides to leave the locality, and he therefore loses contact with what few roots he has: wherever else he goes in society he will be in yet another sense an outsider. Then in the later part of the story we learn that he has been tried and convicted to set a deterrent example to others because of society's fear of social unrest. He just happened to be in the vicinity when a hayrick was set on fire – and even the hangman himself has no doubt of his innocence: 'if ever a young fellow deserved to be let off, this one does'.

So the boy's origins victimise him and set him apart through no fault of his own; the hard life he is subsequently forced to endure reinforces the effect of these influences; and in the end society imposes upon him something which makes him the ultimate 'victim' and 'outsider' – an unjust death penalty.

3 We are actually told that following the death of his son and Gertrude, Farmer Lodge becomes 'chastened and thoughtful' – which suggests that he is reflecting upon his past behaviour. He then removes himself from his home locality – which might mean that he feels guilty and ashamed and does not wish to be seen by his fellow countrymen, or it might be that he is *punishing* himself for his previous behaviour. He sells off his farm and stock (which he formerly wished to pass on to his legitimate heirs) which suggests that he has given up any ambition and any sense of positive growth. And finally, the fact that he bequeaths all his money to a boy's reformatory (with a small annuity to Rhoda) tells us where he thinks most amends need making.

The general impression given therefore is that he regrets his former actions; he behaves in a generally chastened manner; and he makes as large a gesture of recompense as possible before dying.

4 The settings can have a variety of significance, depending upon what they are seen in relation to. But in general the following seem most apposite.

The *dairy* is a place of communal work, which emphasises the social group to which Rhoda belongs, and it is *owned* by Lodge, which connects it with his ambition, success, and later renunciation.

The *cottage* is almost a symbol of Rhoda herself – poor, weatherbeaten, and 'bony'. It reflects the austerity of her life.

The *church* is a place of public assembly in which Lodge shows off his newly acquired wife. His private actions are thereby tied into a larger social context.

Many of the events of the story take place *out of doors*, which places them amongst 'nature' – which in Hardy's world is supremely indifferent to the fate of human beings.

Conjurer Trendle lives in a remote part of *Egdon Heath*, the isolation and historical connexions of which reinforce the old-fashioned superstitions he (almost reluctantly) practises.

The *hangman's cottage* is situated outside the county town – which reflects some possible embarrassment on society's part at acknowledging the unpleasant role he performs for it. And the stream which flows past the cottage also flows through Holmstoke – which connects the events which took place on the farms with what ultimately happens in the town.

Casterbridge itself is the seat of legal authority as home to the assizes in the area, and its jail is a fittingly grim location for the tragic finale which 'imprisons' the four principal characters in their joint fate – though the story actually ends up back where it began, with the enduring Rhoda still milking cows in the dairy.

Chapter Five

1 Opprobrious' means 'conveying reproach, or abusive', and 'epithet' means 'an adjective expressing quality or attribute'. An example might be 'dirty dog' or 'filthy cur'.

2 (a) Alliteration: repetition of 'f' and 'l'.

   (b) Principally by the equal number of stresses and the equal weight of the two clauses on either side of the second comma.

   (c) Adjective ('mute') and abstract noun ('greatness').

3 The statement would normally be written with the two adjectives coming before the noun they qualify ('a ruthless and efficient man').

4 An experienced person or old hand.

5 A simile ('like').

COMPREHENSION

1 Sierra Leone.

2 Beads, cloth, brass wire.

3 Chief in the station's neighbouring villages.

4 Sugar.

5 Richelieu and d'Artagnan are characters from *The Three Musketeers* by the French novelist Alexandre Dumas. Hawk's Eye is a character who appears in *The Last of the Mohicans* and *The Deerslayer* by the American novelist Fenimore Cooper. Father Goriot is the central character in *Père Goriot* by the French novelist Balzac. Conrad had read all these novels when he was a boy.

ANALYSIS

1 Conrad is trying to evoke the dislocation the two characters feel by pointing to the strangeness and the threatening nature of Africa *as they perceive it*. 'Mysterious glimpses' suggests that they have only a partial, impressionistic view, and 'vigorous life' suggests the physical energy which is almost menacing in this context.

2 Eight months.

3 Because he knows that they are slave traders and doesn't want to have to explain what is going on to Kayerts and Carlier.

4 Conrad is implying that Kayerts is just mouthing platitudes in his grovelling response to the director.'

5 Kayerts has hanged himself on the cross which marks the grave of his predecessor. Carlier had earlier in the story re-planted the cross in a more upright position and tested his work by suspending himself 'with both hands to the cross-piece'. Kayerts 'seemed to be standing rigidly to atten-

tion' (appropriate for a subservient before his boss). And 'with one purple cheek *playfully* posed on the shoulder' (my emphasis) is grotesquely ironic – as is the swollen tongue which is poking out at the director. There is also a grim irony created by the contrast between Kayerts as a moral degenerate and the usual rather spiritual connotations of the cross as a Christian symbol of Christ's suffering. All these details are ironic because they point to a level of meaning and a series of connexions which are offered to the reader behind the backs of the characters.

Chapter Six

LANGUAGE

1 Hyperbole (or exaggeration).

2 Violently abusive or fault-finding.

3 'You are there, are you?'

4 Saying very little.

5 Simile. Lot's wife (in the Old Testament) was turned into a pillar of salt.

COMPREHENSION

1 That she is an emotionally passionate woman.

2 Luther.

3 She could not overcome her own desire for him.

4 She felt excited.

5 She did not reveal her intentions.

ANALYSIS

1 The significance of Morley Chapel is at least fourfold. It is the place where Fanny and Harry first met, and their prospective marriage will be held there. It is thus closely linked to the social lives of the characters. But in addition, Harry sings in its choir: he is therefore publicly prominent – which makes the denunciation of him by Mrs Nixon all the more dramatic. It is therefore a location in which all the social forces and tensions of the story are focused.

2 Mrs Goodall thinks that her son has demeaned himself by accepting Fanny's renewed attentions after a number of years in which Fanny has had a chance to roam freely ('gallivantin' round wherever she'd a mind') as a single woman. She has spoiled her son and thinks him less of a man for accepting Fanny. She is also an inverted snob of course – and yet part of her admires Fanny, because she perceives her to be powerful – 'a woman of her own match'.

One clinching detail is that Fanny has money – both an inheritance and her own savings. This would give her an extra degree of social status in addition to that of coming from a slightly higher level in the social hierarchy, and Mrs Goodall would relish the reflected glory. Certainly when there is a danger that Fanny might back away following the public denunciation, we are told that 'It would have annoyed her very much if Fanny had dropped her son at that moment'. Mrs Goodall's thoughts and feelings are therefore interestingly ambiguous.

3   We are presented with the first hymn – 'All is safely gathered in' – from Fanny's point of view, and she sees it as ironic in the sense that the season has been wet and 'half the crops were still out, and in a poor way'. But of course the 'gathering in' applies to Fanny herself. She thinks that decisions about the marriage (a form of 'gathering in') are all settled – an assumption which will be disturbed by Mrs Nixon's public denunciation of Harry.

The second hymn – 'They that sow in tears shall reap in joy' – has also been taken by many readers to apply to Fanny. She is unhappy about the prospective marriage, and yet here is a possible clue that she *might* be happier in the future.

The third – 'Fair waved the golden corn' – seems to be linked to Harry, whose blonde hair is mentioned more than once in the story.

All three hymns are perfectly normal 'harvest festival' songs as well of course, but in subtle and complex pieces of fiction it is common for details to be connected in this metaphoric and referential manner to the main themes of the work.

4   The two most important points it seems to me are the strong sense of physical attraction she feels for Harry (despite herself) when they are in the chapel. We are told that 'his kisses had ... sent roots down into her soul' and 'The thorn of desire rankled bitterly in her heart'. And then Mrs Nixon's denunciation presents Fanny with an image of Harry's sexual connection with another woman. Even if he is not the father of the child, he does not deny that he *might* be. It is interesting to note that after her unhappy thoughts about marriage, Fanny's reaction to the news is '"It's a sudden surprise, that's one thing" said Fanny *brightly*' (my emphasis). Even though she does not commit herself until the last lines of the story, these two incidents seem to reveal the motives underpinning her decision.

5   There has been scandal attached to Harry, who is a member of Reverend Enderby's choir. The clergyman could play safe by asking him to stay away from the chapel, but when Harry asks if he is wanted for the evening service, Enderby says 'Yes, I think we must take no notice'. And this decision comes after some pain and thought. It has not been easy for him, yet he allows Harry to stay within the community.

Similarly, Harry could make life easier for himself in the short term by not showing his face at chapel. Fanny asks him if he will come to the evening service, and he in his turn makes the morally more courageous decision to stay within the community by saying 'Ay, I s'll come'.

Chapter Seven

1 It means 'by means of ...'

2 They are adjectives, but give yourself bonus points if you spotted that 'oozier' and 'wetter' are being used as *comparatives*.

3 Saturnine means 'of sluggish, gloomy temperament' – characteristics which were once thought to be produced by the influence of the planet Saturn – hence the etymology of the term.

4 The study of sciences.

5 As if viewed through the wrong end of a telescope.

COMPREHENSION

1 His interest in the railway system.

2 'A language ... fractions and decimals ... a little algebra.'

3 'A beautiful young lady'.

4 He thinks that there might seem 'something treacherous' in reporting to the Company what the signalman has told him.

5 'just at broad day' – that is, dawn.

6 The implication is that it is chosen as an occupation when nothing else is possible.

ANALYSIS

1 The narrator says 'In me, he merely saw a man who had been shut up within narrow limits all his life.' The signalman has similarly been shut up within the narrow limits of the cutting. We are not told exactly what 'limits' the narrator is referring to, but he could be hinting at a demanding occupation, burdensome responsibilities, or something which has prevented him satisfying his curiosity.

2 Because the signalman has previously been visited by the spectre which shouted to him using the same words as the narrator had used – 'Halloa! Below there!' There is also a close correspondence in their gestures. The narrator shaded his eyes with his hand; the spectre put its arms across its face. The signalman admits 'I took you for someone else yesterday evening.'

3 A state of uneasiness or death. The signalman has resigned himself to having gone down in the world. The narrator tells us 'He had made his bed, and he lay upon it'. This is a sort of social 'death'. Then the beautiful young lady who dies is taken into the signalman's box and laid down on the floor. This reinforces the notion of the box itself as a sort of death trap and a 'coffin' of sorts. In addition the narrator, expressing his disquiet concerning the red danger light, says 'I should have slept but poorly if my bed had been under it'. And finally, when the signalman has been killed,

he is laid out in a little makeshift hut which to the narrator looks 'no bigger than a bed'.

4   The cutting is 'extremely deep and unusually precipitous' and the narrator describes the post as 'solitary and dismal'. The walls are of jagged stone which is 'clammy', 'oozier', and then 'dripping wet'. He calls the location a 'dungeon'. There is almost no natural light, and it has an 'earthy, deadly smell'. The narrator feels 'as if [he] had left the natural world'. All these details suggest a sort of prison or a cold, wet, and oppressive sort of 'hell'.

Index

COALVILLE TECHNICAL COLLEGE
LIBRARY